The EAW Electrical Handbook

List of authors

Chapters 1–11	John D. Hobbs, CEng, MIEE
Chapter 12	John F. Pickup, MIllumES, MAPLE
Chapters 13–15	Marjorie E. Pickford, BSc, editor
Chapter 16	Maureen E. Brook
	Mary Clay
Chapter 17	William R. Lee, MD(Lond), DIH
	John L. Wood, BSc, CEng, FIEE

The EAW Electrical Handbook

prepared by
The Electrical Association for Women
Director: Mary George, MBE

The English Universities Press Ltd

ISBN 0 340 15500 0

First printed 1934
Ninth edition (completely revised) 1971

Copyright © 1971 The Electrical Association
for Women
All rights reserved. No part of this publication
may be reproduced or transmitted in any form or
by any means, electronic or mechanical, including
photocopy, recording, or any information storage
and retrieval system, without permission in
writing from the publisher.

The English Universities Press Limited
St Paul's House, Warwick Lane, London EC4P 4AH

Filmset by Keyspools Ltd, Golborne, Lancashire
Printed and bound in Great Britain by
C. Tinling & Co. Ltd, London and Prescot

Contents

1	Units	1
2	Electric Current	10
3	Direct-Current Circuits	18
4	Alternating-Current Circuits	30
5	Magnetism and Electromagnetism	43
6	Cells, Generators, Motors and Transformers	55
7	Generation, Transmission and Distribution of Electrical Energy	72
8	Tariffs	94
9	Domestic Electrical Installation	107
10	Electric Water Heating	134
11	Electric Space Heating	149
12	Lighting	167
13	Domestic Cookers and Small Cooking Appliances	195
14	Motor-driven Appliances for Domestic Use	214
15	Electric Home Laundry	233
16	Commercial Equipment	245
17	Electric Shock	264

Foreword

The need for a handbook of this kind first became apparent in the early 1930's when the increasing interest in electricity in the home had revealed a whole new subject for study. The impact of electrical science on housecraft had then created a new career for women, which developed into that of Electrical Housecraft Adviser. The training for such a career included instruction both in domestic science and in the applications of electricity to household routines. A textbook was required which would be of use not only to students but to their instructors who, while fully conversant with technicalities, would not necessarily be so familiar with the needs of the home. The Handbook, in its original form and in its eight successive editions, is therefore primarily designed as the textbook for the EAW Certificate, which is awarded to demonstrators and teachers and others with suitable qualifications.

In this edition, for the first time, a chapter has been included on electric catering equipment, so that catering students will find the book has a direct application to their work. Others to whom the book may be useful for reference purposes include those working in institutional management, social welfare, journalism, public relations and advertising. It is also used in some training programmes in the electrical industry.

The information in this edition is as up-to-date as is possible at the time of going to press. Fortunately, the basic principles that have to be mastered by the student remain unchanged and the aim has been to present these in the simplest but yet the most comprehensive way. SI units and metric equivalents are used throughout the book, and further information is supplied in the appendices. The number of illustrations, many of them original drawings, has been increased by 70%.

The Association acknowledges with much gratitude the generous assistance of the contributors to this book whose names are listed on

FOREWORD

page ii, and in particular the work of compilation undertaken by Mrs M. E. Pickford, BSc, EAW Education Officer. It also wishes to record its thanks to the following who have assisted by providing illustrations or other material: AEI Ltd, Electricity Council Appliance Testing Laboratories, Belling Ltd, British Standards Institution, Bulpitt & Sons Ltd, Burco Ltd, Central Electricity Generating Board, Crabtree & Co. Ltd, Design Centre, Dimplex, DoRDEC, Electricity Council, Electrolux Ltd, English Electric Co. Ltd, Faber & Faber Ltd, GEC (Henley) Ltd, G. & R. Gilbert Ltd, Heatrae Ltd, Heatstore Ltd, Hobart Manufacturing Co. Ltd, Imperial Machine Co., Jackson Boilers Ltd, Kenwood Manufacturing Co. Ltd, MK Electric Ltd, Pifco Ltd, Sangamo Western Ltd, Simplex Electric Co. Ltd and to Mr W. J. Jones, MSc, CEng, FIEE, Mr P. A. Rowland, and Mr D. C. J. Thorogood, DFH, CEng, MIEE for assisting with reading of proofs.

Mary George, MBE, BA, Companion IEE,
Director: Electrical Association for Women.

1 Units

Decimalisation and Metrication

It is not generally appreciated that the recent change to a system of decimal currency is linked with another change called metrication. Metrication is the process of changing to a metric system of measurement and we will start by discussing the factors which influenced the Government's decision to make these important changes.

The Imperial or F.P.S. System

A system of units is necessary to enable us to measure time, distance, area, volume, weight, etc. In order that the units which we are using may be checked when necessary, each one must be carefully defined. Furthermore, to make the system as simple as possible there should only be a few 'basic' units. For this reason a system of units often consists of three basic units and all the other units which are required are then built up from these basic units.

Thus in this country we have used as basic units:
 the foot—to measure length,
 the pound—to measure mass (see p. 4),
 the second—to measure time.
Samples of the pound and the foot are kept very carefully in London and there is a very comprehensive definition of the second.

For some measurements, however, these units are not convenient, and 'practical' units are used in these circumstances. For example, if we are measuring the distance between two towns we would normally use the mile as our unit of length, and, if we have to state our age, we do so in years. The mile and the year are referred to as practical units.

Quantities other than mass, length or time may be measured by using one or more of our basic units. Thus we can measure area in square feet and velocity in feet per second, and these units, having been derived from our basic units, are referred to as 'derived' units.

Once again, however, these derived units may not be convenient for a particular measurement. In such cases the corresponding practical units are used, such as the acre for the measurement of area and miles per hour for the measurement of velocity.

C.G.S. and MKS (Metric) Systems

In addition to the Imperial system, two other systems have been used in this country for scientific purposes. The c.g.s. system was adopted in 1873 and used the centimetre, gramme and second as the basic units. However, a number of difficulties arose when electrical quantities were defined in terms of c.g.s. units, so the introduction of a new system became desirable. After considerable discussion among the many countries concerned, it was decided in 1950 to adopt the MKSA system, based on the metre, kilogramme, second and ampere.

Système International d'Unités (SI Units)

In 1954 an international body known as the Conférence Générale des Poids et Mesures adopted a system of units which they later named the Système International d'Unités (SI units). This system, which is very similar to the MKSA system, has now been accepted by many countries and it was considered likely that by 1975 the only major countries not using SI units would be the USA and Canada. Accordingly, in May 1966, following a recommendation in 1965 by the Federation of British Industries, the Government announced their support for metrication and recommended that a considerable degree of conversion should have taken place by 1975. At the present moment British industry, in conjunction with the British Standards Institution (BSI), the Metrication Board and the Ministry of Technology, is making preparations so that the changeover to SI units may take place as smoothly as possible. BSI has introduced a key symbol (see fig. 1.1) for use nationally to symbolise the changeover in the United Kingdom. It is suggested that the symbol should be used on catalogues and trade literature dealing with products conforming to the new metric standards.

SI units differ from the systems they replace in the following ways. The new system has six basic units:

metre (m)—length
kilogramme (kg)—mass
second (s)—time
ampere (A)—electric current
kelvin (K)—temperature
candela (cd)—luminous intensity

These units have been arbitrarily selected and, since they are basic units, they must be carefully defined. For example, the metre is defined in terms of a number of wavelengths of a particular radiation of light, whilst the kilogramme is defined in terms of a standard kilogramme which is carefully stored under controlled conditions at Sèvres near Paris. It should perhaps be stated that, although the second is the basic unit, the minute, hour, day, etc. will continue to be used as the practical units of time, since these units are already in international use. The complete list of the definitions of the basic SI units is given in Appendix 1. A list of the definitions of the derived SI units with which we shall be concerned in this book is given in Appendix 2.

Fig. 1.1 The key symbol used in connection with products and literature conforming to the new metric standards.

In the Imperial system, practical units are usually given a different name from the corresponding basic unit, e.g. the basic unit of length is the foot; one-twelfth of a foot is an inch; three feet are a yard. In SI units, submultiples and multiples are obtained simply by the use of a prefix, e.g. the basic unit of length is the metre; one-hundredth of a metre is a centimetre; one thousand metres are one kilometre. A complete list of these prefixes is given in Appendix 3.

The relative magnitudes of the metre and the foot and the kilogramme and the pound are shown in fig. 1.2.

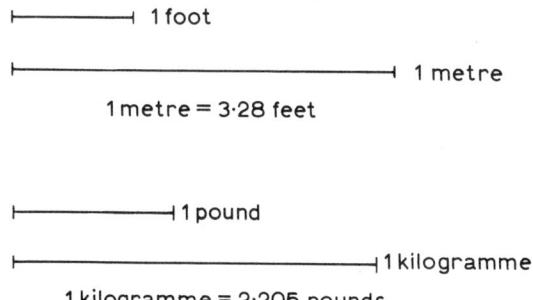

Fig. 1.2 Relative magnitudes of the basic units of length and mass in the Imperial and the SI systems.

3

Mass and weight

At this stage it is necessary to explain the difference between the terms mass and weight, since in the past much confusion has arisen in the use of these quantities.

The mass of an object measures the quantity of matter in that object. The weight of an object measures the force of gravity acting on the mass of that object.

The confusion which has existed in the past has largely been due to the fact that the same unit has been used to measure both these quantities. In the Imperial system, the pound is used as the unit of mass and (incorrectly) as the unit of force, i.e. it is used to measure weight. Comparatively recently, in an attempt to make a distinction between these units, the unit of force was sometimes called the pound-force or pound-weight.

As a simple example, imagine a bag filled with marbles. The mass of these marbles depends only upon the type of glass used in their manufacture and it will have a fixed value. We could measure their mass by placing the bag in one pan of a balance and placing a known mass (or weight as we incorrectly call it) in the other pan so that the two pans exactly balance. Wherever we carried out this measurement on the earth's surface we should get the same answer (see fig. 1.3a).

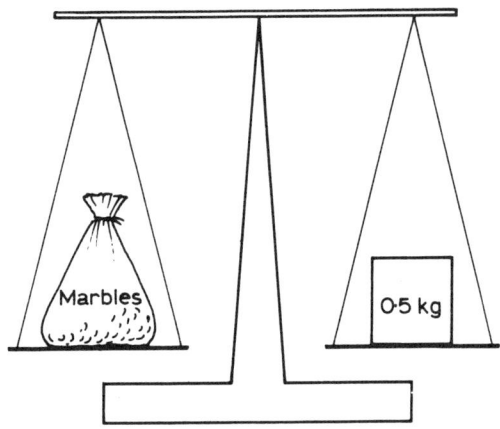

Fig. 1.3a The mass of an object is constant.

The weight of the marbles, however, will vary at different points on the surface of the earth because it is dependent upon the force of gravity and this varies slightly, having a maximum value at the poles and a minimum value at the equator. We could obtain the weight of these marbles by hanging them from a spring balance and we would then find that the indication of their weight shown on the balance was slightly greater at the poles than at the equator. However, on the moon's surface the indication of their weight would be considerably less because the force of gravity there is only about one-sixth of that on the surface of the earth (see fig. 1.3b). The mass of the marbles is constant, the weight is not—it varies at different points on the earth's surface.

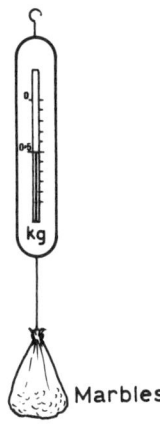

Fig. 1.3b The weight of an object varies at different points on the earth's surface.

In future apples will be bought by the kilogramme and not by the pound or even the pound-force. What is more important, however, is that we should talk about the mass of the apples and not their weight. Perhaps the term weight may in time disappear. There should then be no confusion.

Derived SI Units

Having discussed some of the basic units, we can now build up various derived units.

Velocity

Velocity measures the rate of change of distance, i.e. the distance travelled divided by the time taken to travel that distance. Since distance is measured in metres and time in seconds, the unit of velocity is the metre per second. However, this would not be a convenient unit for measuring the speed of a car, for instance, and the kilometre per hour will be used in such circumstances (30 miles per hour is approximately equal to 48 kilometres per hour or 13 metres per second).

Acceleration

Acceleration measures the rate of change of velocity, i.e. it equals the change in velocity divided by the time in which that change takes place. Since velocity is measured in metres per second and time in seconds, the unit of acceleration is the metre per second per second (or 'metre per second squared'). This is often abbreviated to m/s^2.

Force

Force may loosely be described as a push or pull. Isaac Newton defined a force as 'that which tends to change the state of rest or uniform motion of a body'. If we apply a force to a stationary object, the force will cause the object to accelerate (assuming there are no other factors, such as friction, affecting the situation). This could be demonstrated very simply.

If we dropped a stone from the top of a tall building and stationed observers on each floor of the building, recording the time at which the stone passed them, we should find that the stone travelled approximately 9·8 metres further in each succeeding second. Thus in the first second it would travel approximately 9·8 metres, in the second second 19·6 metres, in the third second 29·4 metres, and so on. The rate of acceleration of the stone is therefore approximately 9·8 m/s^2. Furthermore, we could show that this value remained the same whatever size of stone we used. Because the stone falls due to the force of gravity acting upon it, the value of approximately 9·8 m/s^2 is referred to as the acceleration due to gravity. As described, the experiment would not give a very accurate result because the friction between the stone and the air through which it was falling would reduce the rate at which the stone accelerated. An accurate value for the acceleration due to gravity would only be obtained if the experiment were carried out in a vacuum.

As Newton was responsible for the world-famous experiments on the effects of the force of gravity, it is very appropriate that the unit of force in SI units should bear his name. The unit of force therefore no longer has the same name as the unit of mass.

$$\text{Force} = \text{mass} \times \text{acceleration}$$

where force is in newtons, mass is in kilogrammes and acceleration is in metres per second per second.

We will now calculate the force required to support a bucket of water having a total mass of 20 kilogrammes.

$$\text{Force} = \text{mass} \times \text{acceleration}$$
$$= 20 \times 9 \cdot 81 = 196 \cdot 2 \text{ newtons}$$

Note that the figure we have used here for acceleration is 9·81 m/s², because in supporting the bucket of water we must apply an upward force exactly overcoming the force of gravity. As stated previously, the acceleration due to gravity would be slightly more at the poles (approximately 9·83 m/s²) and slightly less at the equator (approximately 9·78 m/s²). We shall always use the value of 9·81 m/s² in this book.

Energy

When a force is applied to an object, causing it to move, work is done and we calculate the work done from the relationship:

work done = force × distance

where work done is in joules, force is in newtons and distance is in metres.

From this relationship we might deduce that the unit of work or energy would be the newton metre. Although this unit has been used in the past, it has been decided that the joule will be the only unit of energy in SI units. It will therefore replace the various units of energy used for different applications in the past, including the British Thermal Unit, the calorie, the therm and the foot-pound force. The unit of electrical energy—the kilowatt hour, equivalent to $3·6 \times 10^6$ joules— will continue to be used.

Force must be expressed in newtons. The energy required to lift the bucket of water referred to above from the bottom of a well 10 metres deep is therefore:

$$\text{work done} = \text{force} \times \text{distance}$$
$$= 196·2 \times 10$$
$$= 1962 \text{ joules.}$$

Power

Power is defined as the rate of doing work and the unit of power is the watt.

$$\text{Power} = \frac{\text{work done}}{\text{time}}$$

where power is in watts, work done is in joules, and time is in seconds, *or* power is in kilowatts, work done is in kilowatt hours, and time is in hours.

Continuing our earlier example, we will calculate the power required to lift the bucket of water from the bottom of the well in 25 seconds.

THE EAW ELECTRICAL HANDBOOK

$$\text{Power} = \frac{\text{work done}}{\text{time}} = \frac{1962}{25} = 78.48 \text{ watts}.$$

However, if the time taken to lift the bucket was 2 minutes, we must divide by 120, because the work done must be stated in joules and the time in seconds. The answer would then be:

$$\text{Power} = \frac{1962}{120} = 16.35 \text{ watts}.$$

Great care must be taken not to confuse the units of work and power.

Electrical units

All the mechanical units used in this book have now been considered. To define the units used to measure electrical quantities, a fourth basic unit is required which is essentially electrical. As stated earlier, the unit which has been chosen in SI units is the unit of current, the ampere. All the other electrical units may then be defined using the ampere together with some of the units we have discussed, some of these definitions being given in Appendix 2.

Volume (or capacity)

The derived unit of volume will be the cubic metre. When dealing with liquids, however, the litre (equivalent to a cubic decimetre or one-thousandth of a cubic metre) will be used, and this unit will replace the gallon, pint, etc. One pint is approximately equal to 3/5 litre.

Temperature

The unit of absolute temperature—the kelvin—is one of the six basic SI units. However, since the degree Celsius (°C—formerly known as the degree Centigrade) is identical to the kelvin, the degree Celsius will be the customary unit of temperature. The difference between the Celsius and Kelvin scales is only that they have their zeros at different temperatures. Thus 0° Celsius is equivalent to 273 kelvin. 0 kelvin is equivalent to −273° Celsius (see fig. 1.4).

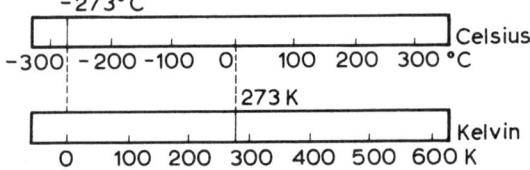

Fig. 1.4 Relationship between the Celsius and Kelvin scales of temperature.

Luminous intensity
This unit is discussed in the chapter on lighting.

Only a few of the SI units have been considered in this chapter. A complete list of SI units and notes on their use is given in the following BSI publications:
BS 3763: 1970—The International System (SI) Units,
PD 5686: 1969—The Use of SI Units,
and also, Changing to the Metric System (HMSO, 1969).

Chapter 1—Questions

1 What units do the following abbreviations represent?
  (i) MW   (ii) mm   (iii) ns   (iv) km/h   (v) cm^3
  (vi) l   (vii) kN   (viii) Mcd   (ix) m/s^2 (x) °C
  (xi) GJ   (xii) m^2

2 Using the list of prefixes given in Appendix 3, carry out each of the following conversions:
  (i) 1723 cm to metres   (ii) 5835 W to kilowatts
  (iii) 25 ms to seconds   (iv) 6 MJ to kilojoules
  (v) 3 m^3 to cubic centimetres   (vi) 18 ns to microseconds
  (vii) 320 mA to amperes   (viii) 158·2 cg to decagrammes
  (ix) 3 dam to decimetres   (x) 250 pF to microfarads
  (xi) 4·73 kN to newtons   (xii) 16 l to millilitres.

3 Using the conversion tables given in Appendix 4, convert the following to SI units.
  (i) 75 mph   (ii) 5 lb 7 oz (mass)
  (iii) 8 yd 2 ft   (iv) 3 lb 6 oz (force)
  (v) 3 h 17 min   (vi) 6 sq ft 70 sq in
  (vii) 14·45 Btu   (viii) 3·5 hp
  (ix) 10 cu ft 1000 cu in   (x) 5 gal 2 pt
  (xi) 200 cal   (xii) 32·18 ft/s^2

4 Calculate the force exerted by gravity acting on a mass of 4 lb, expressing your answer in SI units.

5 Calculate, in SI units, the work done if 20 gallons of water are pumped out of a hole 6 feet deep. Take the mass of 1 litre of water as 1 kilogramme.

6 Discuss the terms 'basic' and 'derived' units. Describe briefly the systems of units used in this country before the introduction of SI units.

7 Explain the difference between the mass and weight of an object.

2 The Electric Current

The introduction of electrons and protons into a book of this nature may seem to be an unnecessary complication. However, it is necessary to know something of the basic principles of electrical engineering before the operation of domestic appliances can be understood.

Molecules and Atoms

The effects of electricity had been observed from early times, but it was not until Rutherford carried out his now world-famous research some sixty years ago that the present-day theory of the structure of the atom was first formulated. This theory suggests that everything—liquids, solids and gases—is made up of a very large number of molecules. These molecules in turn consist of one or more particles called atoms. When the molecules of a substance consist of only one type of atom, the substance is called an element. Examples of elements include copper, aluminium and iron. If the molecules consist of two or more different types of atoms, the substance is called a compound. Examples of compounds include water, paper and plastics. There are about one hundred elements and an almost infinite number of compounds.

Electrons and Protons

Atoms are extremely small and their effective diameter is of the order of one ten-thousand-millionth part of a metre. However, the atom is an extremely complex particle and is often described as a miniature solar system. The centre of this system is called the nucleus and it consists mainly of one or more similar particles, each carrying an equal electric charge. These particles, called protons, are very tightly bound together. Revolving around this nucleus, just as the earth and the other planets revolve around the sun, are a number of particles called electrons. The electrons also carry an electric charge, the magnitude of which is exactly equal to that of the charge on the proton. However, the charges act in different ways so that, if we bring together an equal number of protons and electrons, the resultant group of particles behaves as if it has no electrical charge. To distinguish between the charges on protons and electrons, we call the charge on a proton a positive charge and the charge on an electron a negative charge. It has been shown that if similar charges are brought together they repel each other, whereas if two unlike charges are brought together they attract each other.

O Proton

• Electron

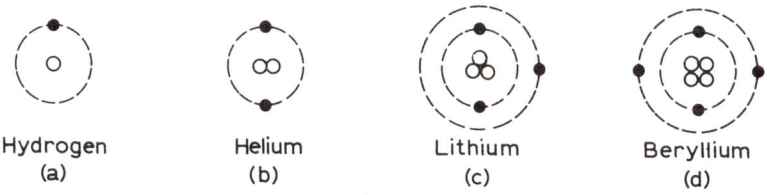

Hydrogen (a)　　Helium (b)　　Lithium (c)　　Beryllium (d)

Fig. 2.1 Simplified diagrams showing the arrangement of the hydrogen, helium, lithium and beryllium atoms.

The electrons are arranged in their orbits (or shells) in a definite pattern. Thus the simplest atom—that of hydrogen—consists of one proton in the nucleus with one electron revolving around it (fig. 2.1a). Helium has two protons in the nucleus and two electrons in orbit (fig. 2.1b). Lithium has three protons in the nucleus and three electrons in orbit (fig. 2.1c). Two of these electrons are positioned closer to the nucleus than the third. Beryllium has four electrons, two in an inner shell and two in an outer shell (fig. 2.1d). The maximum number of electrons in any shell is fixed, i.e. the inner shell cannot contain more than two electrons, the next shell not more than eight electrons, the next not more than eighteen, and so on.

Free electrons

Figure 2.2 is a simplified diagram of the copper atom. It will be seen that there are twenty-nine protons and twenty-nine electrons and that the outer shell contains only one electron. This shell is incomplete (it could contain up to thirty-two electrons) and the electron is very 'loosely' bound to its nucleus. It is referred to as a 'free' or 'conduction'

THE EAW ELECTRICAL HANDBOOK

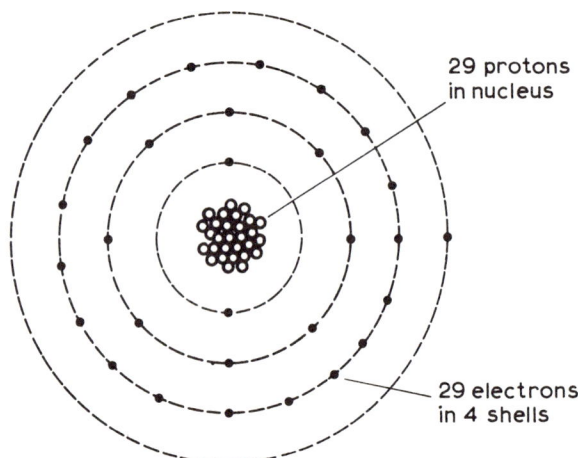

Fig. 2.2 Simplified diagram of the copper atom. Note that it contains 29 protons and 29 electrons. The 29 electrons are arranged in 4 shells containing 2, 8, 18 and 1 electrons respectively.

electron and it may leave its parent atom and attach itself to an adjoining atom. The original atom then becomes positively charged since it possesses twenty-nine protons but only twenty-eight electrons whilst the atom which has accepted the free electron is negatively charged. The original atom then attracts a free electron from another neighbouring atom. In a piece of copper there is, therefore, a random movement of electrons throughout the material (fig. 2.3). It should again be stressed that the atom is an extremely small particle and that the diagrams are therefore greatly enlarged. In a cubic centimetre of copper, for example, there are approximately 85 000 000 000 000 000 000 000 ($8 \cdot 5 \times 10^{22}$) atoms.

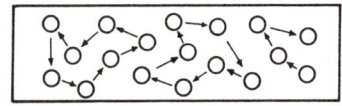

Fig. 2.3 In this diagram, representing a small piece of copper, the circles represent atoms, and the arrows represent the movement of free electrons. It will be seen that this movement is completely random.

In an electric cell or battery (a battery consists of two or more cells connected together) the chemical action which occurs causes electrons to accumulate at the negative terminal of the battery, leaving the positive terminal with a shortage of electrons. If a battery is joined to the ends of a piece of copper, the electrons will move in the same general direction through the copper. Figure 2.4 illustrates this. The movement of electrons is from right to left, i.e. the electrons are being repelled from the negative terminal of the battery (shown by a short thick line on the diagram) where there is an excess of electrons and attracted to the positive terminal (shown by a longer thin line) where there is a shortage of electrons. This movement of electrons constitutes an electric current.

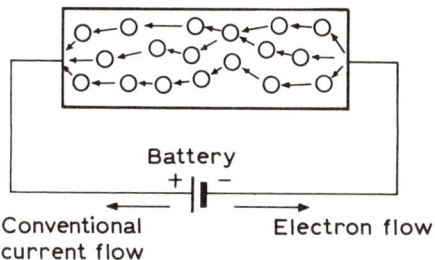

Fig. 2.4 When a battery is joined to the piece of copper shown in fig. 2.3, the free electrons all move through the copper in the same direction. We say, however, that current is flowing in the opposite direction.

Unfortunately the effects of an electric current had been studied long before the existence of the electron was known. It was suggested in those early days that current flowed from the positive terminal of the battery, around the circuit and back to the negative terminal of the battery. Although the discovery of the electron showed this to be an incorrect assumption, it was decided that the direction of current flow as originally suggested should not be altered. For this reason it is often called the 'conventional' direction of current flow.

The individual electrons move around the circuit quite slowly, but the effect of their movement is transferred to all parts of the circuit almost instantaneously. Thus, when we switch on a light, the light comes on as soon as the switch moves to the 'on' position. As an analogy, imagine we have a long row of billiard balls spaced about a quarter of an inch apart. If we roll up another ball so that it hits the first ball in the row, none of the balls will travel very far, but the effect of the impact on the first ball in the row is very quickly transferred down the row (see fig. 2.5).

When the movement of electrons takes place in only one direction, we call the current a direct current (d.c.). With alternating current (a.c.) the movement of electrons through the circuit reverses at frequent intervals, as we shall discuss later.

Fig. 2.5 If the ball on the left hits the row of balls, no ball moves far, but the effect is very quickly transferred to the end of the row.

Conductors and Insulators

It is found that most materials having only one or two electrons in their outer electron shells allow an electric current to flow through them and are therefore referred to as good conductors. On the other hand, if all the electrons are tightly bound to the nucleus (i.e. the outer shells are complete or nearly complete) an electric current will not flow through the substance and it is then termed an insulator. If a generator producing a high voltage were applied to an insulator, it is possible that the outer electrons, although tightly bound to their nucleus, could be dragged away from their atoms so that the insulator becomes a conductor. It is said to have 'broken down' and the effect is accompanied by a chemical change in the substance. It is necessary in all electrical circuits to ensure that the voltage across the insulation does not become so great that breakdown could occur.

Examples of good conductors and insulators are given below. It should be noted that most metals are good conductors.

Conductors	*Insulators*
silver	dry air
copper	paraffin wax
gold	porcelain
aluminium	glass
tungsten	dry paper
brass	rubber

The Simple Electric Circuit

It has been shown that, before an electric current will flow, there must be a complete circuit of conducting materials, providing a supply of free electrons, and a source of electrical energy, such as a battery, to force the electrons around the circuit. It is also necessary to ensure that the current flows through each part of the circuit and does not take a shorter path, or 'short circuit', as it is called. The conductors are therefore covered with a suitable insulating material—the type of insulation used being dependent upon the voltage, as we have already seen. If a break is made in any part of the circuit, the break is referred

ELECTRIC CURRENT

to as an open circuit. It could be due to a broken wire, a loose connection or some other cause.

Figure 2.6 illustrates a simple circuit consisting of a battery, a switch and a lamp. It shows the way we would represent a torch on an electrical circuit diagram. Notice that in circuit diagrams symbols are used to represent the different parts of the circuit, and the insulation around conductors is not shown. It would take too long to represent each item pictorially.

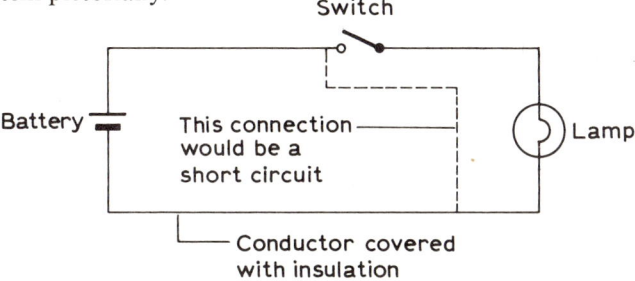

Fig. 2.6 A simple electrical circuit.

Ammeters and Voltmeters

The current flowing through a circuit may be measured by an instrument called an ammeter. The magnitude of the current is determined by the rate at which the electrons are passing around the circuit and the ammeter must therefore be connected so that all the electrons moving around the circuit pass through it, i.e. the circuit must first be 'broken' so that the ammeter may be inserted. However, it may be placed at any point in the circuit, e.g. next to the positive terminal of the battery or next to the negative terminal of the battery. The current is measured in amperes—the ampere being one of the six basic SI units.

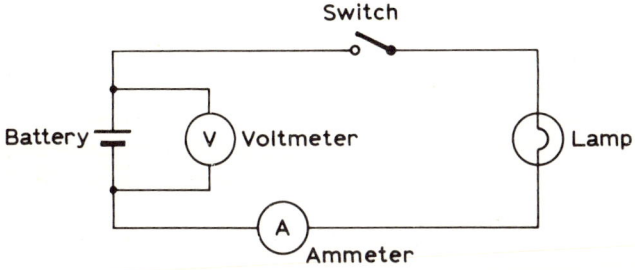

Fig. 2.7 Method of measuring voltage (by a voltmeter) and current (by an ammeter).

15

The 'force', known as the electro-motive force (e.m.f.), required to cause the free electrons to move around the circuit may be measured by another instrument called a voltmeter and, since this e.m.f. is applied between two points in a circuit, the voltmeter must be connected between these points. The e.m.f. is measured in volts (abbreviation V) as also is the potential difference (p.d.) or voltage across any other part of the circuit.

Figure 2.7 illustrates how a voltmeter and an ammeter should be connected into a circuit.

Effects of an Electric Current

When a current flows through a wire, we cannot usually see any change take place either in the wire or in the space around the wire: however, changes do occur.

Heating effect

When electrons move through the wire, a large number of collisions take place and these collisions cause heat to be produced. The temperature of the wire will increase, although normally the increase will be so slight that we cannot easily detect it. The element of an electric fire, however, is specially designed so that it will become very hot when current flows through it. On the other hand, the connecting wire between the socket outlet and an appliance must not become hot or else the heat produced would cause deterioration of the insulation, leading to eventual breakdown. It would also mean that power was being wasted in this part of the circuit.

The size of the conductor must always be chosen so that it will safely carry the required current without becoming excessively hot. As was stated earlier, the insulation must be carefully chosen so that it will withstand the voltage without breaking down.

Magnetic effect

When the switch is pressed in the low-voltage circuit, current flows the wire, just as a magnetic field exists in the space around a magnet. There are very many examples where this magnetic effect is used in electrical appliances, perhaps the most common being the electric motor.

A relay is a simple example. This is a device having many applications, one of which is for controlling a high-voltage circuit from a low-voltage supply. The principle is shown in the simplified diagram (fig. 2.8).

ELECTRIC CURRENT

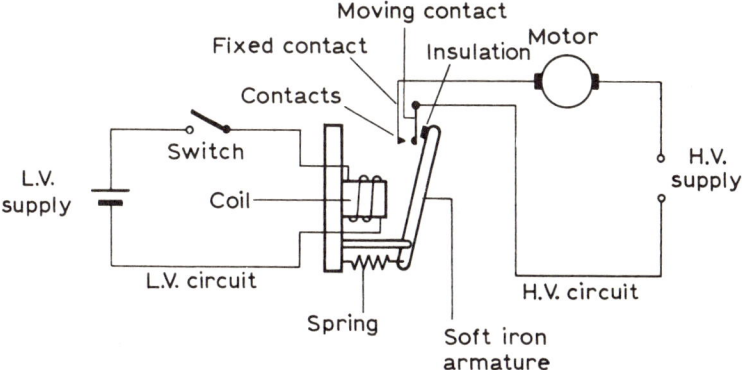

Fig. 2.8 Simplified diagram showing how a relay may be used. Although the motor is connected to a high-voltage supply, it may be safely switched on and off using a low-voltage supply.

When the switch is pressed in the low-voltage circuit, current flows through the coil, causing the piece of iron on which it is wound to become magnetised. It will then attract the soft iron armature, causing the contacts to close and thus connecting the motor to the high-voltage supply.

Chemical effect
When a current flows through certain liquids, changes occur in these liquids and also in any metals placed in the liquids and forming part of the circuit. Two common examples of this chemical effect are electroplating and battery charging.

Chapter 2—Questions

1 What is meant by (i) a conductor, and (ii) an insulator of electricity? Name four good conductors and four good insulators. Describe in simple terms what we understand to happen within a copper wire when an electric current flows through it.
2 Draw a simple electric circuit and label each part of the diagram. What instruments are used to measure current and voltage? Indicate on your diagram how these instruments would be connected. What is meant by a short circuit and an open circuit?
3 Describe the three effects of an electric current, and give one example of the way in which each of these effects is made use of in the operation of domestic electrical appliances.
4 Why do some conductors require a thicker layer of insulation around them than others? Why do some conductors have a much larger diameter than others?

3 Direct-Current Circuits

Ohm's Law

We have seen that it is necessary to apply a voltage to a circuit before a current will flow in that circuit. If the voltage applied to a given circuit is increased, we may reasonably assume that the rate at which electrons will move through the circuit, i.e. the current, will increase. In 1826 Georg Ohm, a Bavarian scientist, showed that for most conductors, providing their temperature remains constant, the voltage applied to the conductor is proportional to the current flowing through it, e.g. if we double the voltage applied, the current flowing will also double; if we halve the voltage applied, the current will also be half its original value.

This relationship is referred to as Ohm's Law and may be stated as

$$\frac{\text{voltage}}{\text{current}} = \text{constant}.$$

This constant is called the resistance of the circuit and it is measured in ohms (the abbreviation Ω is often used). The relationship may be stated in symbols, using V for voltage, I for current and R for resistance.

$$\frac{V}{I} = R$$

where V is in volts, I is in amperes, and R is in ohms.

Alternatively we may write

$$V = IR$$

or

$$I = \frac{V}{R}.$$

As an aid to remembering these relationships, the symbols may be inserted in a triangle, as shown in fig. 3.1. If then, for example, it is

DIRECT-CURRENT CIRCUITS

required to find the current, *I*, we cover *I* and we are left with *V/R*. Similarly, to find the voltage, *V*, we cover *V* and we are left with *IR*.

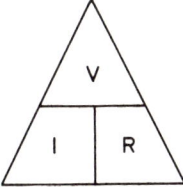

Fig. 3.1 Relationships between voltage, current and resistance in a d.c. circuit.

Example 1
Calculate the current taken by an electric fire having a resistance of 40 ohms if it is connected to a 200 volt supply.

From the Ohm's law relationship

$$I = \frac{V}{R}$$

$$\therefore I = \frac{200}{40} = 5 \text{ amperes.}$$

Example 2
Calculate the resistance of a circuit if a current of 2 amperes flows through the circuit when a voltage of 240 volts is applied.

Since
$$R = \frac{V}{I},$$

$$R = \frac{240}{2} = 120 \text{ ohms.}$$

Series Circuits

When we want to represent on a circuit diagram the resistance of part of a circuit (e.g. the element of a cooker), we usually do so by means of a zig-zag line, although a rectangle is sometimes used. Figure 3.2 represents some cooker elements joined end to end so that the same current flows through each of them.

We say that the elements are joined in series. The total resistance of a number of resistors joined in series is the sum of their resistances. Thus, in fig. 3.2 the total resistance of the two elements is $60+40 = 100$ ohms. We may now calculate the current flowing in the circuit.

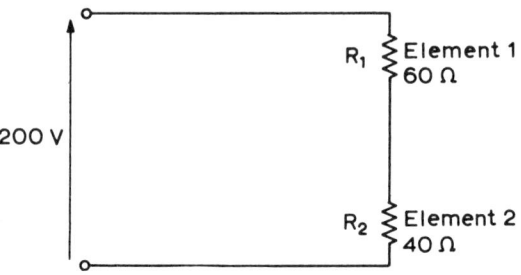

Fig. 3.2 A series circuit—the current through each part of the circuit is the same.

Since
$$I = \frac{V}{R},$$

$$I = \frac{200}{100} = 2 \text{ amperes.}$$

In general, for a series circuit,

$$R_T = R_1 + R_2 + R_3 + \ldots + R_n$$

where R_T = total resistance, and R_1, R_2, R_3 ... R_n = resistance of resistors 1, 2, 3, ... n.

We may now also calculate the voltage across each of the elements in fig. 3.2.

Since $V = IR$, the voltage across the first element will equal the current through that element times its resistance, or, in symbols,

$$V_1 = I_1 R_1$$
$$\therefore V_1 = 2 \times 60 = 120 \text{ volts.}$$

Similarly for the second element

$$V_2 = I_2 R_2$$
$$\therefore V_2 = 2 \times 40 = 80 \text{ volts.}$$

Note that the sum of the two voltages (120V + 80V) equals the applied voltage (200V).

DIRECT-CURRENT CIRCUITS

Parallel Circuits

If we now reconnect the two elements so that the voltage across each element is the same, the circuit diagram will be as shown in fig. 3.3. This is called a parallel circuit and we find the total resistance in this case from the relationship

$$\frac{1}{R_T} = \frac{1}{R_1} + \frac{1}{R_2}$$

$$\therefore \frac{1}{R_T} = \frac{1}{40} + \frac{1}{60} = \frac{3+2}{120}$$

$$\therefore R_T = \frac{120}{5} = 24 \text{ ohms.}$$

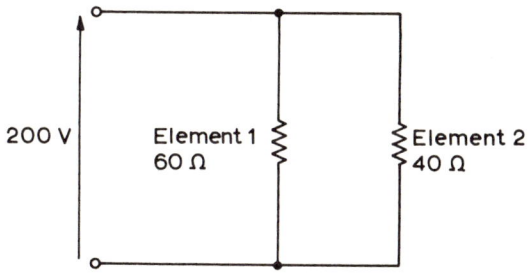

Fig. 3.3 A parallel circuit—the voltage across each branch of the circuit is the same.

Thus, if the elements were connected to a 200 volt supply, the total current taken from the supply would be

$$I_T = \frac{V_T}{R_T} = \frac{200}{24} = 8\cdot33 \text{ amperes.}$$

The current through the 60 ohm element

$$I_1 = \frac{V_1}{R_1} = \frac{200}{60} = 3\cdot33 \text{ amperes}$$

and the current through the 40 ohm element

$$I_2 = \frac{V_2}{R_2} = \frac{200}{40} = 5 \text{ amperes.}$$

Note that the sum of the separate currents ($3\cdot33$A + 5A) equals the total current ($8\cdot33$A).

In general, for a number of circuits in parallel

$$\frac{1}{R_T} = \frac{1}{R_1} + \frac{1}{R_2} + \frac{1}{R_3} + \ldots + \frac{1}{R_n}$$

where R_T = total resistance, and $R_1, R_2, R_3 \ldots R_n$ = resistances of circuits 1, 2, 3, ... n.

Electrical appliances are usually connected in parallel so that any one appliance may be disconnected without affecting the others (fig. 3.4a). On the other hand, the lights on a Christmas tree are usually connected in series (fig. 3.4b). In this case, if one lamp fails, all the other lamps go out because there is no longer a complete circuit: an open circuit has occurred.

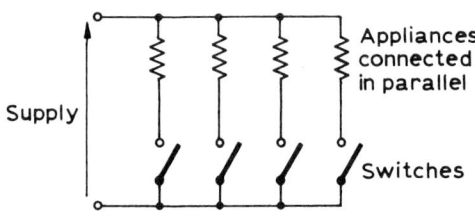

Fig. 3.4a Method of connecting appliances to the electricity supply.

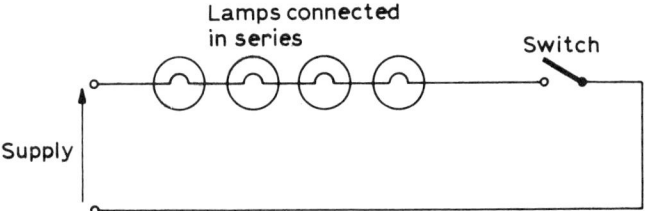

Fig. 3.4b Lamps on a Christmas tree are usually connected in series.

Resistivity

The resistance of a conductor depends upon several factors. We have just seen that, if we have two equal resistances connected in series, their total resistance will be twice their separate resistances. If we consider these two resistances as representing identical lengths of wire, then by connecting them in series we are effectively doubling the length of one of them. Thus, if we double the length of a piece of wire we double its resistance. In other words, resistance is proportional to length, or, in symbols,

$$R \propto l \text{ (see fig. 3.5)}.$$

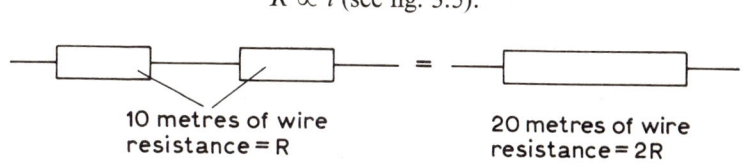

10 metres of wire
resistance = R

20 metres of wire
resistance = 2R

Fig. 3.5 The resistance of a conductor is proportional to its length.

We have also just seen that two identical wires connected in parallel have a total resistance equal to half their separate resistances. Therefore, if we double the cross-sectional area of a piece of wire (which effectively is what we are doing when we join two identical wires in parallel), we halve its resistance. Thus resistance is inversely proportional to cross-sectional area, a.

$$R \propto \frac{l}{a} \text{ (see fig. 3.6)}.$$

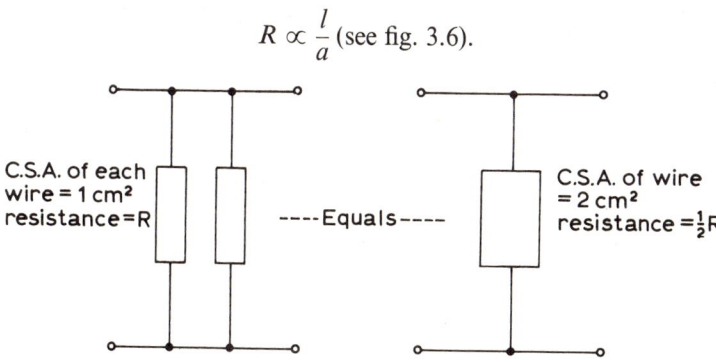

C.S.A. of each wire = 1 cm²
resistance = R

----Equals----

C.S.A. of wire = 2 cm²
resistance = ½R

Fig. 3.6 The resistance of a conductor is inversely proportional to its cross-sectional area (CSA).

Since some materials conduct electricity more easily than others, i.e. they have more free electrons available than other materials, the resistance of a conductor must depend upon a property of the material from which it is made. This property is referred to as the resistivity of the material and it is measured in ohm metres. The symbol ρ is used to represent resistivity. We can now calculate the resistance of any conductor from the relationship

$$R = \frac{\rho l}{a}$$

where ρ = resistivity in ohm metres, l = length in metres, and a = cross-sectional area in square metres.

Example
What is the resistance of a length of copper wire 1 km long having a diameter of 2 mm if the resistivity of copper is $17 \cdot 3 \times 10^{-9}$ ohm metres.

The first thing to note with this type of problem is that our units must be consistent.

If ρ is in ohm metres, l must be in metres, and a in square metres, *or*, if ρ is in ohm centimetres, l must be in centimetres, and a in square centimetres.

$$\text{Cross-sectional area} = \frac{\pi d^2}{4} = \frac{\pi(2 \times 10^{-3})^2}{4} = 3 \cdot 14 \times 10^{-6} \text{ m}^2.$$

$$\therefore R = \frac{17 \cdot 3}{10^9} \times \frac{10^3}{3 \cdot 14 \times 10^{-6}} = 5 \cdot 51 \ \Omega.$$

In addition to resistivity, length and cross-sectional area, the resistance of a conductor is dependent upon its temperature: with the majority of conductors the resistance increases as the temperature increases. The rise in temperature of the conductors with which we are concerned is quite small in most cases, so the change in resistance may be neglected. In our calculations we shall assume the temperature remains constant.

Electrical Energy

We have already noted that the joule is the unit of energy in SI units and that it is defined as the work done when a force of 1 newton moves its point of application through a distance of 1 metre. It was also stated that the joule will be used for all forms of energy, and it therefore follows that it is the basic unit of electrical energy. Using electrical quantities, energy may be calculated from the following relationship.

$$\text{Energy} = \text{voltage} \times \text{current} \times \text{time}$$

where energy is in joules, voltage is in volts, current is in amperes, and time is in seconds.

or
$$\text{energy} = \text{power} \times \text{time}$$

where energy is in kilowatt hours, power is in kilowatts, and time is in hours.

DIRECT-CURRENT CIRCUITS

In symbols,
$$W = V \times I \times t.$$

However, the joule is too small a unit to measure the amount of electrical energy used by electricity consumers, and Electricity Boards will therefore continue to use the kilowatt hour (kW h) when charging for electricity.

1 kW h is the amount of electrical energy used by a 1 kW electric fire in 1 hour, or a $\frac{1}{2}$ kW electric fire in 2 hours, or a 2 kW electric fire in $\frac{1}{2}$ hour.

$$1 \text{ kilowatt hour} = 3 \cdot 6 \times 10^6 \text{ joules}$$

since 1 kilowatt equals 1000 watts and 1 hour equals 3600 seconds. One kilowatt hour is conventionally called a 'unit' of electricity, this being a contraction of the earlier term 'Board of Trade Unit'.

Electrical Power

Since power is defined as the rate of doing work, and the basic unit of power is the watt, then

$$\text{Power} = \frac{\text{energy}}{\text{time}}$$

$$\therefore \text{power} = \frac{\text{voltage} \times \text{current} \times \text{time}}{\text{time}},$$

or

power = voltage × current

where power is in watts, voltage is in volts, and current is in amperes.

In symbols,
$$P = V \times I.$$

Note that a triangle may be used as an aid to remembering power relationships, as was done previously with the Ohm's Law relationship: see fig. 3.7.

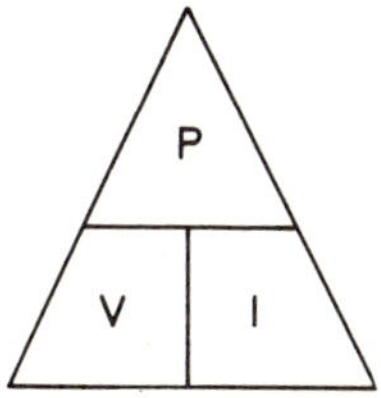

Fig. 3.7 Relationship between power, voltage and current in d.c. circuits.

To obtain any quantity in terms of the other two, cover up the symbol representing that quantity, and the other two appear in the correct relationship.

e.g. $$V = \frac{P}{I}$$

or $$I = \frac{P}{V}.$$

We have previously seen that voltage and current are related to resistance by Ohm's Law, so we may substitute for both voltage and current in the power expression above and obtain the following expressions.

Since $P = V \times I$ and $V = I \times R$,
$$P = (I \times R) \times I = I^2 R.$$

Or, since $P = V \times I$ and $I = \frac{V}{R}$,
$$P = V \times \frac{V}{R} = \frac{V^2}{R}.$$

We may therefore calculate power from any one of these expressions:
$$P = V \times I$$
$$P = I^2 \times R$$
$$P = \frac{V^2}{R}$$

where P is in watts, V is in volts, I is in amperes, and R is in ohms.

Example
What is the rating (i.e. power consumption) of an electric fire which when connected to a 240 volt supply takes a current of 5 amperes?
$$P = V \times I$$
$$= 240 \times 5 = 1200 \text{ watts}$$
$$= 1 \cdot 2 \text{ kW}.$$

Example
If the above fire is switched on for 30 minutes, calculate the energy used.
$$W = V \times I \times t$$

$$= 240 \times 5 \times (30 \times 60)$$
$$= 2\,160\,000 \text{ joules} = 2 \cdot 16 \text{ MJ}$$

As has already been stated, the practical unit of electrical energy is the kilowatt hour. In practical units, then,

$$W = \frac{V \times I}{1000} \times t$$

where V is in volts, I is in amperes, t is in hours, and W is in kW h.

$$\therefore W = \frac{240 \times 5}{1000} \times \frac{30}{60}$$
$$= 0 \cdot 6 \text{ kW h.}$$

Cost of Using Electrical Appliances

The electricity meters in our homes record the number of kilowatt hours (or units of electricity) we have used. To find the cost of using an appliance, we simply require to know the number of units it has used and we then multiply this by the cost per unit.

Example
Find the cost per hour of using a 2 kW fire if electricity costs 0·8p per unit.

Since
$$W = \frac{V \times I}{1000} \times t$$

and in this case the time is 1 hour,

$$\text{kW h used} = 2 \times 1 = 2 \text{ kW h}$$
$$\therefore \text{cost} = 2 \times 0 \cdot 8 = 1 \cdot 6\text{p.}$$

All the calculations we have considered above apply to d.c. circuits, but, as we shall see in the next chapter, in certain circumstances some of them may be applied to a.c. circuits without modification.

Chapter 3—Questions

1 Copy out the following table and insert the missing figures.

	Voltage (volts)	Current (amperes)	Resistance (ohms)	Power (watts)	Time (hours)	Energy (kWh)	Cost (at 0·8p per unit)
(i)	240		48			6	
(ii)	200	10			$\frac{1}{2}$		
(iii)		5	96				19·2p
(iv)	600			6000		2	
(v)	220			3300			39·6p
(vi)		2	50		$\frac{1}{4}$		

2 Name four factors which affect the resistance of a length of wire and state how each of them is related to resistance. The element of an electric fire takes a current of 4 amperes when connected to a 240 volt supply. If the element consists of 360 turns of wire, each having an average diameter of 20 mm, calculate the cross-sectional area of the wire used if it has a resistivity of 110 microhm centimetre at the working temperature.

3 A d.c. motor having an input of 1000 watts is to be fed from a point 100 metres away. If the voltage at the terminals of the motor is 200 volts, calculate the current taken by the motor. If the resistance of the supply cable is 0·005 ohm per metre per conductor, calculate the voltage at the supply point to which the motor is connected.

4 Differentiate between power and energy, and state the units in which these quantities are usually measured. Draw a circuit diagram to represent an electric fire connected to a 240 volt mains supply and indicate the connections of the instruments which would be used to measure the current taken by the fire and the voltage of the supply. If the element of the above fire has a resistance of 40 ohms, calculate the rating of the fire and the cost of using it for 3 hours if electricity costs 0·8p per unit.

5 Two conductors A and B having resistances of $R_A \Omega$ and $R_B \Omega$ respectively are connected in parallel to a 240 volt supply. If the current passing through conductor A is 2 amperes and through conductor B is 3 amperes, calculate the values of R_A and R_B. What would be the equivalent resistance of the two conductors?

6 Explain the difference between series and parallel connections. If three resistors each of 8 ohms resistance were connected in series across a 240 volt supply, how many units would be consumed in 10 hours? How many units would be used in the same time if the same resistors were connected in parallel across the same supply?

7 What quantities are associated with the following units?
(i) volt   (ii) ampere   (iii) kilowatt   (iv) kilowatt hour   (v) joule   (vi) ohm.

Calculate the current taken by a 3 kW appliance when connected to a 240 V supply. What current would be taken if this appliance were incorrectly connected to a 200 V supply, assuming its resistance remains constant?

8 Calculate the cost of using the following appliances for the times stated if electricity costs 0·8p per unit.
  (i) 150 W TV for 6 hours,
  (ii) 400 W vacuum cleaner for $1\frac{1}{2}$ hours,
  (iii) 1 kW fire for 4 hours,
  (iv) 3 kW washing machine for 40 minutes,
  (v) $\frac{1}{4}$ kW refrigerator for 6 hours ('switched-on' time).

4 Alternating-Current Circuits

In Chapter 2 we saw that when electrons move around the circuit in only one direction, we refer to the current as a direct current (d.c.). However, if they reverse their direction at frequent regular intervals, we then refer to the current as an alternating current (a.c.). We can illustrate the difference between direct and alternating current most clearly by drawing two graphs on which we plot the magnitude of the current in each case over a certain interval of time.

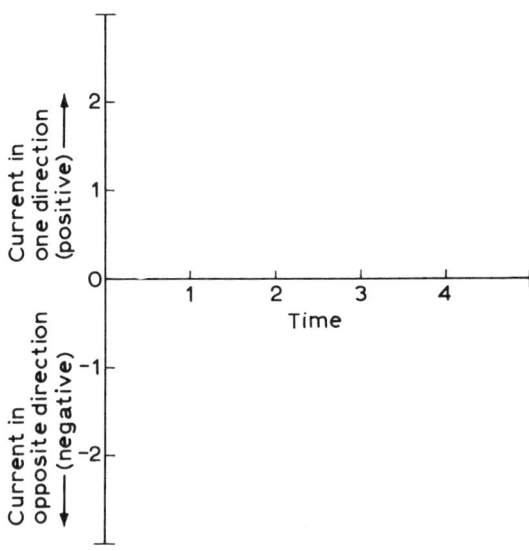

Fig. 4.1 Method of constructing a graph to represent varying values of current.

ALTERNATING-CURRENT CIRCUITS

To construct the graph representing the current we use two lines, or axes, drawn at right-angles to each other. Along the horizontal axis we represent the time for which the current is flowing. Along the vertical axis we represent the magnitude of the current. To distinguish between the two possible directions of current flow we represent current flowing in one direction above the time axis (often called the positive direction), and current flowing in the reverse direction below the time axis (often called the negative direction). The two axes must be marked with scales to indicate on the horizontal axis the length of time being considered in, say, minutes or seconds and along the vertical axis the magnitude of the current in amperes. This is shown in fig. 4.1.

Direct-current waveform

We will now represent a direct current on our current and time axes. Figures 4.2 and 4.3 represent a simple circuit consisting of a battery, a lamp and a switch.

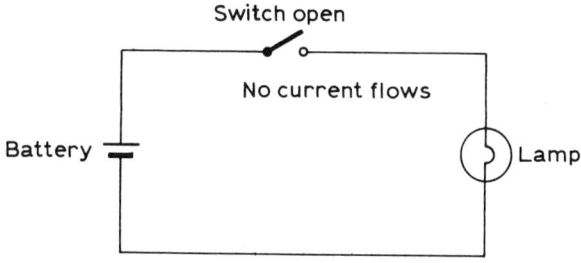

Fig. 4.2 No current flows when the switch is open.

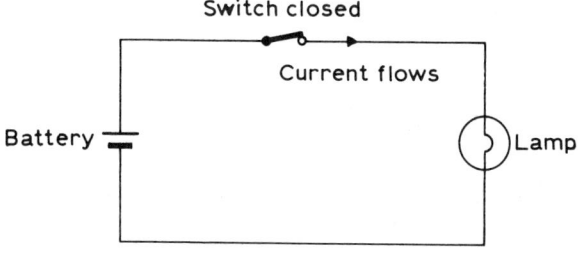

Fig. 4.3 Current flows when the switch is closed.

The current supplied by a battery is a direct current and therefore we shall not require the part of the current axis below the time axis since only one direction of current flow is involved.

31

In fig. 4.2 the switch is open so no current flows, and this is represented on our graph by a line drawn from A to B, see fig. 4.4, where it has been assumed that no current flows for one minute. In fig. 4.3 the switch has been closed so that current flows around the circuit. If this current flows for 3 minutes and if it has a magnitude of 0·3 ampere, it will be represented by the line from C to D. To indicate that the current suddenly increased from zero to 0·3 ampere, we join points B and C. Now, if the switch is again opened so that no current flows for the next minute, we show this by a line from E to F. The sudden fall of current from 0·3 ampere to zero is indicated by the line between D and E.

The graph showing how a current varies is often referred to as the waveform of the current.

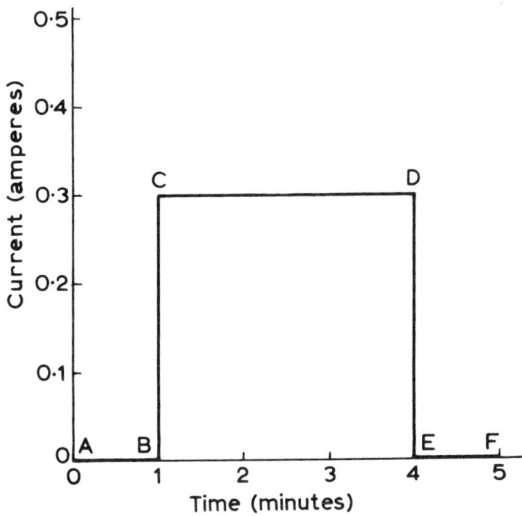

Fig. 4.4 Graph showing the variation of the current for the circuit shown in figs. 4.2 and 4.3 when the switch is opened and closed.

Alternating-current waveforms

In figs. 4.5 and 4.6, a double-pole reversing switch has replaced the single-pole switch shown in figs. 4.2 and 4.3. A reversing switch is used, as its name suggests, to reverse the flow of current through a circuit. It consists essentially of two moving parts (or poles) which open or close the circuit and which both move at the same time. In the single-pole switch there is only one moving part. In a triple-pole switch there are three moving parts.

ALTERNATING-CURRENT CIRCUITS

Although figs 4.5 and 4.6 may appear at first sight to be rather complicated, with a little care the reader should be able to trace the direction of current flow through the circuit. In these diagrams there is no electrical connection between two wires shown crossing thus:

At one time the fact that there is no connection was emphasised by drawing a 'bridge' on one of the wires thus:

but this is not standard practice nowadays. If there is an electrical connection between the wires they would be shown thus:

In fig. 4.5 the two poles of the reversing switch are connected between the centre and left-hand terminals. The arrowheads indicate the direction of current flow in each part of the circuit, and by starting from the positive terminal of the battery, it will be found that the direction of current flow through the lamp is 'downwards'.

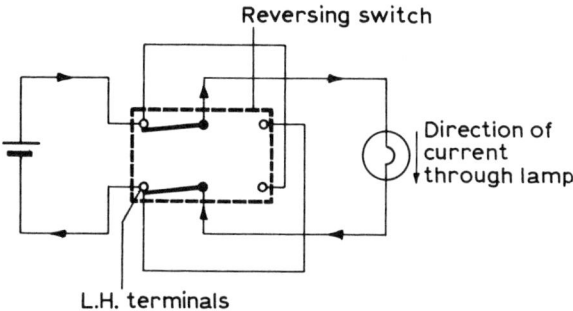

Fig. 4.5 How the direction of the current flowing through a circuit may be reversed by the use of a reversing or changeover switch.

In fig. 4.6 the two poles of the reversing switch have been moved so that they connect the centre and right-hand terminals. Arrowheads have again been used to represent the direction of current in each part of the circuit. It is seen that the direction of the current through the lamp is 'upwards', i.e. it has been reversed.

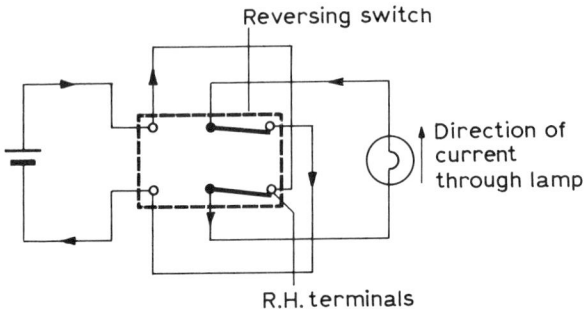

Fig. 4.6 How the direction of the current flowing through a circuit may be reversed by the use of a reversing or changeover switch.

We will now represent the waveform of this current. Since the direction of the current changes, the current axis must be drawn both above and below the time axis, as shown in fig. 4.1. In fig. 4.5 the direction of the current is downwards. We shall call this the positive direction and, if the current flows in this direction for one minute and its magnitude is 0·3 ampere, it will be represented by a line from A to B on the waveform diagram shown in fig. 4.7.

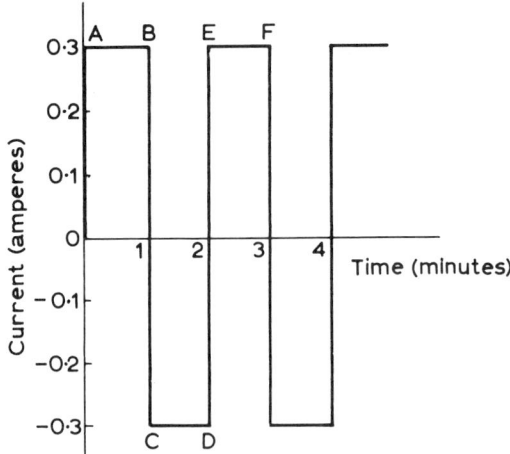

Fig. 4.7 Waveform diagram of alternating current.

ALTERNATING-CURRENT CIRCUITS

If the position of the reversing switch is now suddenly changed so that it connects the centre and right-hand terminals, as shown in fig. 4.6, the direction of the current through the lamp changes, but its magnitude will not change because the voltage applied has not changed. Therefore, if the switch remains in this position for one minute, the current will be represented by a line between C and D. If the reversing switch is returned to its original position for the next minute, the current will be represented by a line between E and F. Thus, by continually changing the position of the reversing switch we would obtain a waveform similar to that shown in fig. 4.7. We have used the reversing switch to convert the direct current from the battery to an alternating current through the lamp.

Now, if the movement of the reversing switch were performed very slowly, the lamp would 'go out' whilst the switch was being changed over. If, on the other hand, the movement of the reversing switch were performed very quickly indeed, the lamp would remain alight even though the direction of the current through it was continually changing.

The electricity supply we receive in our homes varies in much the same way as has been described above, although these variations are not produced by somebody rapidly moving a reversing switch! The waveform of the supply we receive is similar to the waveform shown in fig. 4.8.

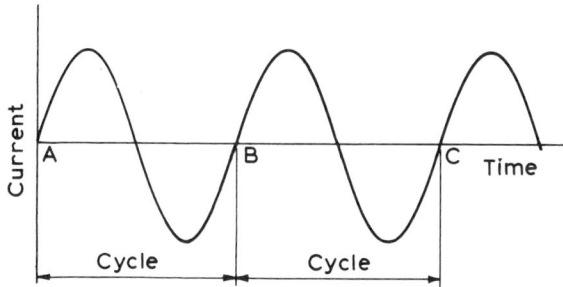

Fig. 4.8 Waveform of the alternating current supplied by the Electricity Boards. The voltage varies in the same way.

Both the current and voltage vary in the same way, so the waveform may represent either current or voltage. This waveform is known as a sine waveform and the supply is said to be sinusoidal. It will be seen that it is slightly different from the waveform we obtained from the reversing switch. The current does not suddenly change from flowing in one direction to flowing in the opposite direction. It gradually builds up to a maximum in one direction and then reduces gradually to zero: it then repeats this process in the opposite direction.

Frequency

The complete sequence from A to B (or from B to C) in fig. 4.8 is known as one cycle, and the number of complete cycles occurring in one second is called the frequency of the supply. The frequency is measured in hertz (abbreviation Hz), although the earlier term 'cycles/second' (c/s) is still sometimes used.

The frequency of the electricity supply in this country is 50 Hz. Because of this extremely rapid reversal of current, we cannot detect any flicker from our lamps. However, if the frequency were reduced to, say, 2 Hz, we would detect a very noticeable flicker. The frequency of the supply in the USA is 60 Hz.

Electrical apparatus is usually marked with the frequency of the supply to which it should be connected. Most appliances, with the important exception of electric clocks, will operate equally satisfactorily from either a 50 Hz or a 60 Hz supply.

Although only the square waveform (produced by a reversing switch) and the sinusoidal waveform have been described, many other types of waveform have applications in electrical engineering. A few of these waveforms are illustrated in fig. 4.9.

In all future references to alternating currents and voltages in this book, it may be assumed that the waveform is sinusoidal.

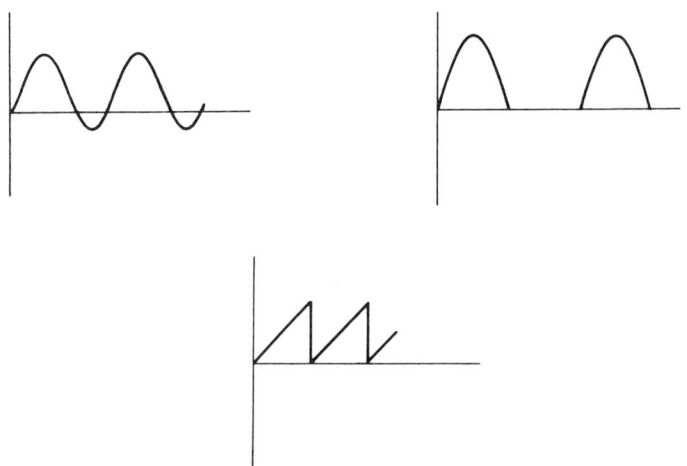

Fig. 4.9 Other waveforms used in electrical engineering.

ALTERNATING-CURRENT CIRCUITS

Maximum and R.M.S. Values of Alternating Currents and Voltages

Although in certain circumstances it is necessary to know the maximum value of an alternating voltage, this value only occurs for two brief instants in each cycle and it is not, therefore, normally used to define the voltage.

The value inferred when defining an alternating current (or voltage) is known as the *root mean square* (r.m.s.) value. The r.m.s. value of an alternating current is the value of that direct current which would generate exactly the same amount of heat as the alternating current in a given resistance. In other words, if an electric fire were connected to a d.c. supply and a direct current of 5 amperes flowed through the element, exactly the same amount of heat would be given off as would be in the case of the same fire being connected to an a.c. supply and an alternating current of 5 amperes flowing through the element.

For a sinusoidal current or voltage, the r.m.s. value is a little more than two-thirds of the maximum value.

More accurately (fig. 4.10):

r.m.s. value of sinusoidal current (or voltage)

$= 0{\cdot}707 \times$ maximum value. (Note: $0{\cdot}707 = 1/\sqrt{2}$.)

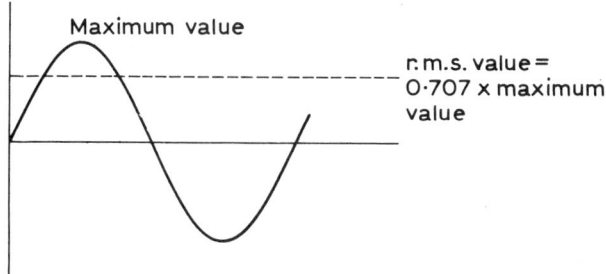

Fig. 4.10 Maximum and r.m.s. values of a sinusoidal waveform.

Since the r.m.s. value is inferred when we are speaking of currents and voltages, a 250 volt supply has a maximum value of $250/0{\cdot}707 = 354$ volts, and a 13 ampere current has a maximum value of $13/0{\cdot}707 = 18{\cdot}4$ amperes.

The importance of the maximum value occurs when the type of insulation is chosen. The insulation must safely withstand the maximum value of the voltage. Thus the insulation used in the cables for the standard 240 volt domestic supply must withstand a maximum voltage of 339 volts.

Phase Difference

If an alternating current flows through a circuit consisting of filament lamps, water heaters, cookers or electric fires, it can be shown that when the current is zero the voltage is also zero, and that when the current is a maximum the voltage is also a maximum. The current and voltage are said to be in phase and these conditions are represented on a waveform diagram in fig. 4.11.

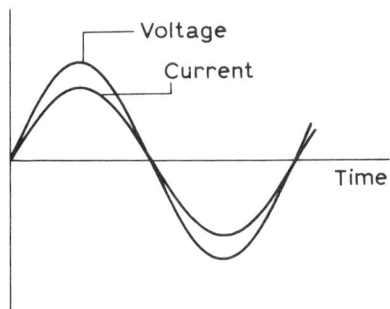

Fig. 4.11 Current and voltage in phase.

The current and voltage are always in phase in a.c. circuits containing only resistance, and this is the case for each of the four items mentioned in the previous paragraph.

For this special case of an a.c. circuit, the relationships we previously discussed still apply:

i.e. $\dfrac{\text{voltage}}{\text{current}} = \text{resistance}$ $\quad\left[\dfrac{V}{I} = R\right]$

and $\text{power} = (\text{current})^2 \times \text{resistance}$ $\quad [P = I^2 R]$

$\qquad\qquad\; = \text{voltage} \times \text{current}$ $\quad [P = V \times I]$

$\qquad\qquad\; = \dfrac{(\text{voltage})^2}{\text{resistance}}$ $\quad P = \dfrac{V^2}{R}$

Example
The rating of an electric fire is stated as 2 kW when used on a 240 volt supply. Calculate the current taken by this fire.

$$I = \frac{P}{V} = \frac{2000}{240} = 8 \cdot 33 \text{ amperes}$$

Impedance

If we took a long length of wire and wound it into a coil consisting of a very large number of turns and introduced this coil into an a.c. circuit, we should find that the voltage applied to the circuit divided by the current flowing did not equal the resistance of the wire. This is because a coil not only possesses resistance but also something else which limits the current which will flow when the coil is connected to an a.c. supply. It is found that the effect is even greater when the coil is wound over an iron core. This additional property of the coil is called inductive reactance and is represented by the symbol X_L. Generally speaking, we still find that

$$\frac{\text{voltage}}{\text{current}} = \text{constant}$$

but, for an a.c. circuit, the constant is called the impedance of the circuit (symbol Z).

Thus, in an a.c. circuit consisting of a coil or a number of coils,

$$\frac{\textbf{voltage}}{\textbf{current}} = \textbf{impedance} \qquad \left[\frac{V}{I} = Z\right]$$

and $\quad$ $(\textbf{impedance})^2 = (\textbf{resistance})^2 + (\textbf{inductive reactance})^2$
$$[Z^2 = R^2 + X_L^2]$$

Like resistance, reactance and impedance are measured in ohms.

More important for our purposes, however, is the fact that in this type of a.c. circuit the current and voltage are not in phase: they do not reach their zero nor their maximum values at the same instants. We find that the current is always lagging behind the voltage, as shown in fig. 4.12.

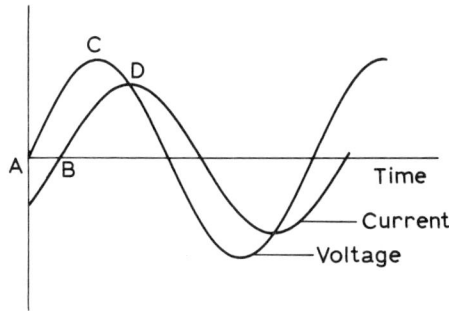

Fig. 4.12 Current lagging voltage.

Here it is seen that the current passes through zero a little while after the voltage passes through zero (points B and A respectively): the current passes through a maximum a little while after the voltage (points D and C respectively). Thus, for an a.c. motor which consists of a large number of coils, the current will lag behind the voltage.

The opposite effect occurs in an a.c. circuit containing a capacitor. A capacitor consists essentially of two plates of conducting material separated by a layer of insulation called the dielectric. Capacitors have a large number of applications in electrical engineering.

If a d.c. circuit contained a capacitor, the insulation between the plates would prevent any current from flowing. However, in an a.c. circuit current will flow, but it is limited not only by the resistance of the circuit but also by a property of the circuit known as its capacitive reactance (symbol Xc).

For this type of circuit

$$\frac{\text{voltage}}{\text{current}} = \text{impedance} \qquad \left[\frac{V}{I} = Z\right]$$

and $(\text{impedance})^2 = (\text{resistance})^2 + (\text{capacitive reactance})^2$
$$[Z^2 = R^2 + X_c^2]$$

As with the coil, the voltage and current are not in phase, but for a circuit with resistance and capacitance the current will lead the voltage as shown in fig. 4.13.

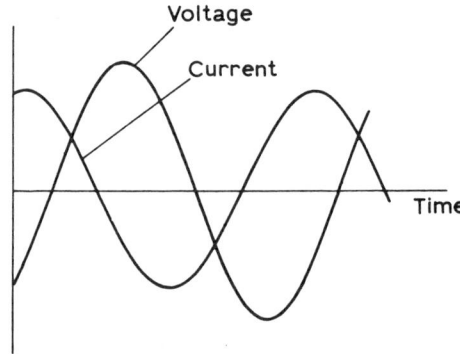

Fig. 4.13   Current leading voltage.

Power in a.c. Circuits

We have seen in Chapter 3 that the power dissipated in a d.c. circuit is given by the product of voltage and current. In an a.c. circuit we

ALTERNATING-CURRENT CIRCUITS

often find that the power dissipated is less than this product. This occurs when the circuit possesses reactance, due to the presence of either coils or capacitors. In these circumstances the power dissipated is given by the expression:

power = voltage × current × power factor $[P = V \times I \times \text{p.f.}]$

This expression applies only to what are referred to as single-phase circuits, the type of circuit with which we have dealt so far. For 3-phase circuits the expression must be modified, as we shall see later.

The maximum value the power factor can have is one (unity), and from what has already been said it may be deduced that this occurs when the circuit contains no reactance. The power factor of domestic installations is very nearly one.

With industrial installations having a large number of motors, the power factor may be 0·7 or even lower. The disadvantages of an installation having a low power factor are discussed in Chapter 8.

Since   **power = current × voltage × power factor,**

$$\text{power factor} = \frac{\text{power}}{\text{voltage} \times \text{current}}.$$

Example

Calculate the full load current taken by a ½ h.p. 240 volt motor having an efficiency of 60%, if the power factor for this condition is 0·7.

(Although the unit of horse-power (h.p.) will disappear when SI units have been completely adopted, this unit has been in such common usage that it is likely to be used for a considerable time. It is, of course, a unit of power, 1 horse-power being equivalent to 746 watts. Efficiency is defined as output/input and percentage efficiency is therefore (output/input) × 100. The symbol for efficiency is η.

A half h.p. motor has a full load output of ½ h.p. The input to the motor must be greater than this because some losses will occur in the motor, e.g. the windings will become warm when current passes through them and this heat requires additional power from the supply. In any machine the input to the machine must be greater than the useful output.)

$$\text{Output of motor} = \tfrac{1}{2} \times 746 = 373 \text{ watts.}$$

$$\text{Input to motor} = \frac{\text{output}}{\% \text{ efficiency}} \times 100 = 622 \text{ watts.}$$

Now, since $P = V \times I \times \text{power factor,}$

$$I = \frac{P}{V \times \text{power factor}}$$
$$= \frac{622}{240 \times 0.7} = 3.67 \text{ A}.$$

Chapter 4—Questions

1 What is meant by the 'power factor' of a circuit?
   A single phase a.c. motor has a full load output of 375 watts, the efficiency then being 80% and the power factor 0·75. Calculate the full load current taken by the motor if it is connected to a 240 volt supply.

2 The following appliances are used on a 240 volt supply: two 150 watt, four 100 watt and two 40 watt lamps for 3 hours a day; two 2 kilowatt fires for 2 hours a day; a 400 watt cleaner for two hours per week.
   Find (i) the total power consumption and the total current taken from the supply if all the appliances are switched on at the same time,
   (ii) the number of units consumed during one week.

3 State an expression for calculating the power dissipated by a circuit in terms of the supply voltage and the resistance of the circuit. It may be assumed that the circuit is purely resistive (i.e. the power factor equals unity).
   An appliance has a resistance of 40 ohms. Calculate the power taken by this appliance when connected to a 240 volt supply. If the supply voltage is reduced by 10%, what is the percentage drop in the power taken by the appliance?

4 Two elements, A and B, are connected in parallel across a supply. The resistance of A is 20Ω and the power dissipated by this element is 2 kW. The current through element B is 5 amperes.
   Calculate:
      (i) the voltage of the supply,
      (ii) the resistance of element B,
      (iii) the power dissipated by element B.
   If the two elements are now connected in series across the same supply, calculate the current taken from the supply.

5 Describe clearly the difference between alternating current and direct current. Draw sketches to illustrate your answer.

6 Write short notes on four of the following:
   (i) a reversing switch, (ii) frequency, (iii) sinusoidal waveform, (iv) r.m.s. value of alternating current, (v) phase difference, (vi) impedance.

5 Magnetism and Electromagnetism

In 1831 Michael Faraday demonstrated that, when a magnet was moved into and out of a coil of wire, a 'wave of electricity' was generated in the wire. This simple experiment, which could be performed by any schoolboy today, demonstrated the principle upon which the design of all alternating current generators (or alternators) and direct current generators (formerly called dynamos) built since that time is based. He also showed that, providing there was relative movement between the magnet and the coil, it did not matter which of the two moved and which was held stationary. Before we can discuss the construction of an a.c. or d.c. generator, it is necessary to consider the basic ideas associated with magnets and what is called electromagnetism, i.e. the relationship between electricity and magnetism.

Elementary Theory of Magnetism

Having demonstrated the generation (or the induction) of an e.m.f. in a circuit, Faraday described his experiment in terms which could be easily understood by introducing an idea which is still used today, in both elementary and advanced textbooks. He suggested that the space around a magnet—called the magnetic field—could be represented on diagrams by means of 'lines of force'. Where the field is strongest these lines are drawn close together, and where the field is weaker the lines are drawn correspondingly further apart. Such a diagram cannot represent the magnetic field in three dimensions—it can only be drawn in two dimensions—but it must always be remembered, when representing the magnetic field in this way, that it actually exists throughout the space around the magnet.

'Properties' of lines of force

It has been shown by experiment that magnetic fields behave in such a way that we can imagine these lines of force to possess certain properties, and we can use these imaginary properties to help us visualise what will happen under given conditions. The 'properties' we shall give to lines of force are:
(i) they never cross each other,
(ii) they repel each other sideways when they are in the same direction,
(iii) they act like bands of stretched elastic,
(iv) their 'direction' is always from a North pole to a South pole (see below).

Magnetic Field around a Bar Magnet

Using these ideas, we can now represent the magnetic field around a bar magnet, as in fig. 5.1.

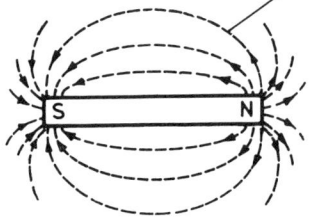

Fig. 5.1 Magnetic field around a bar magnet. The arrows indicate the direction of the field, i.e. leaving the North pole and entering the South pole.

It is seen that the lines of force are symmetrical about the centre lines of the magnet and that they are closest together at the ends of the magnet. These regions are called poles and, to differentiate between them, one is called a North (N) pole and the other a South (S) pole. If the magnet were suspended so that it was free to rotate in a horizontal plane, it would come to rest so that the North pole of the magnet pointed towards the earth's magnetic North pole—the earth itself behaving as though it had a giant magnet inside it with one pole near the earth's North pole and the other near the earth's South pole.

Poles always exist in pairs: if we cut a magnet into halves we should find that each half now possessed a North and a South pole (fig. 5.2).

Fig. 5.2 If a magnet is broken in two, each half still possesses a North pole and a South pole, as shown.

The arrows on the lines of force indicate the direction of the magnetic field. This has already been stated as being from the North pole around through the magnetic field to the South pole. The direction of a magnetic field can be determined by placing a small compass needle in the field—the direction in which it comes to rest will be the direction of the field at that point.

Magnetic Field between Two Magnets

It is found that, when similar poles of two magnets are brought together, as the distance between the magnets decreases there is a definite force trying to keep the magnets apart. We can explain this force in terms of the imaginary properties we have already given to lines of force. As the magnets approach each other, the lines of force between them are being compressed (fig. 5.3).

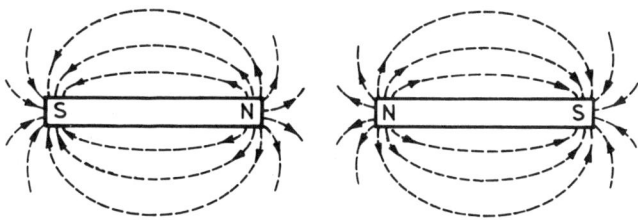

Fig. 5.3 Magnetic field between two magnets arranged with similar poles close together.

Since we may imagine that the lines cannot cross each other and also that they repel each other sideways, there will be a force acting between the poles trying to keep them apart. Conversely, if the two magnets are brought together so that dissimilar poles are close together, a force exists between them tending to draw them closer together. In this case, illustrated in fig. 5.4, the lines of force are joining the North and South poles. If they were bands of stretched elastic they would draw the magnets together.

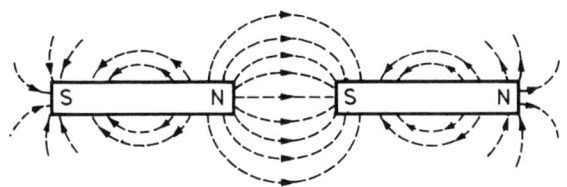

Fig. 5.4 Magnetic field between two magnets arranged with dissimilar poles close together.

This suggests a simple rule of magnetism:
> **like poles repel,**
> **unlike poles attract.**

Magnetic Field around a Conductor carrying a Current

About eleven years before Faraday's demonstration, a Danish scientist named Oersted made another very important discovery. He found that, when a current flows through a piece of wire, a magnetic field exists around the wire. The presence of the magnetic field could be indicated by the use of a compass needle. For a straight conductor this field is circular and at right-angles to the conductor, as shown in fig. 5.5.

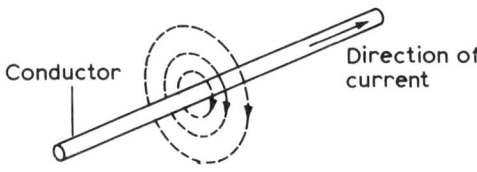

Fig. 5.5 The magnetic field around a straight conductor is at right-angles to the conductor, and is circular.

If we look from the left-hand end of the conductor, we can represent the magnetic field by a series of circles. Notice in fig. 5.6 that the spacing of the circles increases as the distance from the conductor increases, since the magnetic field is strongest immediately next to the conductor.

The cross inside the conductor indicates that the current is flowing away from us, i.e. into the paper. The direction of the magnetic field when the current is flowing could be checked with a small compass, and it would be found to be clockwise.

If we now look at the conductor shown in fig. 5.5 from the right-hand end, the current would now be flowing towards us. This direction, i.e. out of the paper, is indicated by a dot in fig. 5.7. The direction of the magnetic field when the current is flowing towards us is anticlockwise.

As an aid to memory, the dot and the cross may be thought of as being the end-on views of the point or the flights of an arrow moving respectively towards or away from us, in the same direction as the current.

MAGNETISM AND ELECTROMAGNETISM

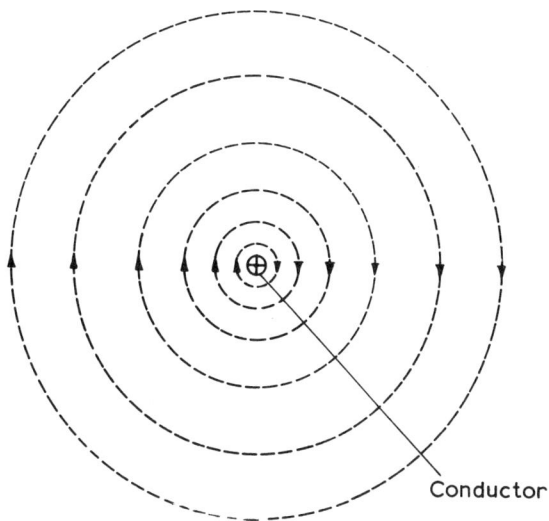

Fig. 5.6 Magnetic field around a straight conductor carrying a current 'into the paper'.

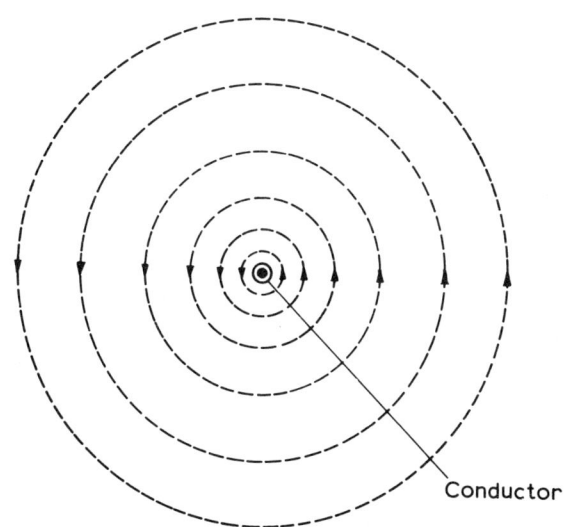

Fig. 5.7 Magnetic field around a straight conductor carrying a current 'out of the paper'.

Corkscrew rule

From this we can deduce a very simple yet useful and important rule known as the corkscrew rule. If we imagine that we screw a corkscrew into a cork in the direction of the flow of current, the direction in which the corkscrew is twisted will be the corresponding direction of the magnetic field. The reader should check the directions shown in figs 5.6 and 5.7 using this rule.

Magnetic Field around Two Parallel Conductors both carrying a Current

If the two parallel conductors A and B shown in fig. 5.8 are both carrying a current, the direction of which in each case is into the paper, the directions of their respective magnetic fields will both be clockwise. Now, at a point halfway between A and B, the line of force from A is in the opposite direction to the line of force from B. We may therefore consider that the lines of force cancel each other in this region. However, lines of force must form complete loops, so the more distant lines of force will link both conductors, as shown.

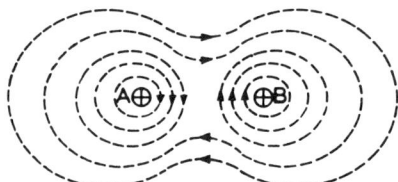

Fig. 5.8 Magnetic field around two straight conductors, both carrying current in the same direction.

Now, remembering that lines of force may be considered to act like bands of stretched elastic, these common lines of force will tend to bring the conductors together. There will be a force of attraction between the conductors when the current flow in the two conductors is in the same direction. This could be demonstrated by suspending two conductors about a centimetre apart and passing a current of several amperes through them.

The reader may remember that the basic SI unit of current is the ampere and that it is defined in terms of the force exerted between two conductors each carrying a current of one ampere.

Magnetic Field around a Coil

We will next examine the magnetic field associated with the coil shown in fig. 5.9, where a current is entering at end A and leaving at end B.

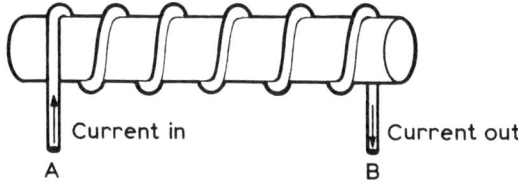

Fig. 5.9 A simple electromagnet, formed by winding a wire around an iron core.

We first redraw the coil as it would appear if we cut it in half (fig. 5.10a).

The direction of the current in the conductors shown at the top of the coil in fig. 5.10a will be into the paper, indicated by crosses. In the conductors at the bottom of the coil it will be out of the paper, indicated by dots. Now, as shown in the previous section dealing with parallel conductors, some of the lines of force between the conductors will cancel, giving a resultant field as shown. The field arrangement will be seen to be similar to that for a magnet.

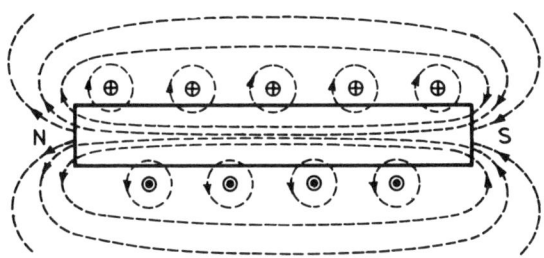

Fig. 5.10a Magnetic field of the electromagnet shown in fig. 5.9.

The coil, known as a *solenoid*, behaves as though it is a magnet, as could be demonstrated by bringing up the North pole of a magnet to the North pole of the coil: there would be a force of repulsion between the two. If the direction of the current through the coil were reversed, the North and South poles of the coil would interchange, i.e. the direction of the field would reverse.

If the coil were wound on an iron bar (using insulated wire) we would obtain a magnetic field of greatly increased strength. This arrangement is called an electromagnet and is used to provide the magnetic field in a large generator. It also has many other applications in electrical engineering.

Right-hand grip rule

This is a useful rule which may be used to determine the polarity of an electromagnet or solenoid. Imagine the right hand to be used to grip the coil, the fingers pointing in the same direction as the current flowing around the coil (fig. 5.10b). The thumb will then point to the North pole of the electromagnet.

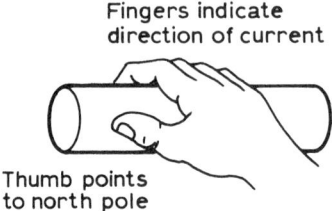

Fig. 5.10b Right-hand grip rule to determine the polarity of an electromagnet. The fingers grip the coil in the direction of current flow, and the thumbs then point to the North pole.

Faraday's Law

In an extension of his experiment with a magnet and a coil, Faraday showed that the magnitude of the e.m.f. generated in the coil was dependent upon the rate at which the magnet was moved, i.e. the rate at which the lines of force from the magnet cut the coil. The magnitude of the e.m.f. was greatest when the rate at which the lines of force cut the coil was greatest.

We have previously seen that an e.m.f. will be generated in a coil, or a single conductor, moving through a stationary field. Figure 5.11 represents a single conductor moving with constant speed through a magnetic field. The e.m.f. generated in the conductor will be greatest

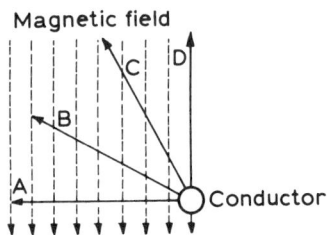

Fig. 5.11 The e.m.f. generated in a conductor is greatest when it moves in direction A. There will be no e.m.f. generated when it does not 'cut' the magnetic field (i.e. direction D).

when the conductor cuts the field at right-angles (i.e. direction A) because, in a given time, more lines of force will be cut by the conductor when moving in this direction than when moving in direction B. Similarly, more lines of force are cut in the same time when moving in direction B than when moving in direction C. Finally, no lines of force are cut when moving in direction D, so no e.m.f. is generated in the conductor in this case.

Lenz's Law

A German scientist named Lenz discovered that the direction of the e.m.f. induced in a conductor moving through a magnetic field is such that it tends to cause a current to flow so as to oppose the motion producing it. This statement is now called 'Lenz's Law'. Stated in words it sounds complicated, so let us now see how it can be applied.

In the following two examples we shall consider a conductor moving through a magnetic field. The conductor forms part of a complete circuit, as shown in fig. 5.12, so the e.m.f. generated in the conductor as it moves through the field will cause a current to flow around the circuit. We wish to determine the direction in which this current will flow.

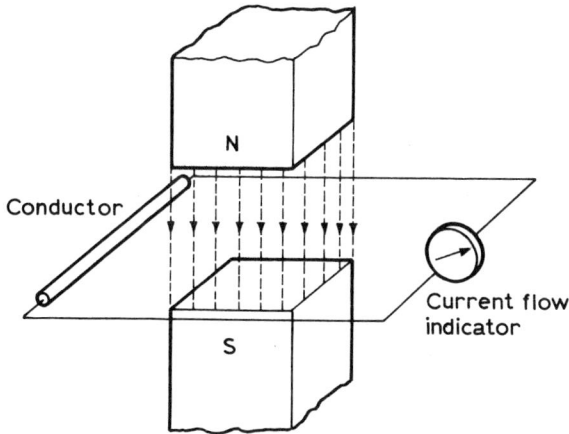

Fig. 5.12 Conductor moving through a magnetic field.

We first redraw fig. 5.12, representing the conductor by a circle (i.e. as if we are looking directly at one end of it). We also show the direction of the magnetic field and the direction in which the conductor is moving (fig. 5.13).

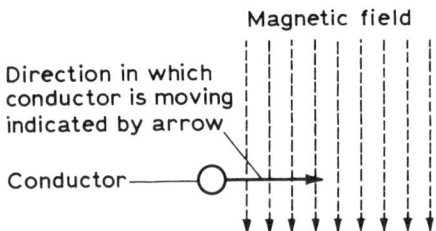

Fig. 5.13 Diagram to illustrate Lenz's Law.

Now the direction of the current flow may be into or out of the paper. We will draw the resultant field for each of these possibilities and then use Lenz's law to determine which is correct.

In fig. 5.14 the current is shown flowing out of the paper. Using the corkscrew rule, this would cause an anticlockwise field around the conductor, shown at fig. 5.14a.

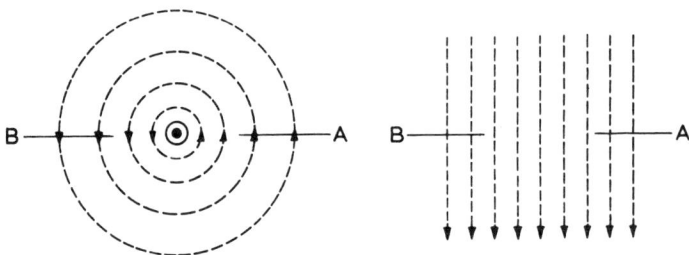

Fig. 5.14a Direction of magnetic field for current flowing in a straight conductor. Note regions A and B indicated by arrows.

Fig. 5.14b Direction of main magnetic field shown in fig. 5.12. Note regions A and B indicated by arrows.

The main magnetic field, as shown in fig. 5.12 and redrawn in fig. 5.14b, is downwards. Now, since lines of force cannot cross each other, when the conductor is moving through the field the two fields will combine, giving the resultant field shown in fig. 5.15a. This is obtained as follows. In regions A in figs 5.14a and 5.14b it will be seen that the two fields are in opposite directions and will therefore tend to cancel out. In regions B, however, they are in the same direction and will therefore make a stronger field. Now, using the idea of bands of stretched elastic, the conductor is being urged to the right, i.e. in the same direction as it is already moving. This must be incorrect since Lenz's law says that the current direction must oppose the motion.

MAGNETISM AND ELECTROMAGNETISM

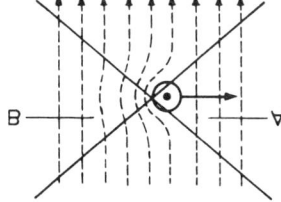 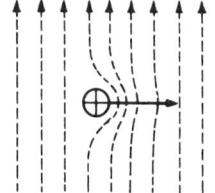

Fig. 5.15a Diagram to show that the assumed direction of current flow does not agree with Lenz's Law, and is therefore incorrect.

Fig. 5.15b Diagram to show that the assumed direction of current flow agrees with Lenz's Law, and is therefore correct.

If the current flows into the paper, the direction of the field due to the current will be clockwise. Considering this field with the main field, as in the previous case, we obtain the resultant field shown in fig. 5.15b. This time we see the field opposes the motion of the conductor. The lines of force are trying to push the conductor back in the opposite direction to that in which it is moving. This direction agrees with Lenz's law.

Summarising, then, we may say that the direction of the generated e.m.f., and therefore the current, will be such that it will make a stronger field ahead and a weaker field behind the conductor as it moves through the magnetic field.

In the next chapter we shall see how the ideas we have discussed in this chapter are used in the design of alternating and direct current generators and motors.

Chapter 5—Questions

1 What is meant by a 'line of (magnetic) force' and for what purpose are lines of force used?
   Describe the effect noticed when:
   (i) similar poles of two magnets are brought close together,
   (ii) dissimilar poles of two magnets are brought close together.
2 Make a sketch of the magnetic field associated with a current flowing through a long straight conductor. Indicate on your diagram the direction of the magnetic field and describe a simple rule which may be used to determine this direction. At what point is the field strongest?
3 Sketch the magnetic field associated with a coil. Explain the convention of using a cross and a dot to indicate current flow.

4 Make a diagram of a conductor moving at right-angles to a magnetic field. Show on your diagram the direction of the e.m.f. induced in the conductor. Explain how you have obtained this direction.

What happens when a conductor is moved parallel to a magnetic field?

6 Cells, Generators, Motors and Transformers

The Primary Cell

The simplest form of generator is the primary cell. It consists essentially of two different metals (known as *electrodes*), both of which are in contact with a liquid (the *electrolyte*) which permits electric current to flow through it. In the early primary cells the two electrodes and the electrolyte were contained in a glass jar. Although the electrodes and electrolyte could easily be replaced as they became exhausted, the arrangement was not convenient, particularly for portable applications. Consequently the dry cell, the construction of which is shown in fig. 6.1, was developed.

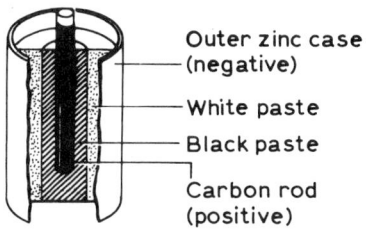

Fig. 6.1 The construction of a dry cell, as used in many torches.

The outer case of the cell is made of zinc, often surrounded by a cardboard cover. Within this case is an electrolyte, in the form of a white paste, and a carbon rod, which is usually provided with a brass cap. This rod forms the positive terminal of the cell and the zinc case forms the negative terminal.

A chemical reaction takes place within the cell, as a result of which electrons accumulate at the negative terminal, leaving the positive terminal with a corresponding shortage of electrons. A voltage then exists between the terminals and, if they are connected through an external circuit, a current will flow around the circuit.

It will be seen that a black paste separates the carbon rod from the white paste. This is provided to prevent hydrogen bubbles accumulating on the carbon rod, as they would act as an insulator and stop the flow of current.

The most common use of this cell is in the torch, but it has a wide range of applications in other portable appliances. It has a voltage of approximately 1·5 volts and a maximum current of about one-tenth of an ampere. It cannot be recharged, as the chemical reaction is irreversible, and it must therefore be discarded when the voltage falls to about one volt.

When higher *voltages* are required, a number of cells may be joined in series to form a battery, as shown in fig. 6.2, where three cells are connected in series to form a 4·5 volt battery. A 9 volt battery consists of six cells connected in series. Note that to connect cells in series the negative terminal of the first cell must be connected to the positive terminal of the second cell, and so on.

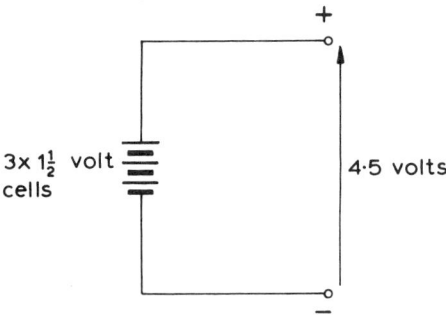

Fig. 6.2   Three cells connected in series provide a total voltage of 4·5 volts.

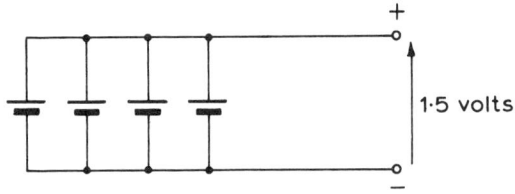

Fig. 6.3   Four cells connected in parallel provide a total voltage of 1·5 volts, but they can supply four times the current supplied from a single cell.

CELLS, GENERATORS, MOTORS AND TRANSFORMERS

If a higher *current* is required, a number of cells may be joined in parallel (fig. 6.3). In this case, all the positive terminals are connected together to the positive terminal of the battery, and all the negative terminals are similarly connected to the negative terminal.

Cells may also be connected in a series–parallel arrangement to give both an increased voltage and current output (fig. 6.4).

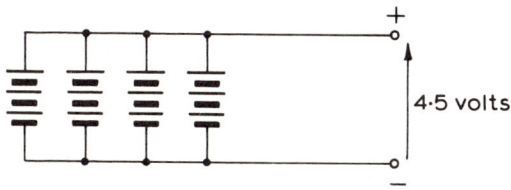

Fig. 6.4 Cells connected in a series-parallel arrangement.

The Secondary Cell

The use of dry cells is restricted to small appliances operating at low voltages and currents. When a large current is required, a secondary cell is used (fig. 6.5).

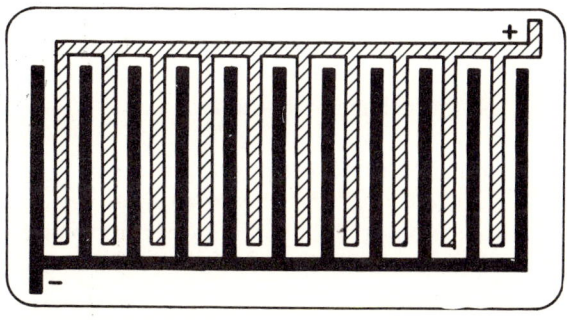

Fig. 6.5 Top view of a battery, showing how the positive and negative plates are connected to their respective terminals.

In the secondary cell, several lead plates covered with a lead peroxide paste are connected together to the positive terminal of the cell. These plates are interleaved with a second set of lead plates covered with a spongy lead paste—this second set of plates being connected to the negative terminal. The two sets of plates are immersed in a solution of sulphuric acid and water, and are held apart by insulators.

When the cell is connected to an external circuit, current will flow, due to the chemical action taking place between the lead plates (electrodes) and the sulphuric acid solution (electrolyte). As a result of this chemical action, the paste on the plates gradually changes to lead sulphate, and at the same time the voltage at the terminals of the cell falls from about 2 volts to 1·85 volts. The time taken for this change to occur is determined by the average current supplied by the cell. When the voltage falls to 1·85 volts, the cell must not be used again until it has been recharged by connecting it to a suitable d.c. supply and passing a current through the cell in the reverse direction to that of the current flow when it is being discharged, as shown in fig. 6.6.

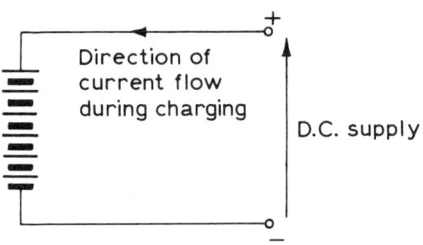

Fig. 6.6 Secondary cells may be recharged by passing a current through them in the reverse direction, as shown.

This results in a chemical change which causes the paste on the plates to change back to lead peroxide and spongy lead respectively. When this occurs, the voltage at the terminals of the cell rises to 2 volts again.

Secondary cells may be charged from an a.c. supply, provided a transformer is used to reduce the voltage to a suitable value and a rectifier is supplied to convert the alternating current to direct current.

Secondary cells have a long life, provided they are promptly and correctly recharged when the voltage falls to 1·85 volts. An indication of the state of a cell may be obtained by measuring the 'strength', or specific gravity, of the electrolyte by means of a hydrometer.

These cells have a wide range of applications, but their most common use is in the motor car where either three cells connected in series are used for a 6 volt battery or six cells connected in series are used for a 12 volt battery. The current supplied by the battery when the car is started is of the order of several hundred amperes. Another important application is their use as a standby supply in public buildings, to provide lighting in the event of a failure of the normal mains supply.

CELLS, GENERATORS, MOTORS AND TRANSFORMERS

The energy which may be stored by a secondary cell, although considerably greater than that for a primary cell, is very limited. To provide a public supply of electricity, it is necessary to use rotating machines operating upon the principles first demonstrated by Faraday.

The Simple Alternator

In Chapter 5 we saw that an e.m.f. is generated in a conductor when it moves through a magnetic field. We saw also that the magnitude of the e.m.f. generated in the conductor is proportional to the rate at which it cuts the lines of force in the magnetic field. Thus the maximum e.m.f. is generated in the conductor when it is cutting the field at right-angles. However, it would be very difficult to design a machine in which conductors always moved at right-angles to the field. For this reason, the conductors are placed on the surface of the moving part of the machine (called the *rotor*), and they move through the field along a circular path.

Figure 6.7 illustrates a simple alternator. The magnetic field is produced by electromagnets which, as we have seen earlier, will provide a very strong field. The electromagnets may be bolted to the case (or frame) of the machine to form the *stator*.

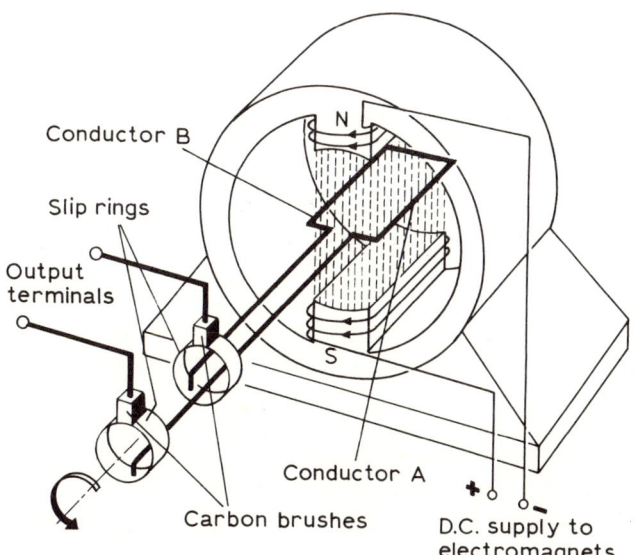

Fig. 6.7 A simple alternator, showing two conductors forming one coil rotating in a magnetic field. The output terminals are connected to the coil by stationary carbon brushes.

59

The direction of the direct current flowing through the coils may be arranged to give a North or a South pole as required. The reader should check the polarities shown on fig. 6.7 by using the right-hand grip rule described in Chapter 5.

Two conductors (A and B in fig. 6.7) are joined together in series to form a coil, and each end of the coil is connected to a copper ring (called a *slip-ring*). In contact with each slip-ring is a small carbon block (known as a *brush*) and each brush is connected to an output terminal of the alternator. The coil and the slip-rings rotate, whilst the brushes and the output terminals remain stationary.

We will now consider how the e.m.f. generated in conductor A varies as A rotates through one revolution. Four positions of the conductor are shown in figs. 6.8a, b, c and d, where we are looking directly at the end of the conductors.

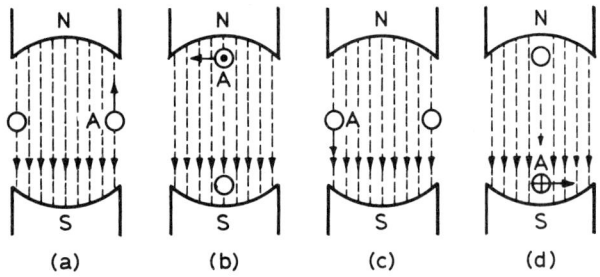

Fig. 6.8 Generation of an alternating e.m.f. in a conductor as it rotates in a magnetic field.

Figure 6.8a At this instant the conductor is not cutting any lines of force, so there will be no induced e.m.f.

Figure 6.8b The conductor is now cutting lines of force at right-angles, so the e.m.f. will be a maximum. The direction of the induced e.m.f. (by Lenz's law, see Chapter 5) will be out of the paper.

Fig 6.8c The conditions are similar to those in fig. 6.8a

Figure 6.8d The e.m.f. will again be a maximum, but the direction of the e.m.f. will be opposite to that shown in fig. 6.8b, i.e. it will be into the paper.

Now, between the positions shown in figs 6.8a and b, the generated e.m.f. will rise gradually from zero to a maximum, so an e.m.f. having

CELLS, GENERATORS, MOTORS AND TRANSFORMERS

a sinusoidal waveform will result (see fig. 4.8). With the aid of fig. 5.11, it should be possible for the reader to understand how this waveform is derived.

Practical Alternators

This simple alternator would generate a very low voltage. It is therefore necessary in a practical machine to make certain modifications, the more important of which are as follows.

(i) A large number of coils must be provided and these must be connected in series so that the e.m.f.'s generated in the conductors will all add up to give the required voltage output.

(ii) The magnetic field must be very strong, to make the generated voltage as high as possible. This may be achieved by making the gap between the underside of the poles and the conductors very small indeed. Furthermore, the conductors must be placed on a rotor constructed of a special type of steel. Steel, however, is a conductor, so an e.m.f. would be generated in the rotor itself, as it rotated in the magnetic field, and also in the stator. This would, of course, represent a loss of power, and so, to prevent this, the rotor and stator are laminated, i.e. they are built up of thin slices or laminations of steel insulated from each other. This considerably reduces the power loss which would otherwise occur, and this method of reducing power losses is commonly used in all alternating current machines and transformers.

(iii) Considerable design problems would occur with high voltage alternators if the e.m.f. were generated in the moving part of the machine. It is very much more convenient to place the coils in which the e.m.f. is to be generated on the fixed part of the machine, and the coils for the electromagnets on the rotating part of the machine, as we have seen in Chapter 5 that an e.m.f. will still be generated provided there is relative movement between the coils and the electromagnet.

The alternator described above is a single-phase alternator. Almost all large alternators generate a three-phase supply.

Simple 3-Phase Alternator

The output of a simple 3-phase alternator is shown in fig. 6.9. Instead of one coil, as was used in the simple single-phase alternator described above, three coils are equally spaced around the rotor. Each coil is connected to a pair of slip-rings, so that six slip-rings, six brushes and six terminals are required. Now, since the coils have identical dimensions, the e.m.f.s generated in them will be identical, having the same maximum values and the same waveform. In each revolution, the e.m.f. generated in each of the coils will complete one cycle, but, since the coils are equally spaced around the rotor, the three e.m.f.'s will be out of phase by an interval of time corresponding to one-third of a revolution. Since the e.m.f.'s vary through a complete cycle in one revolution, they will be displaced by one-third of a cycle, as shown in fig. 6.9.

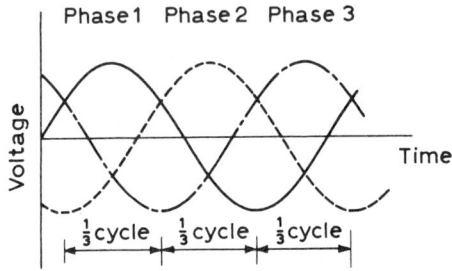

Fig. 6.9 Variation of the e.m.f.'s in the three coils of a simple 3-phase alternator. Note that the e.m.f.'s are each displaced by one-third of a cycle.

Practical 3-Phase Alternator

In a high-voltage 3-phase alternator, as in a high-voltage single-phase alternator, the coils in which the e.m.f.'s are generated are placed on the stator, with the electromagnet coils on the rotor. For each phase, a large number of coils must be provided and connected in series to give the required voltage. Also, the gap between the rotor and the stator is made as small as possible, and both the rotor and the stator are laminated.

Furthermore, the three coils are usually connected together so that only four output terminals are required, as shown in fig. 6.10.

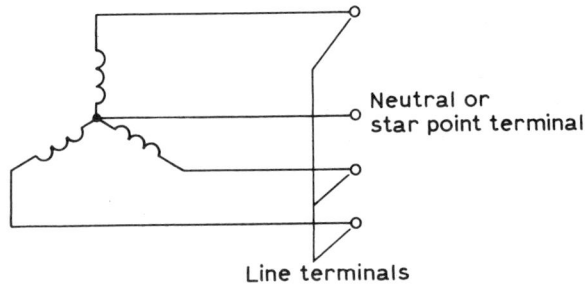

Fig. 6.10 Coils connected in star.

It will be seen that one end of each of the coils is connected together to form a star-point (or neutral), and the other ends of the coils are connected to line terminals. This type of 3-phase connection is known as the *star connection*. It is widely used in 3-phase circuits, another application being the low-voltage connection in transformers supplying the mains cables laid in the streets, referred to in figs. 7.18 and 7.19.

An alternative method of connecting the 3-phase coils is shown in fig. 6.11, this method being frequently used for 3-phase motors. This method is referred to as the *delta* or *mesh connection*, and it will be seen that in this case there is no neutral or star-point.

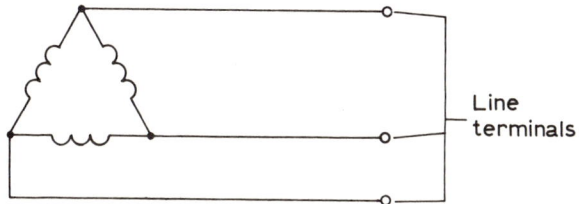

Fig. 6.11   Coils connected in delta or mesh.

Motors

Although a few d.c. motors are used for special purposes, such as cranes and electric trains, where their special characteristics are particularly suitable, the majority of motors used in this country are a.c. motors. Probably more than 90% of all the a.c. motors used are induction motors. Surprisingly, the principle of the 3-phase induction motor is easier to describe than that of the single-phase induction motor.

3-Phase Induction Motor

The 3-phase induction motor is similar to the 3-phase alternator, in that it consists essentially of a motor and a stator.

The motor may be of either the *squirrel-cage* or the *wound* type. The squirrel-cage motor consists of a number of aluminium or copper bars placed in slots around the periphery of the laminations, the ends of these bars being connected to aluminium or copper end-rings, as shown in fig. 6.12. In the wound motor, three sets of coils joined together at one end are used. These coils, like the bars in the squirrel-cage motor, are placed in slots near the surface of the laminations, and the free ends of the coils are connected to slip-rings, as previously described. These coils are often short-circuited automatically when the motor is running.

The stator contains the three sets of coils to which the 3-phase supply is connected. These coils are usually placed in slots around the inside of the stator, the coils being delta-connected.

The wound motor has some important advantages, especially during starting, but the squirrel-cage motor is cheaper and more robust, and for these reasons is commonly used where conditions are suitable.

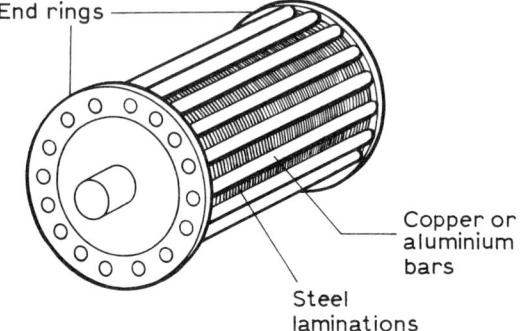

Fig. 6.12 Construction of squirrel-cage rotor.

When the motor is connected to a 3-phase supply, a magnetic field is set up due to the current flowing in the coils. However, because the supply consists of three alternating voltages which are not in phase, the resultant magnetic field is pulsating. The effect of the pulsations is similar to the effect which would be produced by the magnet system shown in fig. 6.13 rotating around the rotor. It must be stressed that,

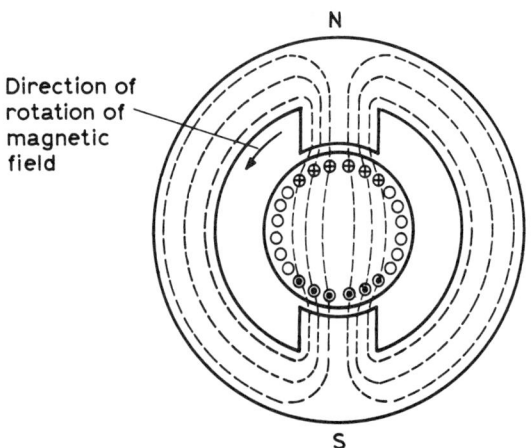

Fig. 6.13 Principle of the 3-phase induction motor. It is important to realise that it does not represent the actual construction of the motor.

CELLS, GENERATORS, MOTORS AND TRANSFORMERS

in a 3-phase motor, the supply coils are stationary—it is only the magnetic field which is effectively rotating. Figure 6.13 does not, therefore, correctly represent the construction of a 3-phase motor—it is drawn to illustrate and explain the principle involved. Some of the rotor bars are shown immediately under the two poles and the direction in which the magnetic field is rotating is also indicated.

The conditions under the North pole are redrawn in fig. 6.14, where one stationary conductor is shown, and the field is moving from right to left, causing an e.m.f. to be induced in the conductor. The direction of the induced e.m.f. will be the same as would be the case if the conductor moved from left to right and the field remained stationary, as illustrated in fig. 6.15.

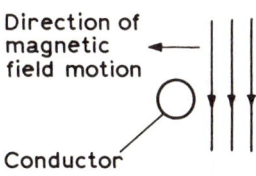

Fig. 6.14 Stationary conductor and a moving magnetic field.

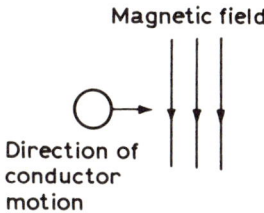

Fig. 16.15 Moving conductor and stationary magnetic field. This arrangement is equivalent to that shown in fig. 6.14.

From Lenz's law the reader should be able to deduce that the direction of the induced e.m.f., and therefore that of the current which will flow, will be into the paper. We thus get the distorted magnetic field shown in fig. 6.16, and this will result in a force acting on the conductor, because, as we can see, the lines of force are bent around the conductor, tending to cause it to move to the left. As the

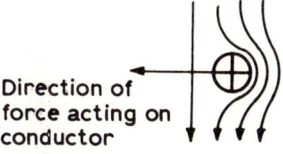

Fig. 6.16 The conductor represented in figs. 6.14 and 6.15 will experience a force tending to move it to the left.

rotor is free to move, the combined forces acting on all the conductors around the rotor will cause the rotor to rotate in the same direction as the magnetic field is rotating. The reader should check that, although the direction of the current flowing in the conductors under the South

65

pole is in the opposite direction, the forces acting on them also make the rotor turn in an anticlockwise direction.

The motor may therefore be used to drive a machine, the shaft of the rotor being connected to the machine.

The 3-phase induction motor is very simple in construction, robust in use and is cheaper than other comparable forms of 3-phase motor. Furthermore, it will start to rotate immediately the supply is connected to the stator coils.

Single-Phase Motors

All the motors used in domestic appliances are single-phase motors because domestic consumers normally are connected to only a single-phase supply. The general construction of many of these motors is similar to that of the 3-phase induction motor previously described, a squirrel-cage rotor being used, but the stator coil has only one winding, instead of three.

When an alternating supply is connected to a single-phase winding, the magnetic field is also alternating but it does not pulsate or rotate as is the case with a 3-phase winding. The motor will, therefore, not start to rotate when the supply is connected, unless special arrangements for starting are provided.

Several methods of starting employ an auxiliary stator winding in addition to the main stator winding. The current in this winding is made to differ in phase from that in the main winding so that the supply to the motor effectively becomes a 2-phase supply. Provided a sufficient difference in phase is achieved, the motor will start and will continue to run even when the auxiliary winding is disconnected.

The most common domestic single-phase induction motors are the *split-phase, capacitor* and *shaded-pole* types.

In the split-phase motor, the difference in phase between the currents in the main and auxiliary windings is obtained either by increasing the resistance of the auxiliary winding (e.g. by using wire with a smaller diameter) or by increasing its reactance (e.g. by using more turns of wire). This type of motor is cheaper than other types and is often used in washing machines.

In the capacitor type, the difference in phase is due to the presence of a capacitor in the auxiliary circuit. The effect of a capacitor was discussed in Chapter 4. This type of motor is usually employed in refrigerators.

The shaded-pole motor is frequently used for very small motors, such as are found in record-players, tape-recorders and small fans.

The principle of this type is rather more complicated than that of the split-phase and capacitor types. The stator often has poles projecting inwards, as described for the simple alternator. Each of these poles is in two parts, the flux in one part reaching particular values before the flux in the other part.

Apart from these induction motors, another common type of single-phase a.c. motor is the *universal* (or *commutator*) *motor*. In this case, windings are provided on both the stator and the rotor, and carbon brushes are used to provide the electrical connection to the rotor. These are high-speed motors and they are used in vacuum cleaners, sewing machines and portable drills.

It is most important that the motor used in an electric clock should operate at a constant speed. The type of motor used for this purpose is the *synchronous motor*, the speed of which is determined by the frequency of the supply. Under normal conditions, in this country, this remains constant at 50 Hz.

The Transformer

In a single-phase transformer, two windings are wound, one over the other, on a steel core built up of a large number of laminations. One winding is called the *primary* (or input) winding and the other is the *secondary* (or output) winding (fig. 6.17).

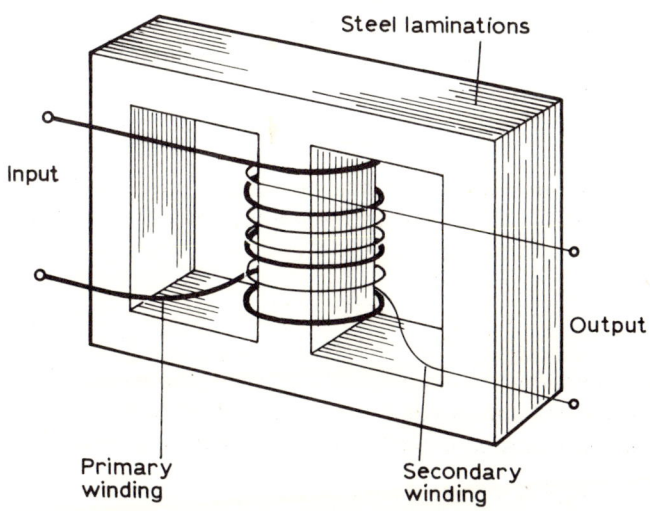

Fig. 6.17 Simple single-phase transformer.

If the primary winding is connected to an alternating voltage supply, the current which will flow will set up an alternating magnetic field. This alternating field is continually building up to a maximum in one direction, collapsing, and building up to a maximum in the opposite direction, following the variations of the voltage and current. As the secondary winding is close to the primary winding, this changing field will cut the secondary winding and an e.m.f. will be induced in it. If the secondary is connected to a circuit, current will flow in that circuit. The transformer may be represented by either of the methods shown in fig. 6.18.

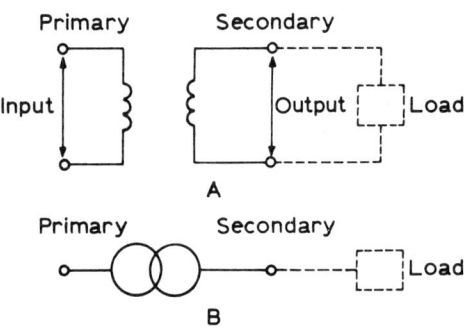

Fig. 6.18 Method of representing a transformer (A) on a circuit diagram and (B) on a single line diagram.

It can be shown that the current flowing in the secondary winding multiplied by the number of turns on the secondary winding is equal to the current flowing in the primary winding multiplied by the number of turns on the primary winding. In symbols:

$$I_1 \times N_1 = I_2 \times N_2$$

where I_1, N_1 are the current and number of turns for the primary winding, and I_2, N_2 are the corresponding values for the secondary winding.

$$\therefore \frac{N_1}{N_2} = \frac{I_2}{I_1}.$$

As the transformer is almost 100% efficient, the power supplied to the primary will almost equal the power output from the secondary. This may be expressed in the form of an equation, as follows.

$$V_1 \times I_1 \times \text{power factor} = V_2 \times I_2 \times \text{power factor}$$

where V_1, V_2 are the voltages across the primary and secondary

CELLS, GENERATORS, MOTORS AND TRANSFORMERS

windings, and I_1, I_2 are the currents through the primary and secondary windings.

Now, we may consider the power factor to be the same for each winding so that:

$$V_1 \times I_1 = V_2 \times I_2$$

$$\therefore \frac{V_1}{V_2} = \frac{I_2}{I_1}.$$

Combining this equation with the equation above we get:

$$\frac{V_1}{V_2} = \frac{N_1}{N_2} = \frac{I_2}{I_1}.$$

It therefore follows that, if an increase in voltage is required, the number of turns on the secondary winding must be greater than that on the primary. This is called a *step-up* transformer. Similarly, if a reduction in voltage is required, the number of turns on the secondary must be less than that on the primary. This is called a *step-down* transformer.

One special type of transformer has the same number of turns on each winding. This is known as an *isolating* transformer, since it electrically isolates the appliance connected to its output from the supply, thus reducing the risk of shock. This type of transformer is used in a bathroom electric-shaver socket, as described in Chapter 8.

Example

A transformer is required to supply an output of 12 volts when the input terminals are connected to a 240 volt supply. (This would be known as a 240/12 volt transformer.) If there are 300 turns on the primary winding, calculate the number of turns on the secondary. Also, if the secondary supplies a current of 4 amperes, calculate the current taken from the supply. The circuit is shown below.

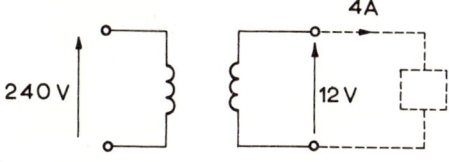

Now $$\frac{V_1}{V_2} = \frac{N_1}{N_2}$$

$$\therefore N_2 = N_1 \frac{V_2}{V_1} = 300 \times \frac{12}{240}$$

$$= 15 \text{ turns.}$$

and
$$\frac{V_1}{V_2} = \frac{I_2}{I_1}$$

$$\therefore I_1 = I_2 \frac{V_2}{V_1} = 4 \times \frac{12}{240}$$

$$= 0.2 \text{A.}$$

The transformer is one of the most efficient and most useful items of electrical equipment. 3-phase transformers have three sets of primary and secondary windings, each set being situated on a separate limb (fig. 6.19). The windings are, in fact, placed one on top of the other, as in the single-phase transformer, but in fig. 6.19 they are shown side by side, for the sake of clarity.

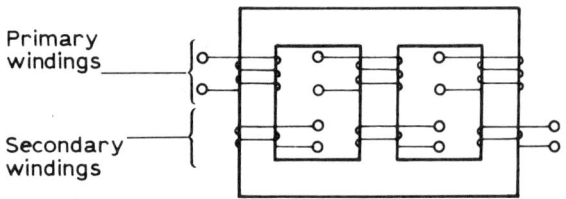

Fig. 6.19 Diagrammatic representation of a 3-phase transformer.

Chapter 6—Questions

1 Describe the construction and principle of operation of a transformer. The input voltage to a single-phase transformer is 240 volts, and the output voltage is 8 volts. If there are 1500 turns on the input winding, calculate the number of turns required on the output winding.

2 Describe, with diagrams, the principle of operation of a 3-phase induction motor. What are meant by the following terms:
(i) squirrel-cage motor,
(ii) stator,
(iii) rotor?

3 Describe (i) a primary cell, (ii) a secondary cell, and give two examples of the use of each type of cell. How should cells be connected to give (i) a higher voltage-output, (ii) a higher current-output?

CELLS, GENERATORS, MOTORS AND TRANSFORMERS

4 Describe the essential features and principle of operation of a simple alternator. Discuss briefly the modifications which must be incorporated in the design of a large alternator.

5 Name three different types of single-phase induction motor used in domestic appliances. What is associated with the starting of single-phase motors which does not apply to 3-phase motors? State one use for each of the different types of single-phase motor you have listed.

6 In what circumstances is an isolating transformer used? A 240/8 volt transformer takes a current of 0·1A from the supply. Calculate the current flowing in the secondary winding. If there are 180 turns on the primary winding, how many turns will be required on the secondary?

7 Generation, Transmission and Distribution of Electrical Energy

Structure of the Electricity Supply Industry

As recently as one hundred years ago there were no public electricity supplies available anywhere in the world. The first lighting system carried out by a public authority in this country was at Billingsgate Fish Market. This was in 1876 and, surprisingly, a French company was responsible for the installation. Several other isolated installations soon followed, mainly in London, each consisting of a generator, an engine to drive the generator, and cables, which were often supported by iron posts on the roofs of houses. As the number of installations increased, it became obvious that generating plants should be grouped together in a building near the centre of the area supplied. In 1882, Edison from America and Swan from Newcastle, England, built the world's first public steam power station at 57, Holborn Viaduct, London. This station had a capacity of less than 100 kW. The steam power stations now being commissioned in this country have capacities of 2 000 000 kW.

In the same year, the first *Electricity Lighting Act* was passed by Parliament. The conditions laid down in this Act favoured Local Authorities at the expense of the private companies so much so that in 1888 it became necessary to amend the Act. The number of supply systems throughout the country then rapidly increased, most of these being owned by private companies. By 1924 there were nearly five hundred power stations throughout the country, many of these stations being small and containing inefficient plant. Also at this time there were seventeen different frequencies being used throughout the country. As a result of this state of affairs, an *Electricity Supply Act* was passed in 1926. This Act led to the setting up of the Central Electricity Board (CEB) who were to be responsible for organising the supply industry. The frequency of the supply was standardised at 50 cycles/second (hertz) and standard voltages for transmission lines

GENERATION, TRANSMISSION AND DISTRIBUTION OF ELECTRICAL ENERGY

were also established. Between 1928 and 1933, the 132 kV grid system was constructed, leading to greatly increased efficiency as much of the older plant was scrapped.

In 1947, when the electricity supply industry was nationalised, there were nearly 550 supply authorities, of which approximately two-thirds were owned by local authorities and one-third by private companies. Ten years after nationalisation, in the light of the experience gained, the original proposals were slightly modified by the *Electricity Supply Act* of 1957. As the organisation for Scotland is different from that applying to England and Wales, the two areas will be considered separately.

Electricity Supply—Scotland

In Scotland the generation, transmission and distribution of electricity is the responsibility of the North of Scotland Hydro-Electric Board and the South of Scotland Electricity Board. These two Boards are responsible to the Minister of State for Scotland for an efficient, coordinated and economical system of supply. When necessary, they must consult with the Electricity Council, the Generating Board and the Area Boards in England and Wales to ensure that these conditions are fulfilled. The North of Scotland Board has an additional duty to collaborate in any schemes for economic and social development which are proposed within its area of supply.

Electricity Supply—England and Wales

The major difference between the organisation in Scotland and that in England and Wales is that, whereas the Scottish Boards are responsible for the generation, transmission and distribution of electricity, in England and Wales these duties are shared between the Central Electricity Generating Board (CEGB) and the Area Boards. The division of responsibility is shown in fig. 7.1.

Electricity Council
The duties of the Electricity Council are to advise the Secretary of State for Trade and Industry—to whom it is responsible—on all matters relating to the electricity supply industry in England and Wales, and also to ensure that an efficient, coordinated and economical system of supply is provided. The Council also have certain specific responsibilities, particularly in matters of finance, research and industrial relations.

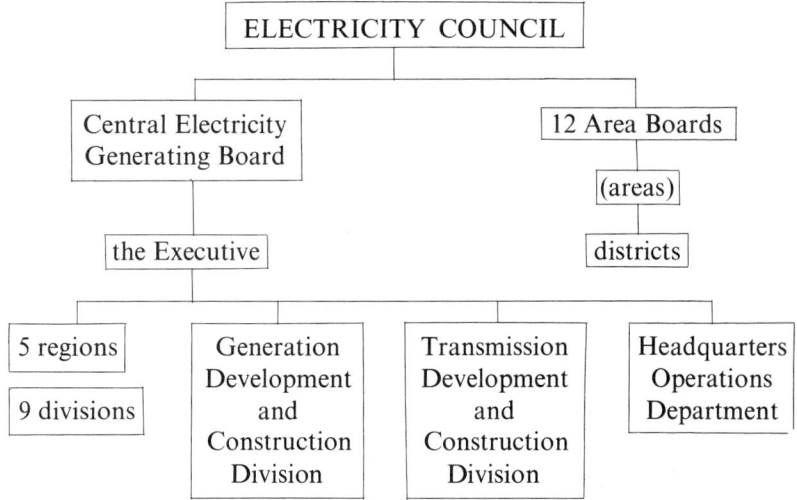

Fig. 7.1 Organisation of the Electricity Supply Industry in England and Wales.

The members of the Council include the Chairman and two other members from the Generating Board, and the Chairmen of the twelve Area Boards, together with other members who are directly appointed by the Secretary of State. Once a year, in October, the Council is required to produce a Report reviewing the previous year's activities within the supply industry.

Central Electricity Generating Board

The CEGB is responsible for the generation and transmission of electricity. By transmission we mean the conveying of the electricity produced at the power stations to substations within the area where the electricity is to be used. At these substations the electricity is purchased in bulk by the local area Electricity Board, which then assumes responsibility for making it available to the consumers in that area. England and Wales is divided into five regions for these purposes, the regions being further subdivided into a total of nine divisions, as shown in fig. 7.2. The two Scottish Boards are also indicated on this diagram.

Following a reorganisation of the CEGB in January 1971, the Executive is now responsible for approving all operating policies, plans

GENERATION TRANSMISSION AND DISTRIBUTION OF ELECTRICAL ENERGY

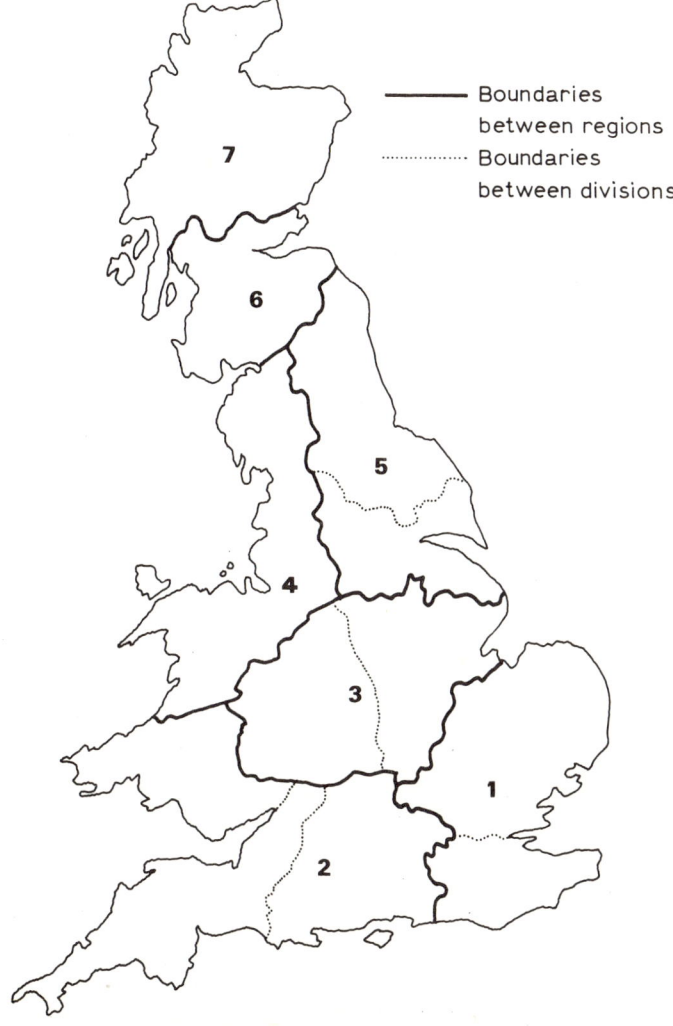

Fig. 7.2 Boundaries of the Regions and Divisions of the CEGB. 1—South Eastern Region; 2—South Western Region; 3—Midlands Region; 4—North Western Region; 5—North Eastern Region; 6—South Scotland Region; 7—North Scotland Region.

and budgets, and the two Development and Construction Divisions have been established.

The CEGB also operates three large laboratories where research work into more efficient methods of generation and transmission is undertaken.

Area Boards

As was mentioned above, the Area Boards purchase electricity in bulk from the CEGB and are responsible for distributing it to consumers. In England and Wales there are twelve Area Boards operating in the areas shown in fig. 7.3. Nearly all the Boards are divided into areas, each area being further sub-divided into districts. However, the London and South Western Boards are divided directly into districts, there being no areas in these Boards.

In addition to the distribution of electricity, the Boards have powers to sell, hire, repair or install fittings. To enable consumers to take advantage of these facilities, and also to accept payment of accounts, shops, formerly called service centres, are provided in most towns. To prevent landlords and other persons making unreasonable charges for electricity supplied through a prepayment meter, the Boards may fix maximum prices for the resale of electricity.

Consultative Councils

Consultative Councils, each consisting of about twenty-five members, have been set up in each of the twelve Area Boards in England and Wales, and also in the two Scottish Boards. The members of these Councils are appointed by the Secretary of State for Trade and Industry (or Minister of State for Scotland, in the case of the Scottish Boards). About half the members are representatives of the local authorities, and the remainder represent other consumer groups.

The duties of the Councils include the investigation of any matter relating to the supply of electricity in the area, which has been brought to their attention either by consumers, the Area Board, or the CEGB. After discussions, the Consultative Council may report the matter to the Electricity Council for appropriate advice or action.

Any variation of the tariffs offered to consumers, or of the bulk supply tariff for electricity bought by the Area Boards from the CEGB, must first be discussed by the appropriate Council.

Steam Power Stations

The list below shows the approximate percentages of the total electricity generated in England and Wales for each of the different types of station.

Coal-fired	78% approx.	} 88.9%	Gas turbine	0.51%
Oil-fired	10.9% approx.		Hydro-electric	0.11%
Nuclear		10.44%	Diesel	0.04%

GENERATION, TRANSMISSION AND DISTRIBUTION OF ELECTRICAL ENERGY

Boundaries of the area boards

Fig. 7.3 Boundaries of the Area Boards.

1—London; 2—South Eastern; 3—Southern; 4—South Western; 5—Eastern; 6—East Midlands; 7—Midlands; 8—South Wales; 9—Merseyside and North Wales; 10—Yorkshire; 11—North Eastern; 12—North Western.

In the North of Scotland almost all the electricity is generated at hydro-electric stations, whilst in the South of Scotland all types of station are used. Oil- and coal-fired stations produce more than 75% of the total electricity, nuclear about 20%, and hydro-electric and gas turbine the remainder.

It will be seen that coal, oil and nuclear stations produce about 99% of the total energy generated and we shall consider these stations (which are similar in many respects) and hydro-electric stations in detail.

However, we shall first briefly discuss the use of gas turbines, as this type of plant has a very important application.

Gas turbines

Most readers will be aware that electricity cannot be stored in large quantities, and consequently there must always be sufficient plant available to meet the maximum demand which is likely to arise, even though this demand will only occur for short periods during the winter months. As generating plant is very expensive, this would mean that costly plant could be standing idle for long periods. In 1962 the CEGB and the South of Scotland Board estimated that there would be a serious shortage of plant available to meet the maximum demand for the winter of 1964–65. As modern power stations take about seven years to complete from the preliminary design stage, it was necessary to find a method of providing plant rapidly. The method adopted was to utilize aircraft jet engines to drive conventional generators. The installations proved to be successful, and it is now general policy to install up to four gas turbines at each modern power station. Thus, about 100 MW of gas-turbine plant may be installed in a modern 2000 MW power station.

The more important advantages of gas-turbine plant may be summarised as:

(i) they are less costly to install than conventional plant,
(ii) they may be started up and connected to the network much more quickly than conventional plant,
(iii) they may be used to keep the voltages of main transmission lines constant.

Against these advantages must be set the fact that their running costs are higher than for conventional plant, and their use is therefore mainly restricted to the periods when the demand for electricity is greatest. We will now discuss in some detail the principles of the most important types of power station.

Types of Power Station

Figure 7.4 is a simplified diagram showing the general arrangement of a steam power station. This type of station may use coal, oil or nuclear fuel to produce the very high temperatures required in the boiler.

It will be seen that there is a closed circuit on the left side of the diagram, formed by the pipes drawn with dots in them and the turbine and condenser. The pipes within the boiler are heated to a temperature between 350 and 550°C, causing the water in them to turn to steam. The pressure of the steam will be between 40 and 160 times the pressure of the atmosphere, the lower figure referring to nuclear stations and the upper figure to oil- or coal-fired stations. The steam passes to the

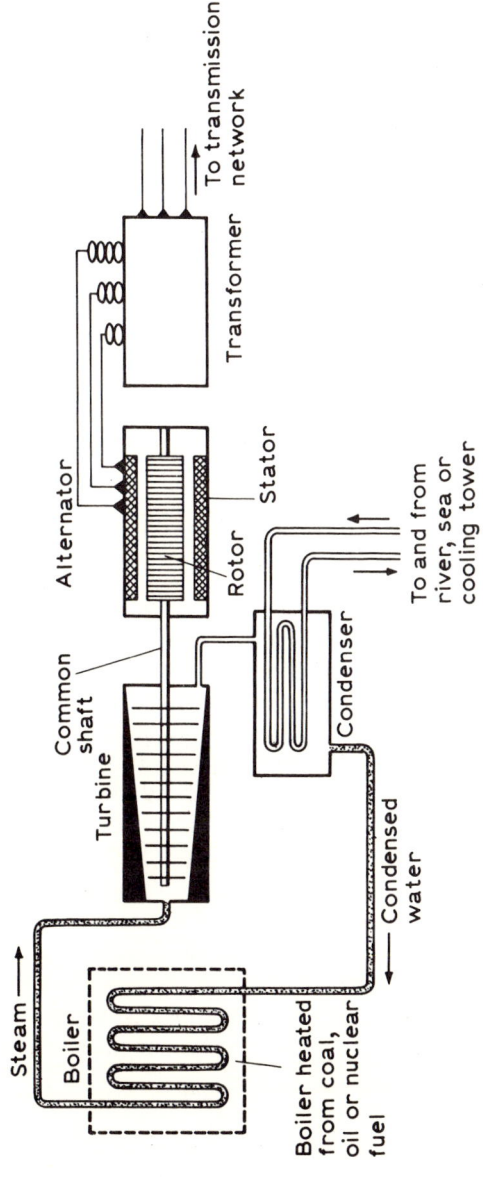

Fig. 7.4 Principal items of plant in a steam power station.

turbine where it impinges against a series of blades attached to the main shaft, causing it to rotate in much the same way as water can be used to turn a water wheel. The speed of the shaft must be carefully adjusted so that it remains constant at 3000 rev/min (revolutions per minute), though in some cases the speed is 1500 rev/min.

After passing through the turbine, the steam enters the condenser, which is basically a large container inside which is another set of tubes through which cold water is circulating. The cold water is usually pumped from the sea or a large river, but, where these facilities are not available, the water is cooled by passing it downwards through one of the large cooling towers which are commonly associated with power stations. When the steam passes around the cold tubes in the condenser, it condenses to become water again, and is pumped back to the boiler to repeat the process. When condensation occurs, the volume of water produced is very much less than the volume of steam from which it has been condensed, and this creates a vacuum in the condenser. This vacuum increases the rate at which the steam passes through the turbine. The water used for these purposes must be very pure if it is not to give rise to corrosion or deposition in the system, and it is therefore chemically treated to remove all impurities.

The alternator is shown on the right of fig. 7.4. As was explained in Chapter 6, the alternator consists basically of a rotor and a stator. The rotor, to which are attached the coils of the electromagnet, is an extension of the shaft of the turbine and therefore rotates at the same speed. The speed of the shaft must be maintained at precisely 3000 rev/min (or 1500 rev/min) as the frequency of the supply is directly related to this speed, i.e. any variation in speed will mean a corresponding variation in the supply frequency. The stator houses the coils, in which electricity is generated at a voltage of about 11 000 to 15 000 volts (11 to 15 kV). The stator coils are arranged to give a 3-phase supply, and this is connected through switchgear to transformers for transmission to the areas where the electricity is to be used, as described below.

We shall now discuss the special features associated with the different types of steam station—coal, oil and nuclear—and also the principles of the hydro-electric stations.

Coal-fired stations

The majority of the CEGB's power stations are of this type, and they burn between them almost 70 million tons of coal a year. A single 2000 megawatt (2000 MW) station on full load will require more than 20 000 tons of coal per day, and if all this coal is to be delivered by

Fig. 7.5 A 500 MW turbo-generator at West Burton, Notts, power station. The turbine is seen on the left, the alternator in the centre (with double doors), and the exciter for the d.c. supply to the rotor on the right. The overall length is almost 170 feet, and the station contains three other similar machines.

Fig. 7.6 A 2000 MW coal-fired power station at Ratcliffe-on-Soar, Notts. In front of the eight cooling towers, to the left centre of the picture, is the 400 kV switchroom. The low building in the centre is the turbine hall, and behind this are the tall boiler-house and a 650 feet high chimney. To the right can be seen the large coal storage area.

rail, facilities must be provided to receive, unload and dispatch some twenty trains daily. In addition, a large area must be set aside to store a three months supply of coal, and equipment must be provided to move the coal from the store to the boiler-house as it is required. To reduce fuel transport costs, many coal stations are sited near the large coalfields.

A further problem arises in the disposal of the ash which remains when this coal is burnt. The CEGB have established a special department to undertake the sale of this ash for civil engineering purposes, including its use in the foundations of new roads. Nevertheless, a considerable amount must still be dumped. Great care is taken to ensure that this dumping does not lead to the formation of the unsightly slag heaps associated with coal mines.

A modern 2000 MW coal-fired station costs about £80 000 000 and generates electricity for about 0·25p per unit. It has an efficiency of about 36%—most of the losses unavoidably occurring in the condenser. Very approximately, we may say that one unit of electricity is generated from one pound of coal.

Oil-fired stations
One of the main disadvantages of the oil-fired station is that we purchase our oil supplies from overseas countries. Consequently, there is always a risk that supplies may be interrupted or curtailed due to the international situation, and that the cost of oil may vary considerably for the same reason. However, at the present time the oil-fired stations situated near the refineries are slightly cheaper to construct and they generate electricity slightly more cheaply than comparable coal-fired stations. The efficiencies of the two types of stations are about equal. The CEGB would like to build more of this type of station, but the Government has decided that, for the time being, the number of new oil-fired stations must be limited. This is to prevent a sudden reduction in the CEGB's coal requirements, which would leave the Coal Board with large stocks of unwanted coal.

Several stations can, in fact, burn either coal or oil.

Nuclear stations
After the promising results obtained from the experimental nuclear power station at Calder Hall, the Government decided that the CEGB could proceed with the building of eight nuclear stations. These stations are often referred to as the 'magnox' stations, because the uranium—which is the basic fuel for a nuclear station—is contained in cans made of magnesium alloy.

GENERATION, TRANSMISSION AND DISTRIBUTION OF ELECTRICAL ENERGY

Fig. 7.7 A 2000 MW oil-fired power station at Fawley, Hampshire. On the left is the boiler house, in the centre is the turbine-hall and to the right the circular control room. The oil is fed by pipe line direct from the adjacent large oil refinery.

Fig. 7.8 A 500 MW nuclear power station at Trawsfynydd, North Wales. This was the first nuclear station to be built inland. The tall buildings contain the reactors, and in front of these buildings is the turbine hall.

The cost of building these stations has gradually been reduced, the cost of the early stations being four and a half times the cost of a similar coal- or oil-fired station. The later stations were only about two and a half times as expensive. The cost of the electricity produced has also been higher at nuclear stations, ranging from about 0·54p per unit at the first to 0·29p per unit at the last of the magnox stations. This last station was not completed until 1971, but in 1965 the CEGB decided to follow the magnox programme with a second programme for three more nuclear stations having an improved design. This type is referred to as the Advanced Gas-cooled Reactor (AGR) station and, although the building costs are about twice those of a coal-fired station, the generating cost will be slightly less, at about 0·23p per unit.

One big advantage of the nuclear station is that the amount of uranium required is very much less than the amount of coal required at a comparable coal station. At the later AGR stations, one ton of enriched uranium will produce as much electricity as 56 000 tons of coal.

Now that the magnox stations have been operating satisfactorily for many years, it has been decided that the possibility of an accident resulting in the release of radio-active material is so slight that new stations may be built close to centres of population. The siting of the nuclear station at Hartlepool is the first result of this change of policy.

The CEGB would like to build more nuclear stations, but is prevented from so-doing by the same restriction which limits the number of oil-fired stations, i.e. the undesirability of suddenly reducing the national demand for coal.

Hydro-electric stations

There are two types of station using water instead of steam to drive the turbines, and these are referred to as pure hydro-electric and pumped-storage stations.

In the pure hydro-electric station, a reservoir is built at a level high above the power station, the difference in height varying from a few hundred to a thousand or so feet.

When the station is required to generate, valves are opened and water is allowed to fall from the reservoir through large pipes. It is directed on to shaped blades attached to the shaft of the turbine in much the same way as water is used to turn a water wheel. The shaft, however, is normally vertical, and the rotor of the alternator, which is connected to the turbine shaft, is therefore situated above the turbine (fig. 7.9). Thus the arrangement of the turbine and alternator is similar

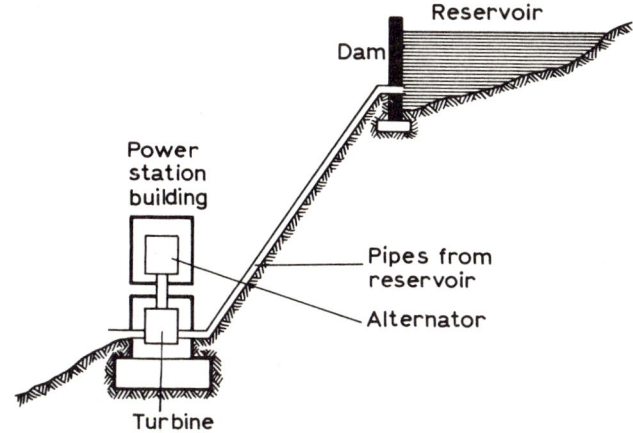

Fig. 7.9 Principle of a hydro-electric power station

to that in a steam station, but the two are installed vertically instead of horizontally.

As one would expect, there are very few hydro-electric stations in England and Wales but a large number in the North of Scotland Electricity Board area. The generating costs per unit are very low, but the construction costs are high—largely owing to the remoteness of suitable sites and the considerable amount of civil engineering work required for the reservoir construction.

It is impossible to store large quantities of electricity, but the pumped-storage type of station provides a novel method of overcoming this difficulty. Here two reservoirs are provided, one at a high level and one at a lower level (fig. 7.10).

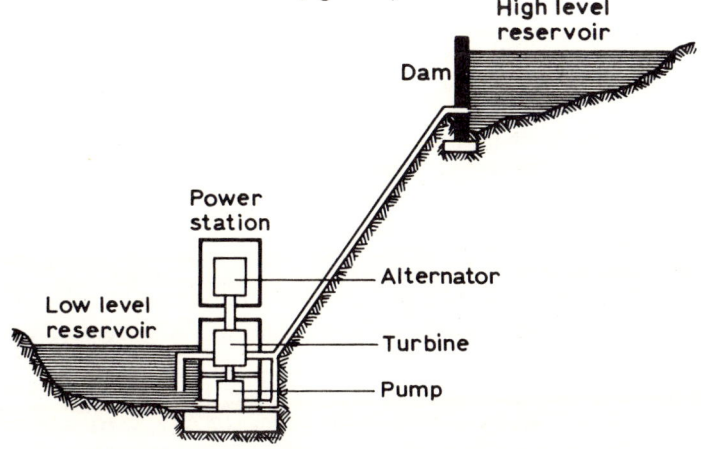

Fig. 7.10 Principle of a pumped-storage power station.

The generation of electricity is carried out during peak-load periods, exactly as described for the pure hydro-electric station. However, instead of the water from the high reservoir passing through the turbines once only, it is retained in the lower reservoir. It is then pumped back at night to the upper reservoir to repeat the process the following day.

Fig. 7.11 A 360 MW pumped-storage power station at Ffestiniog, North Wales. The dam of the high-level reservoir can be seen towards the top of the picture.

The advantages of a pumped-storage station may be explained as follows. At night time the demand for electricity throughout the country is small, and there is plenty of efficient plant available to meet this small demand. The cost of generation at night is therefore small.

During the day, when the demand for electricity is high, most of the available generating plant throughout the country must be used. Some of this plant is inefficient and the generating cost is therefore higher.

In the pumped-storage station the water is pumped up to the high level reservoir at night, and the cost of doing this will be low. The energy stored in the water while it is in the high level reservoir may then be converted back to electricity the following day by allowing it

GENERATION, TRANSMISSION AND DISTRIBUTION OF ELECTRICAL ENERGY

to fall—through the turbine—to the low level reservoir. The effect of this is that the total cost of the electricity produced at the pumped-storage station by day is less than it would be if it were necessary to produce this electricity by the less efficient plant which would otherwise have to be used. Thus the pumped-storage method effectively provides a means of storing cheap electricity.

The number of sites providing suitable conditions for this type of station in England and Wales is very limited. There is, however, one large station, having a capacity of 360 MW, at Ffestiniog in North Wales.

The Transmission System

For reasons discussed earlier, power stations are often sited at long distances from the areas in which the electricity they generate is to be used. It is therefore necessary to convey large quantities of electrical energy from the stations to the distribution centres. This is most commonly achieved by the use of overhead lines having bare conductors suspended from steel towers by glass or porcelain insulators.

Since the conductors of transmission lines possess resistance, some power will be lost in the lines when current flows through them. The power lost in the lines is shown in Chapter 4 to be given by

$$P = I^2 R$$

where I = current, and R = resistance.

It follows that the power lost in this way could be considerably decreased by reducing the current flowing in the line. The total power supplied by a 3-phase line is three times the power supplied for one phase,

$$\therefore P = 3 \times V \times I \times \text{power factor}$$

where V = phase voltage, and I = phase current.

If the power and power factor remain the same, a decrease in current can be achieved by making a corresponding increase in voltage. We saw in Chapter 6 that the transformer provides a very easy and efficient method of varying the voltage. For this reason, the voltages used for transmission lines have steadily increased as the amount of electricity produced has increased. Thus the voltage has risen from the early 132 kV system to the 275 kV and 400 kV systems of today, and development work is proceeding for transmission voltages up to 1500 kV.

These transmission lines are frequently, and rightly, criticised because they involve the erection of unsightly pylons through areas of beautiful countryside, and the question of why underground cables are not used is often asked. Unfortunately, the fact is that the cost of laying a 400 kV underground cable is nearly twenty times greater than the cost of the equivalent overhead line. Cost is not the only consideration, however, and there are both technical and constructional difficulties associated with cables which do not apply to overhead lines. One consoling fact is that a modern 400 kV heavy duty line can carry as much power as eighteen of the earlier 132 kV lines.

Fig. 7.12 A 400 kV overhead line carrying one 3-phase circuit on each side of the tower. Each phase consists of four conductors, and is supported from the cross-arms by two porcelain insulator strings.

One further development should be mentioned at this stage. A transmission line is very similar to a capacitor (as described in Chapter

4) since it consists of a number of conductors separated by insulation (air in the case of an overhead line, or paper in a cable). We have seen that, if an alternating voltage is applied to a circuit containing resistance and capacitance, a current will flow given by

$$I = \frac{V}{\sqrt{(R^2 + X_c^2)}}$$

where R = resistance and X_c = reactance.

As the voltage applied to a line increases, this 'capacitance current' will also increase. This current is in addition to the 'useful' current flowing to the consumers at the end of the line.

Now the maximum current a line can carry is largely determined by the size of the conductors. It follows that, as the capacitance current becomes greater, the current which can be supplied to consumers will become smaller. In fact, a point could be reached when no current at all was available for the consumers. Under certain circumstances this could occur with a cable only about 25 miles long. Although there are methods of reducing the capacitance current, it can be eliminated altogether if a direct current supply is used, since direct current will not flow in a circuit containing an insulator. There are also several other advantages of using high-voltage direct current and, consequently, several systems of this type are now in operation in various parts of the world. Of particular interest is the connection between Kingsnorth power station, in North Kent, and the London Area network. It must be emphasised that the alternators at the power stations still produce alternating current, but this is converted to direct current at the power station and inverted back to alternating current by special equipment at the far end of the line.

Fig. 7.13 Construction of one of the 266 kV d.c. cables used between Kingsnorth power station, Kent, and London.

Fig. 7.14 A 400 kV transformer. The transformer is on the left. The square structure, with the cylindrical tank on top, contains the oil which flows through the transformer to keep it cool.

Fig. 7.15 Six 400 kV circuit breakers (or switches). Each switch consists of three similar sections, and is mounted on a cylinder containing compressed air, which is used to blow out the arc formed when the switch contacts open.

GENERATION, TRANSMISSION AND DISTRIBUTION OF ELECTRICAL ENERGY

The Distribution System

The high-voltage transmission lines terminate at substations within the areas where the electricity is to be used. It is at these points that the Electricity Boards buy the electricity from the CEGB and assume responsibility for its distribution to the consumers (fig. 7.14). For this purpose the supply voltage is reduced to 66 kV, 33 kV or 11 kV, and very large factories may be supplied at one of these voltages. Cables operating at 132 kV, 66 kV and 33 kV usually contain channels parallel to the conductors through which oil circulates under pressure. This reduces the possibility of breakdown in the cable (figs. 7.15 to 7.17).

Fig. 7.16   33 kV 3-core oil-filled cable with a corrugated aluminium sheath. The oil circulates, under pressure, inside the sheath, and reduces the possibility of faults occurring in the cable.

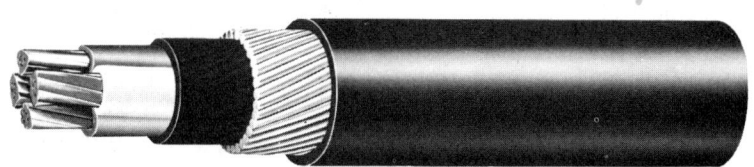

Fig. 7.17   440/250 V 4-core cable. The layer of wires immediately under the exterior sheath is provided to prevent mechanical damage to the cable.

For most commercial and all domestic consumers the supply is further reduced to 415/240 volts at small substations, usually called transformer chambers (fig. 7.18). These are sited about a quarter of a mile apart in residential areas, but closer together in business or industrial areas.

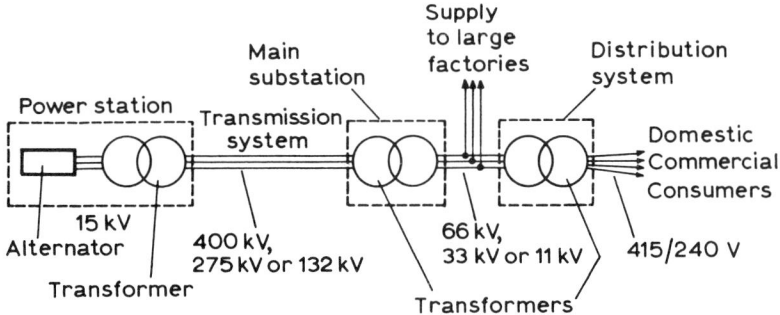

Fig. 7.18 How electricity is conveyed from the power station to the consumer.

Up to about ten cables are laid from these transformer chambers to the surrounding streets to provide a supply to small industrial, commercial and domestic consumers. Figure 7.19 represents one of these cables. It will be seen that there are four conductors, three of these being called *line conductors* and the fourth being the neutral conductor, which is earthed at the transformer chamber. If we measure the voltage between any two lines (called the *line voltage*), we should find that it is 415 volts, whereas the voltage between one line conductor and the neutral (called the *phase voltage*) would be 240 volts. Hence this is termed a 415/240 volt supply. Small industrial and commercial consumers normally receive a 3-phase supply—all four conductors being connected to their premises. Domestic consumers take a single-phase supply, i.e. their supply is connected between any one of the lines and the neutral conductor.

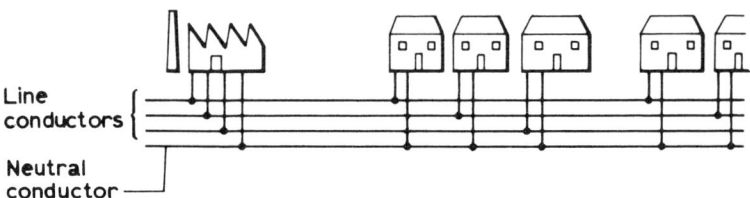

Fig. 7.19 How small industrial, small commercial and domestic consumers are connected to the low-voltage network.

GENERATION, TRANSMISSION AND DISTRIBUTION OF ELECTRICAL ENERGY

To ensure the most efficient use of their cables and plant, the Electricity Boards connect an approximately equal number of domestic consumers to each of the three lines so that the currents flowing in the three lines are nearly equal. This is often referred to as balancing the load.

The terminals on 3-phase switchgear, transformers etc. are often painted red, yellow and blue, so that the phases may readily be identified, or, alternatively, the numbers 1, 2 and 3 may be used.

Chapter 7—Questions

1. What are the advantages of using alternating rather than direct current for the transmission and distribution of electricity? Why does the able used for low voltage distribution normally contain four conductors? Discuss how (i) domestic premises, (ii) small factory premises would be connected to the low-voltage supply cable.

2. Describe briefly, with a diagram, how electricity is generated at a modern coal-fired generating station. State the approximate efficiency of such a station, and name the process which gives rise to most of the losses. Approximately how many pounds of coal are required to produce one unit of electricity?

3. Write brief notes to explain the duties of the following:
   (i) the Electricity Council,
   (ii) the Central Electricity Generating Board,
   (iii) the Area Electricity Boards,
   (iv) the Electricity Consultative Councils.

4. Name three different types of power station used in this country, and describe briefly the operating principles associated with one of the types you have named.

5. Why has the voltage of the main transmission lines steadily increased as the amount of electricity supplied has increased? What disadvantage arises with high-voltage alternating current lines which has lead to the construction of several high-voltage direct current lines?

6. How can two different voltages be obtained from a 3-phase supply? What names are given to the voltages? Draw a diagram representing a low-voltage mains cable and indicate how consumers' installations are connected to the cable.

8 Tariffs

An electricity tariff is the scale of charges used by an Electricity Board when charging consumers for the electrical energy consumed. At the time of nationalisation in 1947, many different tariffs existed throughout the country, but each Area Board has now standardised the tariffs for each class of consumer within its own area.

The Area Boards are autonomous—each Board must ensure that its overall costs are recovered, and that a reasonable surplus is obtained to provide for future improvements. However, their commitments differ widely. For example, the London Electricity Board has about 7000 consumers per square mile, the South Wales Electricity Board has less than 170 consumers per square mile, and the North of Scotland Board has about 20 consumers per square mile. It will obviously be very much easier for the London Board to provide a new consumer with a supply than it would be for the North of Scotland Board. On the other hand, in the North of Scotland the costs of generation (using mainly hydro-electric stations), and also the cost of land for buildings or substations, will be much less than in the London area.

Purposes of a Tariff

The main purposes of the electricity tariffs offered by the Area Boards may be summarised as follows:
  (i) to recover to the Area Board both the cost of the electrical energy purchased from the CEGB, and also the distribution costs involved in making the supply available to consumers,
  (ii) to encourage the use of electricity, since, if more electricity is used, the cost of producing and distributing it may be reduced,
  (iii) to provide a reasonable profit margin for future improvements and extensions to the existing system.

We shall see later how these aims are reflected in the types of tariff available.

TARIFFS

Costs of a supply undertaking
The costs of a supply undertaking may conveniently be considered as falling under three headings, i.e. capacity, varying costs, and consumer-related costs.

The 'capacity costs' are those costs which are related to the capacity of the plant installed (kilowatt related). Some of the costs included under this heading would be the annual interest paid on the money borrowed to buy plant and equipment, the money set aside annually to replace the plant when necessary (sinking-fund or depreciation cost), and rents, rates and insurances on plant and buildings.

The 'varying costs' are the costs which are affected by the amount of electricity supplied (kilowatt hour related). The obvious example in this category is the cost of fuel used in the power stations.

The 'consumer-related costs' are those which are dependent upon the number of consumers supplied. Examples would include the costs of meter reading, the producing of accounts for consumers for electricity supplied, and the provision of services.

Bulk-supply Tariff

The Bulk-supply Tariff, used by the CEGB when charging Area Boards for the electricity they purchase, is essentially a two-part tariff and varies slightly from one Board to another. Two charges are specified in this tariff—a 'capacity charge' and a 'running-rate charge'.

The capacity charge is dependent upon the maximum and basic demands of each of the Area Boards.

The running-rate charge specifies the cost of each unit supplied—these costs varying according to both the time of day and the time of year when the units are supplied. Thus the costs per unit are much lower for electricity supplied at night throughout the year than they are for peak demand periods.

In addition, there is a fuel-cost adjustment-factor applying to coal, coke and oil fuels. This varies the above running-rate charges by a factor which is determined by the local cost of fuel.

Load curves
It is well known that the load on the CEGB's network varies considerably during the day, and that the winter load is much greater than the summer load.

Curve A in fig. 8.1 shows the variation of the national load for a typical winter's day, whilst curve B shows the variation for a typical summer's day.

THE EAW ELECTRICAL HANDBOOK

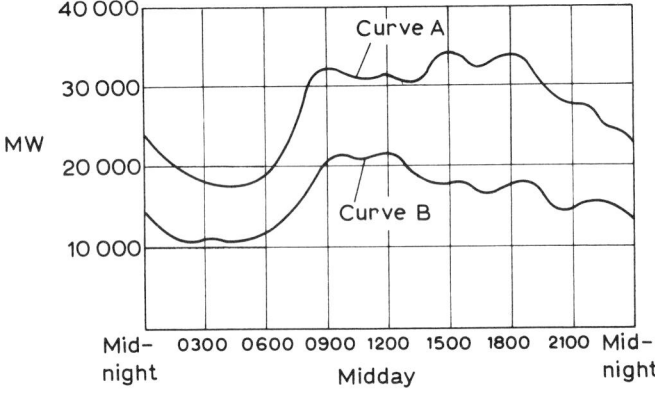

Fig. 8.1 Typical load curves for the CEGB network. Curve A is for a winter's day, and curve B is for a summer's day.

These curves are called *load curves* and the 'dips' in the curves are called valleys. They are important to the supply engineer because they clearly indicate certain characteristics. For instance, the big valley between midnight and 0600 hours indicates that at that time there is a considerable amount of plant lying idle. There are much smaller valleys during the daytime and between 1600 and 1700 hours. In fact, not many years ago, the load curves would have shown quite a large valley during the afternoon, but this valley has now almost disappeared. The tariffs offered by the CEGB to the Area Boards, and by the Area Boards to their consumers, reflect the variations in these load curves. We have seen that the CEGB Bulk-supply Tariff offers a cheaper rate for electricity supplied during the night period. The Area Boards pass on to their consumers these lower costs in the various Off-peak Tariffs.

Area-Board Tariffs

The factors discussed in the previous sections, together with any special local circumstances, are taken into account by the Area Boards when they formulate their tariffs. Each Board offers a separate range of tariffs for domestic, commercial and industrial consumers, and, in addition, there may be special tariffs for other categories of consumers, e.g. for churches and chapels, farms, public lighting, crop drying, etc.

It would be impossible to discuss every type of tariff in a book of this size, and therefore only the more common domestic and commercial tariffs will be mentioned.

Domestic Tariffs

Block tariff

This is the most common type of domestic tariff. It consists essentially of a fixed charge and a unit charge. The fixed charge is in the form of a block (or blocks) of units charged at a comparatively high rate. The number of units in the block (or blocks) is the same for all consumers. All other units after the block units are charged for at a reduced rate.

The Midlands Electricity Board offer a domestic block tariff which is fairly typical. This tariff takes the following form:

each of the first 52 units per quarter	3·13p
each of the next 65 units per quarter	1·46p
each additional unit per quarter	0·73p

Example

A domestic consumer in the Midlands Electricity Board area uses 2040 units in one quarter. Calculate the cost of the electricity consumed.

In this case, 52 units will be charged at 3·13p, 65 units at 1·46p and the remainder $(2040-(52+65) = 1923$ units) at 0·73p. The cost may therefore be calculated as follows.

	£
52 units at 3·13p =	1·63
65 units at 1·46p =	0·95
1923 units at 0·73p =	14·04
	16·62

Two- or three-part tariff

The London, South-Eastern, and Eastern Boards all offer tariffs of this type. It is very similar to the Block Tariff in that it consists of one (or two) fixed charges and a unit charge. In the case of the South-Eastern and Eastern Boards, the fixed charge is the same for all consumers, but in the London Board area the standing charge is based upon the floor area of the premises, and there is also a fixed block of units. The rates are as follows.

(i) A standing charge per quarter based on the floor area of the premises, as follows:

for the first 800 ft^2	90p
for each additional 200 ft^2 of the next 1200 ft^2	20p
for each additional 200 ft^2 of the next 1000 ft^2	15p
for each additional 500 ft^2 in excess of 3000 ft^2	35p

(ii) A primary unit charge: each of the first 195 units per quarter—1·225p.

(iii) A secondary unit charge: each additional unit—0·8p.

Example
A domestic consumer in the London Electricity Board area uses 2040 units in one quarter. If the floor area of his premises for the purposes of the tariff is 1500 ft^2, calculate the cost of the electricity consumed.

In this case, in addition to the standing charge, the first 195 units will be charged at 1·225p per unit, and the remainder (2040−195 = 1845 units) at 0·8p per unit. The cost may therefore be calculated as follows.

$$\text{Area} = 1500 \text{ ft}^2 = 800 + 3 \times 200 + 1 \times 100 \text{ ft}^2.$$

	£
∴ standing charge = 90p + 4 × 20p =	1·70
195 units at 1·225p =	2·39
1845 units at 0·8p =	14·76
	18·85

Flat-rate tariff
This tariff is often more suitable for premises where the consumption of electricity is small. As its name suggests, a standard rate is charged for all units consumed. Sometimes it is possible to obtain a cheaper rate for units supplied for purposes other than lighting. In this case it will, of course, be necessary for the wiring in the premises to be divided, so that electricity used for lighting passes through one meter, and electricity used for all other purposes passes through a second meter.

In the London Electricity Board, electricity used for lighting is charged at 3·125p per unit, and electricity used for all other purposes, and separately metered, is charged for at 1·35p per unit.

Example
A consumer living in the London Electricity Board area uses 30 units for lighting and 64 units for other purposes in a quarter. If the area of the premises is less than 800 ft^2, calculate the cost for electricity supplied using (i) the flat-rate tariff, and (ii) the 3-part tariff.

(i) Flat-rate tariff

	£
30 units at 3·125p =	0·94
64 units at 1·35p =	0·86
	1·80

(ii) 3-part tariff

$$\begin{aligned} &&&& £ \\ \text{Standing charge} &= 0\cdot 90 \\ \text{94 units at } 1\cdot 225\text{p} &= \underline{1\cdot 17} \\ &&&& \underline{2\cdot 07} \end{aligned}$$

Note —no units are charged at 0·8p, since 195 units must be used before the reduced cost per unit applies.

Restricted-hours tariff
This tariff takes into account the fact that the cost of electricity supplied to Area Boards is cheaper during the periods when the demand on the system is small. Thus, three rates are offered—a very cheap rate for electricity used during the night, and two slightly more expensive rates, both of which include the use of electricity during an afternoon period, in addition to the night period. The tariff applies only to consumers using electricity for water heating, or for space heating using storage radiators. However, as has been seen on the load curves, the afternoon valley has practically disappeared at this time, due to the increased use of electricity by industrial and commercial consumers, and also domestic consumers using this tariff. The concession which allowed the use of cheap electricity during the afternoon period is, therefore, no longer being offered to new consumers.

The restricted-hours tariff available to consumers in the area of the Midlands Electricity Board is as follows.

Rate A—supply restricted to not more than eight consecutive hours between 2300 and 0730 hours—0·3p/unit.

Rate B—supply restricted to not more than eight consecutive hours between 2300 and 0730 hours, and up to three hours between 0730 and 2300 hours—0·34p/unit.

Rate C—applies to consumers with floor-warming installations. Supply restricted to not more than twelve consecutive hours between 1830 and 0730 hours, and up to three hours between 0730 and 1830 hours—0·38p/unit.

In all cases, the actual hours during which the supply may be used for the purposes of this tariff are specified by the Board, and there is an additional charge of 50p per quarter for the time switch provided by the Board. As stated earlier, rates B and C are no longer available to new consumers.

White-meter tariff

To obviate the necessity for the afternoon 'topping-up' charge, manufacturers have designed a range of high-capacity storage radiators which only require a night charge. These are discussed in more detail in the chapter on heating. The successful design of these heaters has enabled the Boards to offer a tariff with a considerably reduced charge for electricity used at night. In addition to the use of the cheap-rate electricity for space-heating purposes, it may be an advantage to use it also for water heating. It will, however, be necessary to ensure that the hot-water cylinder has a suitable capacity for the hot-water requirements of the premises in which it is installed. This tariff is known as the 'White-meter Tariff' because a special meter (having a white case) is used (fig. 8.2).

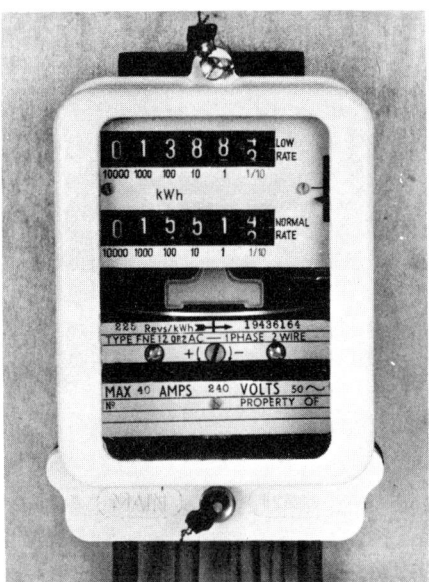

Fig. 8.2 The White Meter used in conjunction with the White-meter Tariff. In this tariff, units used during the off-peak period are charged at a low rate, so two sets of dials are necessary.

The meter has two dials instead of one, as on an ordinary meter. One of the dials records the units used between 2300 and 0700 hours (these are called night units), and the other records the units used between 0700 and 2300 hours (these are called day units). The cost of the night units is less than half the cost of the day units. A standing charge is also made, in addition to the charge for units used.

TARIFFS

The White-meter Tariff for the Midlands Electricity Board is as follows:

> Fixed charge per quarter £2·50,
> Day units 0·8p/unit,
> Night units 0·8p/unit.

For the London Electricity Board the tariff is more complicated, and is made up as follows:

1st standing charge per quarter—based on the floor area of the premises, the charges being the same as for the 3-part tariff given earlier,	
2nd standing charge per quarter	£1·40,
for each unit supplied between 2300 and 0700 hours	0·32p,
for each of the first 195 units supplied per quarter at other times	1·225p,
for each additional unit per quarter	0·8p.

Example

A consumer living in the area of the Midlands Electricity Board uses 2000 units in one quarter. Of these units, 1200 are used during the day period, and 800 are used during the night. Calculate the cost of electricity supplied for this quarter if the tariff used is (i) the White-meter tariff, and (ii) the Block tariff.

(i) White-meter tariff

	£
Fixed charge	2·50
Day units (1200 at 0·8p)	9·60
Night units (800 at 0·30p)	2·40
	14·50

(ii) Block tariff

	£
52 units at 3·13p	1·63
65 units at 1·46p	0·95
1883 units at 0·73p	13·75
	16·33

Example

Calculate the cost of the electricity supplied for the conditions given in the previous example, but assuming the consumer lived in the area of the London Electricity Board in premises having a floor area of 1500 ft².

White-meter tariff

	£
1st standing charge	1·70
2nd standing charge	1·40
800 units at 0·32p	2·56
195 units at 1·225p	2·39
1005 units at 0·8p	8·04
	16·09

3-part tariff (no Block tariff for LEB)

	£
Standing charge	1·70
195 units at 1·225p	2·39
1805 units at 0·8p	14·44
	18·53

If a consumer uses a fairly high number of units at night, the White-meter tariff will probably be better than the Block tariff. To simplify the calculations, all the above examples have been based on the costs for one quarter. However, it must be emphasised that a true comparison of the different tariffs available can only be made on an annual basis, because, although standing charges will be the same for each quarter, the number of units used will vary considerably.

In concluding this section, it must be remembered that there are usually certain provisions applying to most tariffs. Not all these provisions have been discussed in this book. Furthermore, the Electricity Boards reserve the right to withdraw or amend any tariff at any time. Any consumer may easily obtain full details of all tariffs by asking for this information at his or her local Electricity Shop. The staff will also advise consumers on the most suitable tariff for given circumstances.

Commercial Tariffs

It is not proposed to discuss commercial tariffs in the same detail as has been done with domestic tariffs. Generally speaking, the principles discussed at the beginning of this chapter also apply when commercial tariffs are formulated. The most common types of commercial tariff are as follows.

(i) *Block tariff* This is similar to the domestic block tariff. The method of assessing the number of units in the block (or blocks) varies, but a figure based on floor area is used by several Boards.

(ii) *Maximum-demand tariff* This tariff consists of a charge based on the maximum demand recorded at the intake point to the consumer's installation, plus a charge for the units used.

(iii) *Restricted-hours tariff* This is similar to the corresponding domestic tariff, and also applies to electricity supplied exclusively for thermal-storage purposes, i.e. water and space heating.

(iv) *Flat-rate tariff* This is similar to the corresponding domestic tariff, but reduced rates for electricity used only for motors, cooking, or water heating may be offered.

Power Factor Improvement

Both industrial and commercial maximum-demand tariffs often incorporate what is known as a power-factor penalty clause. This clause applies to consumers who operate their installations at a low power factor, and it has the effect of increasing the cost of electricity supplied to such consumers.

The power factor may vary between zero and unity, but is frequently about 0·7 for an industrial installation. When the power factor is unity, the current and voltage are in phase. If the power factor is less than unity, this will normally indicate that the current values are lagging the corresponding voltage values. If a capacitor is connected across the supply, however, the current taken by the capacitor will lead the supply voltage. For this case also, the power factor is less than unity. The power factor thus gives an indication of the phase difference between the current and voltage—the nearer its value is to unity, the more nearly the current and voltage approach the in-phase condition.

We saw in Chapter 4 that the power supplied to a single-phase load is given by

power supplied = voltage × current × power factor.

We may therefore deduce that

$$\text{current} = \frac{\text{power supplied}}{\text{voltage} \times \text{power factor}}.$$

We will calculate the current taken by a motor having an input of 2 kilowatts, if it has a power factor of 0·7, and is connected to a 250 volt supply.

$$I = \frac{P}{V \times \text{power factor}}$$

$$= \frac{2000}{250 \times 0 \cdot 7}$$

$= 11\cdot 4$ amperes.

Now, if the power factor could be improved to unity, the current required from the supply would be

$$I = \frac{2000}{250 \times 1} = 8 \text{ amperes.}$$

It follows that, the nearer the power factor is to unity, the less will be the current required to supply a certain load. Exactly the same conclusion can be deduced in the case of a 3-phase load.

If the current required to supply the load can be decreased in this way, it will mean that the size of the alternators required to provide the current may be reduced. Also, the size of the transformers, cables, switchgear, etc., can all be made smaller, and therefore their cost will be less than would be the case if the power factor were low.

There are other advantages obtained by reducing the current, however. The loss occurring along the cables, which we have seen is given by $I^2 R$, will be reduced, as will be the voltage drop along the cable, given by IZ. The reduced losses will mean a greater efficiency of transmission, and the reduced voltage drop will mean that the voltage at the load will be higher. In addition, as was stated at the beginning of this section, the cost to the consumer for electricity used will be less if the power factor is high.

For all these reasons, then, it will probably pay a consumer having an installation with a low power factor to install power-factor improvement equipment to bring the power factor nearer to unity.

Since, in an industrial installation, the current will usually be lagging the voltage, it is necessary to introduce across the circuit a capacitor, which, as we have seen, will take a current leading the voltage. By choosing a suitable capacitor, the power factor may be improved to any desired value. This is the usual method of power-factor improvement. Since motors are the most important causes of low power factor, individual capacitors are sometimes fitted to motors. The same method is used with fluorescent tubes, which also operate at a low power factor. With large installations, the power-factor improvement equipment may be centrally positioned at the consumer's intake substation.

Domestic installations operate with a power factor close to unity, and special arrangements are not required for improving the power factor.

Chapter 8—Questions

1 (i) What domestic tariffs operate in your area of electricity supply?
(ii) How does the consumer contribute towards the 'fixed costs' of the Electricity Board?
(iii) What is meant by 'off-peak' load?

2 A certain consumer living in a house having a floor area of 1350 ft^2 in the London Electricity Board area uses the following amounts of electricity in a quarter, for the purposes stated.

150 units—lighting
800 units—heating
1250 units—cooking

From the information given in this chapter, calculate the costs of the electricity used by this consumer for both 3-part and flat-rate tariffs. Under what circumstances is the flat-rate tariff likely to be cheaper to a consumer than the 3-part tariff?

Why should a comparison of tariff costs be based on the annual consumption of electricity and not on a quarterly figure?

3 The electrical installation in a flat comprises of the following, used during a quarter for the hours indicated or units assessed:
heating—5 kW for 200 hours,
lighting—1 kW for 100 hours,
cooking—assessed at 300 units,
water heating—assessed at 500 units.
A vacuum cleaner of 450 watts is used for 20 minutes a day.
If the quarterly standing charge is £1·40 and the unit charge 0·71p per unit, what is the quarterly bill, based on 90 days in the quarter?

4 Discuss the essential features of the following types of domestic tariff:
(i) block tariff,   (ii) 2- or 3-part tariff,
(iii) flat-rate tariff,   (iv) white-meter tariff.

5 A family uses the following average amounts of electricity:
cooking—30 units per week,
lighting—500 watts for 4 hours per day,
heating—one 2 kW fire for 3 hours per day,
water heating—50 units per week.

How many units are consumed per week? If a consumer pays a standing charge of £1·50 per quarter, 1·225p for the first 195 units and 0·8p for each additional unit, calculate the cost of the electricity supplied per quarter.

6 Make a sketch of the dials of an electricity meter, clearly showing all markings. The sketch should show five main dials and the hands are to be drawn so that the meter is reading 10693 kilowatt hours. If the value given above relates to the meter reading at a consumer's house, and a subsequent reading three months later showed 11993 kilowatt hours, calculate the average weekly consumption.

7 What factors must be considered in formulating an electricity tariff? What are the main costs associated with the supply of electricity? How are these costs reflected in the tariffs offered by Electricity Boards?

9 The Domestic Electrical Installation

The Electricity Board's Equipment

In a previous chapter it was stated that, in England and Wales, the Central Electricity Generating Board is responsible for the generation and transmission of electricity, but that the responsibility for its distribution to consumers is shared by twelve Electricity Boards. Consumers' installations are connected to the Electricity Boards' cables by means of service cables, and these are terminated within the premises at a mutually agreed position. Where the length of a service cable is excessive, the consumer may be required to contribute towards its cost.

At the service termination position, the Board connect the service cable to a house service fuse. This fuse, which normally has a rating of 60, 80 or 100A, will ensure that no damage occurs to the Board's cables or equipment in the event of a fault occurring on the consumer's premises. Connections are made from the service fuse to the meter, which is supplied to record the amount of electricity used by the consumer (sometimes more than one meter is necessary for this purpose, as, for example, is the case with some of the 'off-peak' tariffs discussed in Chapter 8). Originally, consumers were responsible for supplying their own meters and ensuring that they remained accurate. However, because of the difficulties involved, most Supply Authorities sold or hired meters to their consumers. Soon after nationalisation, this practice was abandoned and, although the meter remains the property of the Electricity Board, no charge is normally made for its installation or use. The house service fuse and the meter (or meters) are sealed by the Electricity Board and consumers are not allowed to interfere with this part of the installation.

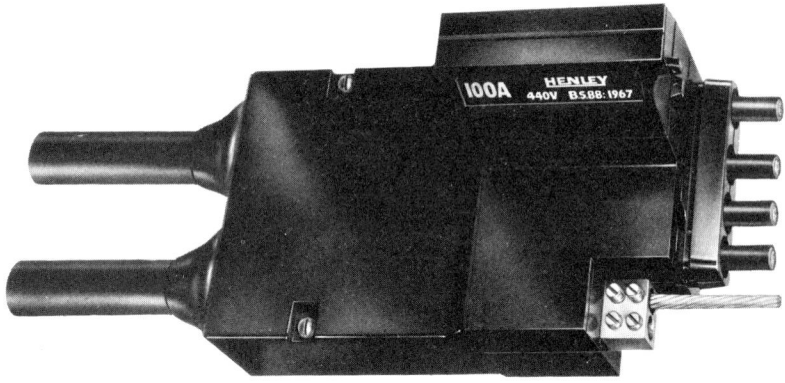

Fig. 9.1 Double-pole house service fuse.

The Consumer's Installation

Connections are made from the meter (or meters) to one or more main switches, and it is at this point that the consumer's responsibility for the installation begins. The main switches must be provided so that the installation may be isolated from the supply when, for example, alterations or extensions are made. They will, therefore, be double-pole switches, i.e. they have two blades—one breaking the line conductor and the other the neutral conductor. A single-pole switch has only one blade and it is used to break the line conductor only—never the neutral. This type is commonly used in lighting circuits.

What has been described so far relates particularly to domestic installations, but the same principles apply to large industrial and commercial installations, except that the equipment will be more complex. Several service cables may be provided or, in the case of very large consumers, a high-voltage supply at 11 kV, 33 kV or an even higher voltage may be provided.

In this book we shall deal mainly with the domestic installation typical of that found in many modern homes. We may summarise the requirements of an electrical installation by saying that it must provide a safe and adequate supply to wherever it is required.

The safety aspect is, of course, of prime importance and we will start by looking at the precautions a consumer should take to ensure that his appliances are safe. We will then discuss the safety requirements associated with the installation itself.

Safety
Choice and maintenance of appliances
There are various organisations which test appliances, and they may issue reports on safety, construction, cost of operation, and so on.

The British Electrical Approvals Board for Domestic Appliances (BEAB), who are sponsored by the various branches of the electrical industry and the British Standards Institution, test appliances in accordance with the requirements of BS 3456. The appliances which they approve bear the yellow and black BEAB mark. Some of these tests check that the appliance can be handled normally without the risk of electric shock, that portable appliances cannot easily be overturned, that boiling water cannot easily be spilled from kettles and steam irons, and that guards on electric fires provide reasonable protection against clothes catching fire. Even after an appliance has been approved, visits are made to the manufacturer's factory to ensure that the required standards are being maintained, and, in addition, random checks are carried out from time to time.

The Consumers Association select the types of appliance which they wish to test, and report on them in their monthly publication *Which*.

Yet another scheme which has been introduced to assist shoppers in this country is the 'Teltag' scheme. This was sponsored by the late Consumer Council and applies to all types of products. A blue and white label (Teltag) is attached to certain appliances, giving, in the case of electrical appliances, details of performance, size of fuse and plug required, and, in conjunction with the BEAB, confirmation that the appliance has been tested for safety. The Teltag does not, however, imply that an appliance has been approved other than from the safety point of view.

Where consumers require further assistance in the choice of appliances, this may always be obtained from any of the Electricity Boards' service centres or from the Electrical Association for Women.

Whilst it is most important to ensure that an appliance has been approved before purchasing it, it is equally important to ensure that it remains safe during the whole of the time it is in use. This is only possible if the appliance is tested at regular intervals—in some cases, e.g. electric blankets, once every year. Whenever a lead becomes frayed, a plug damaged, or the appliance itself damaged in such a way that it reduces its electrical safety, permanent repairs should be carried out before the appliance is used again. Manufacturers' instructions must always be carefully observed, e.g. the flow of air through convector heaters must not be impeded. Provided that these elementary precautions are observed, appliances will be perfectly safe.

Wiring and wiring accessories

The most important guide to the standard of safety required for wiring and wiring accessories is a book issued by the Institution of Electrical Engineers (IEE) entitled *Regulations for the Electrical Equipment of Buildings*. The regulations are detailed and will not be easily understood by the layman. However, all reputable organisations concerned with electrical installation always ensure that their work is carried out in accordance with these regulations. Such work is then guaranteed, and any defects will be rectified without charge.

The standard of workmanship required by the IEE Regulations may not be provided by some of the firms who offer a cheap installation. Substantial reductions are normally possible only at the expense of safety, either in the type of material used or in the method of installation. It cannot be too strongly emphasised that a consumer should only engage the services of a reputable contractor, i.e. a member of the Electrical Contractors' Association, the Electrical Contractors Association of Scotland, or an approved contractor on the roll of the National Inspection Council for Electrical Installation Contracting (NICEIC). In case of any doubt, the advice of the local Electricity Board should first be obtained. As has been mentioned elsewhere in this book, Electricity Boards themselves undertake this type of work.

The requirements of the IEE Regulations may be summarised by the first regulation which says 'All conductors and apparatus must be sufficient in size and power for the work they are called upon to do, and constructed, installed and protected so as to prevent danger as far as is reasonably practicable.' Area Boards may refuse to give a new supply or to maintain an existing supply to a consumer whose installation does not meet the minimum regulation requirements.

To ensure that wiring installations remain in a safe condition, they should be inspected by a qualified electrician at regular intervals not exceeding five years.

In the event of a fault occurring in an installation, whether in an appliance, or in part of the wiring, it is essential that the faulty section be disconnected from the supply immediately, but that the remainder of the system should remain in operation. This can be achieved by an adequate system of fuses or circuit breakers, and by the provision of earthing.

Fuses and circuit breakers

A fuse consists of three parts—the fuse element, the fuse carrier and the fuse base. What we really mean when we speak about a fuse is the fuse element, and it is this which is frequently described as the weak

DOMESTIC ELECTRICAL INSTALLATION

link in the circuit. It is designed to carry the normal full-load current for the circuit it is protecting without overheating. If a short-circuit occurs, there will be a considerable increase in current which will cause the fuse element to become very hot and melt. When this happens, the fuse is said to have 'blown'. If a circuit is slightly overloaded, the fuse element will overheat, but may not 'blow' for several hours—the current required to cause it to 'blow' immediately usually being about twice that of its current rating. Thus a 5 ampere fuse will blow if the current exceeds about 10 amperes. It would be impossible to design, at a reasonable cost, a fuse element which had a rating of 5 amperes but which blew at $5\frac{1}{2}$ amperes.

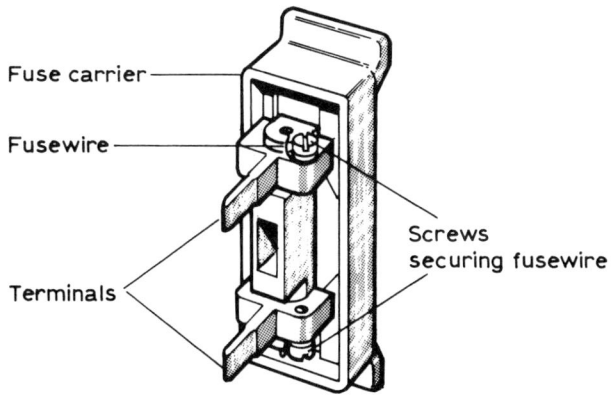

Fig. 9.2 Rewirable fuse.

The fuse element often consists of a piece of tinned copper wire, and it is most important that the correct size is chosen when the element is replaced. There are two methods of connecting the fuse into the circuit. In the first method the fuse element is wrapped around two brass terminals on the fuse carrier, as shown in fig. 9.2, and is known as the rewirable type. In the other method, the wire is enclosed in a cartridge. This cartridge has two brass caps, one at each end of a hollow cylindrical ceramic body filled with quartz powder, the wire being connected internally to the brass caps. The cartridge fits into clips provided on the fuse carrier. This type of fuse is more convenient

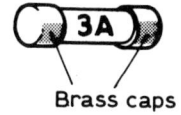

Fig. 9.3 Cartridge fuse.

111

to replace than the rewirable type and, as the rating is clearly printed on the body, there is no difficulty in selecting the correct size. It is more costly than the rewirable type, however.

The fuse carrier is inserted into a base on which terminals are provided for the wiring connections. The fuse carrier and base are commonly made of porcelain. In a fused plug, the carrier and base are combined, as described later, and are made of plastic or tough rubber.

Every circuit must be controlled by a fuse having a suitable rating—the fuse being located at the point where that circuit is connected to the supply. In addition, to prevent several appliances being disconnected when a fault occurs, it is now the usual practice to fuse each appliance separately, by providing a fuse in the plug. The size of this fuse must be correctly related to the rating of the appliance to which it is connected.

Fuses must always be connected in the line conductor so that the circuit or appliance is disconnected from the live terminal of the supply. If it were placed in the neutral conductor, although the circuit would be broken when the fuse blew, the appliance would still be connected to the live terminal and the risk of shock would still be present.

Another device which is sometimes used to protect a circuit from excess current is a miniature circuit breaker (MCB). This is an automatic switch which disconnects a circuit immediately a fault occurs on that circuit. When the fault has been repaired, the circuit breaker can again be switched on in the same way as a light switch is operated, so the restoration of the supply is much simpler than is the case when fuses are used.

Earthing

We have now seen that the fuse or MCB performs an extremely important function in the safety requirements of an installation. Of equal importance, however, is the provision of efficient earthing, as it is possible for an appliance to be faulty and yet still remain connected to the supply because it has not been properly earthed. This may occur in the following circumstances, which are illustrated in the simplified diagram (fig. 9.4).

When an appliance is switched on, it is connected to one of the three windings on the secondary of the Electricity Board's transformer (see fig. 7.18). One end of each of these windings (that connected to the neutral conductor) is connected to earth—this connection being necessary for technical reasons. In fig. 9.4, the normal current path is from A to B, through the appliance to C, to D and back to A. Current

DOMESTIC ELECTRICAL INSTALLATION

will still flow along this path if for some reason the connection at B touches the metal framework of the appliance. This may occur externally (e.g. if the lead becomes damaged at the point where it enters the appliance) or internally (e.g. if a connection becomes loose). It is important to appreciate that, although the metal framework is now live, the appliance operates normally.

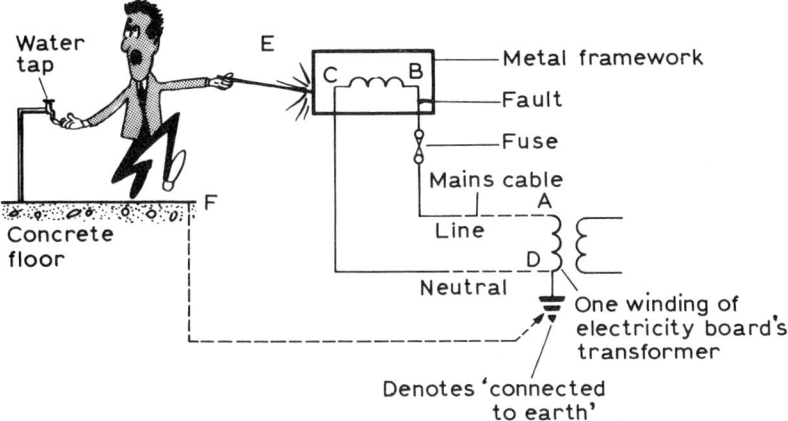

Fig. 9.4 How a person may receive a shock from a faulty appliance.

The danger arises if the metal framework is now touched by a person who is standing on a concrete floor, or touching anything which is connected to earth. It will be seen that, under these circumstances, a second path is formed from A to B, through the metal framework of the appliance to E, through the person's body to earth (F), and back through the earth to D. The person will receive a shock which may prove to be fatal.

This danger can easily be avoided by ensuring that, where appropriate, the metal framework of all appliances is connected to earth by means of an earth wire. This earth wire must be provided not only at socket outlets but also at all lighting points and switches, as nowadays metalwork is often used in the construction of these items. The earth wire must be connected to earth in a manner approved by the Electricity Board.

The effect of the earth wire is shown in fig. 9.5. Immediately the fault occurs and the framework becomes alive, there is a low resistance path around the circuit A to B, through the framework of the appliance to the earth terminal at G, to the earth connection at H, and back through the earth to D. Because of the low resistance of this path, a very high current will flow and blow the fuse, automatically disconnecting the appliance from the supply. Even if a person were touching the appliance when the fault occurred, they would not receive a shock as their body resistance would be considerably greater than that of the earth wire.

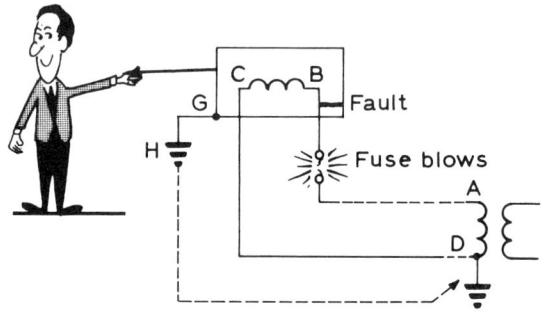

Fig. 9.5 How an earthed appliance is immediately disconnected from the supply when a fault occurs.

Most fixed appliances have exposed metalwork which must be earthed. Portable appliances, however, fall into one of the following categories.

All-insulated appliances, whose exposed parts are made of an insulating material, and metal screws, where used, are covered with an insulating material. These appliances do not, therefore, have to be earthed (e.g. small hairdriers).

Double-insulated appliances, having exposed metalwork which is separated from all live parts by two insulating barriers, so earthing is not required (e.g. electric clocks).

Metal-clad appliances, where only one insulating barrier is provided. As it is possible that this insulation may break down, the appliance must be earthed (e.g. electric fires).

It follows that 2-pin socket outlets should never be fitted. Their use must be restricted to appliances which do *not* require earthing.

When connecting an appliance to the supply, the maker's instructions must always be followed carefully. If there is any doubt as to whether or not an appliance should be earthed, the advice of a qualified electrician should be obtained.

Adequate provision of socket outlets and lighting
The necessity for fuses and earthing is usually recognised when safety is being considered. What is not so often appreciated is that an ade-

quate number of socket outlets must be provided if an installation is to be safe under all conditions. Apart from the convenience of being able to use appliances in any required position, a reasonable number of socket outlets will avoid both the long lengths of trailing flex that one sees all too frequently, and the use of adaptors. Long lengths of flex are dangerous not only because they constitute a hazard to people moving about the room but also because there is a real danger of the flex becoming damaged, resulting either in a fire or in someone getting a shock. It is also important that good lighting is provided, since poor lighting constitutes another common cause of accidents in the home. This can be achieved not only by providing an adequate number of lighting outlets but also by ensuring that those provided are suitably positioned. This is discussed in detail in Chapter 12.

Various suggestions have been made regarding the number of socket outlets which should be installed to give an adequate supply. Most authorities would agree that in a modern six-roomed house the total number should be about twenty-five. These would be positioned as follows:

living and dining rooms and kitchens	4 to 6
double bedrooms	3 to 5
single bedrooms	2 to 4
halls, landings, etc.	1 to 2.

Cables

Before looking at the layout of a wiring installation, we will first consider the three main types of cable now used in domestic installations. These are:

(i) multi-core p.v.c. or rubber insulated cables,

(ii) single-core p.v.c. or rubber insulated cables drawn into conduit,

(iii) mineral insulated cables.

All cables consist of one or more conductors, each surrounded by an insulating material with possibly a further layer of sheath insulation to provide protection from mechanical damage. The material which has been used for conductors in the past has been copper, but it is possible that, for economic and other reasons, it will gradually be replaced by aluminium in the future. The low-voltage mains cables installed by the Electricity Boards generally use aluminium conductors. Except for the smallest sizes, conductors are stranded, i.e. they consist of several wires twisted together to provide flexibility in handling.

The material used for insulation in the earlier cables was usually rubber, but nowadays the use of polyvinyl-chloride (p.v.c.) is much more common. The earth conductor is not covered with insulation, although it may be enclosed within the outer covering of insulation (fig. 9.6).

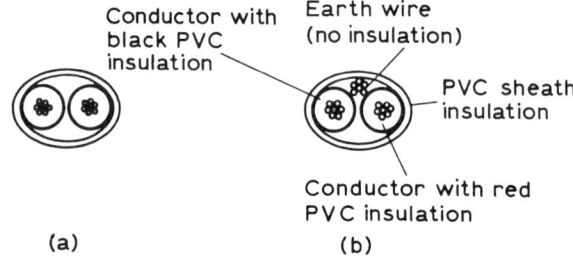

Fig. 9.6 (a) Cross-section of a 2-core (twin) cable, (b) cross-section of a 2-core cable with earth conductor (twin and earth).

Sometimes, where it is required to provide greater mechanical protection, sheath insulation is not used, but instead the separately insulated conductors are pulled into steel or plastic conduit having a diameter of $\frac{5}{8}''$ or $\frac{3}{4}''$. Another type of cable which also gives considerable mechanical protection is the mineral-insulated metal-sheathed (m.i.m.s.) cable. In these cables, the single-strand copper or aluminium conductors are enclosed within a sheath of the same material. The conductors are insulated from each other, and from the sheath, by a filling of magnesium oxide—compressed to ensure good insulating qualities but, at the same time, flexible (fig. 9.7). This type of cable is much more expensive than the p.v.c. insulated cable, and is only used where it is necessary to provide the special protection it affords.

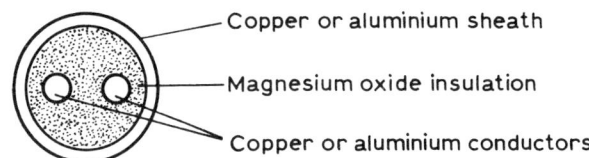

Fig. 9.7 Cross-section of a mineral-insulated, metal-sheathed cable.

In the past, cables have been manufactured in a range of standard sizes described by the number of strands and the diameter of each strand in inches. Thus a 7/·029 cable consists of seven strands, each strand having a diameter of 0·029 inch. Occasionally, especially with larger sizes, the cross sectional area of the conductor is given instead, and for a 7/·029 cable this would be 0·0045 in^2.

DOMESTIC ELECTRICAL INSTALLATION

Since January 1970, all manufacturers have been using metric sizes and describing the cables by their cross-sectional area in square millimetres.

The insulation around the conductors in a cable is coloured either red or black. Red is used for the live conductor and black for the neutral conductor. If, for some reason, it is not possible to adhere to this convention, an electrician will mark one conductor with tape for the purposes of identification.

The current rating of cables depends upon several factors relating to the circumstances in which the cables are used. The following tables give the current rating for some common sizes of cables used in domestic installations. The ratings are those for single-circuit twin cables with copper conductors, p.v.c. insulated and sheathed, and not enclosed in conduit.

Imperial units

No. and dia. of wires (in)	Cross-sectional area (in^2)	Current rating (amperes)
1/0·044	0·0015	12
3/0·029	0·002	15
3/0·036	0·003	19
7/0·029	0·0045	23
7/0·036	0·007	31
7/0·044	0·01	37

SI units

No. and dia. of wires (mm)	Cross-sectional area (mm^2)	Current rating (amperes)
1/1·13	1·0	12
1/1·38	1·5	15
1/1·78	2·5	21
7/0·85	4	27
7/1·04	6	35
7/1·35	10	48

Table 9.1 Current rating of domestic cables.

Conduit

As was mentioned previously, steel or plastic conduit is sometimes used to provide greater protection for the cables: it also facilitates the installation of new or additional wiring, if required at a later date. The conduit is buried in the floor or walls of buildings during construction, or laid over the rafters in the roof space. Cables can then be pulled in after construction work is complete. Lengths of conduit may be screwed or clamped together and, in the case of metal conduit, must be earthed.

Wiring accessories

The cables terminate at accessories such as ceiling roses, switches, socket outlets, etc., which are secured to a suitable fire-resisting enclosure. The usual method is to terminate the cable in a metal box fitted flush with the wall surface. The accessory is then screwed to the box, providing a neat and unobtrusive arrangement.

Diversity factor

When choosing a suitable size of cable for, say, a lighting circuit, it is unnecessary to select the size of cable which would carry the current taken from the supply if every lamp-holder were fitted with the largest size of lamp. Similarly, in cooker circuits, it is unnecessary to connect to the cooker a cable which would carry the total current taken if every part of the cooker were switched on at the same time.

The reason for this is that it is unlikely that the circuits will ever be fully loaded. From experience it is possible to estimate the probable maximum load as a percentage of the possible maximum load which could be supplied. We are allowing for diversity in the use of appliances.

As an example, the cable rating for a cooker is obtained as follows. The cable must be capable of supplying

(i) the first 10A of total rated current,

plus (ii) 30% of the remainder,

plus (iii) 5A for a control unit socket outlet, where provided.

Thus, if a cooker has a total loading of 12 kW, this is equivalent to 50 A at 240 V.

The cable must safely carry

(i) 10 A, plus (ii) 30% of 40 A = 12 A, plus (iii) 5 A—a total of 27 A.

There is no danger of the circuit being overloaded, as the rating of the fuse used would be chosen to suit the current which could safely be carried by the cable.

Flexible cords

When referring to the fixed wiring in an installation, we used the term 'cables'. When referring to the connections between the socket outlet, or lighting point, and the appliance, the term 'flexible cord' is used. A flexible cord is a flexible cable having a cross-sectional area per conductor of up to 0.007 in^2 (4 mm^2).

The current ratings of the most commonly used flexible cords with copper conductors are given below.

	Imperial units	
No. and dia. of wires (in)	Cross-sectional area (in^2)	Current rating (amperes)
14/0·0076	0·0006	3
23/0·0076	0·001	6
40/0·0076	0·0017	13
70/0·0076	0·003	18

	SI units	
No. and dia. of wires (mm)	Cross-sectional Area (mm^2)	Current rating (amperes)
16/0·20	0·5	3
24/0·20	0·75	6
32/0·20	1·0	10
30/0·25	1·5	15
50/0·25	2·5	20

Table 9.2 Current rating of flexible cords.

The Traditional Wiring Installation

Earlier in this chapter we said that we would be concerned mainly with the installation provided in modern houses. However, as many houses are wired according to what is sometimes called the traditional system, we will first look at this type of installation (fig. 9.8). We shall then discuss its disadvantages and the reasons why the modern ring-circuit system was introduced.

We have seen that the service cable terminates at the house service fuse, and that this in turn is connected, through the meter, to one or more main switches. In domestic premises wired by the traditional system, one main switch is provided for each type of circuit (i.e. lighting, power, cooking and water heating). This main switch sometimes incorporates fuses (when its correct name is a switch-fuse), the rating of the switch and of the fuses being determined by the maximum current which may be conveyed by the wiring used for the circuit it is controlling.

The power and lighting circuits are each connected to their own distribution (or fuse)-boards, which contain fuses for each circuit. With power circuits, separate fuses are required for each 15 A socket outlet. Several 5 A socket outlets may be provided from the same 5 A fuses in the lighting circuit fuse-board, and the 2 A socket outlets are often wired from 5 A fuses which also supply lighting points—the principle of diversity being applied in each case.

In the case of the cooker circuit, the wiring is taken from the cooker main switch to a control unit positioned close to the cooker, and a similar arrangement applies for the water-heating circuit.

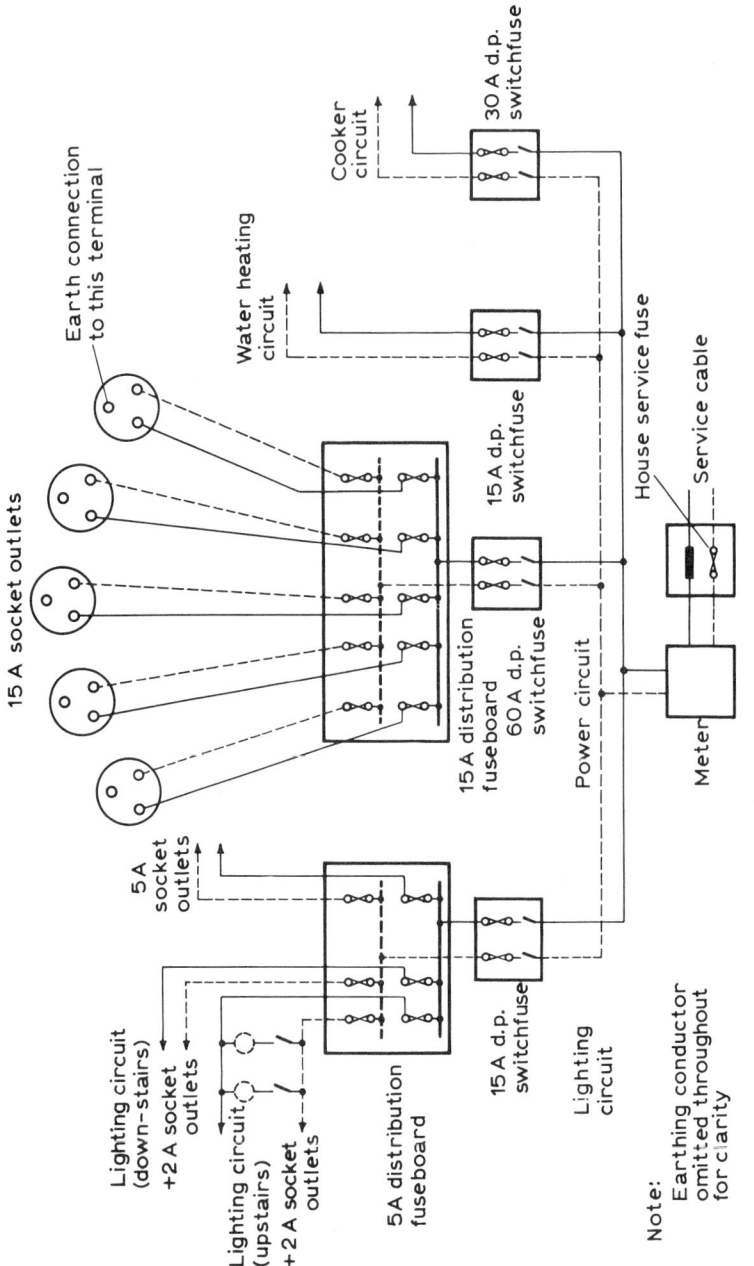

Fig. 9.8 The traditional wiring system.

DOMESTIC ELECTRICAL INSTALLATION

This traditional system has several disadvantages. For example, several main switches are required in addition to two or three distribution boards. This is extravagant in both cost and space. Also, three sizes of socket outlet, 2 A, 5 A and 15 A, are provided so that appliances can only be plugged into the corresponding size of outlet. Assuming a 240 V supply, appliances having a rating of up to 500 W may be connected to a 2 A socket outlet, for a 5 A socket outlet the rating may be between 500 W and 1200 W, and any portable appliance having a rating greater than 1200 W may be connected to a 15 A socket outlet. Furthermore, this system requires an excessive amount of wiring for the provision of a reasonable number of socket outlets and it will also be seen from fig. 9.8 that fuses were often incorporated in both line and neutral conductors.

The Ring-Circuit Wiring System

This system was introduced in the early 1950's. Although it is commonly referred to as the ring-circuit system, the ring circuit is, in fact, only one of the circuits provided. The arrangement is shown in fig. 9.9.

The service termination arrangements are as previously described. One advantage is that all the main switchfuses and distribution boards of the traditional system are replaced by one single piece of equipment called a consumer's unit, or switchfuse control unit, which may contain fuses (as shown in fig. 9.9) or MCB's as described earlier and shown in fig. 9.10. This unit takes up much less space, and is much cheaper than the switchfuse and distribution boards it replaces, besides looking very much neater. So much so, in fact, that it could be installed in a hall, to provide easy access, rather than in the conventional dark inaccessible position under the stairs.

This unit, then, contains one main switch (60 A or larger) and a suitable number of fuses or MCB's (often four or six). The case is made of wood, plastic or metal. As the earth wires from the various circuits terminate on the earth bar in the consumer's unit, a connection from the unit must be made to the earth connection for the installation. This may be to the water pipe, at the point where it enters the premises, or to the sheath of the incoming service cable. In any case, as stated earlier, the method of earthing must be approved by the Electricity Board. At the position where the connection to earth is made—by whatever method—it is essential that a label is fitted reading SAFETY ELECTRICAL EARTH—DO NOT REMOVE. If this connection were removed, and a fault occurred on an appliance, making the metal framework live, then the metal framework of every other appliance

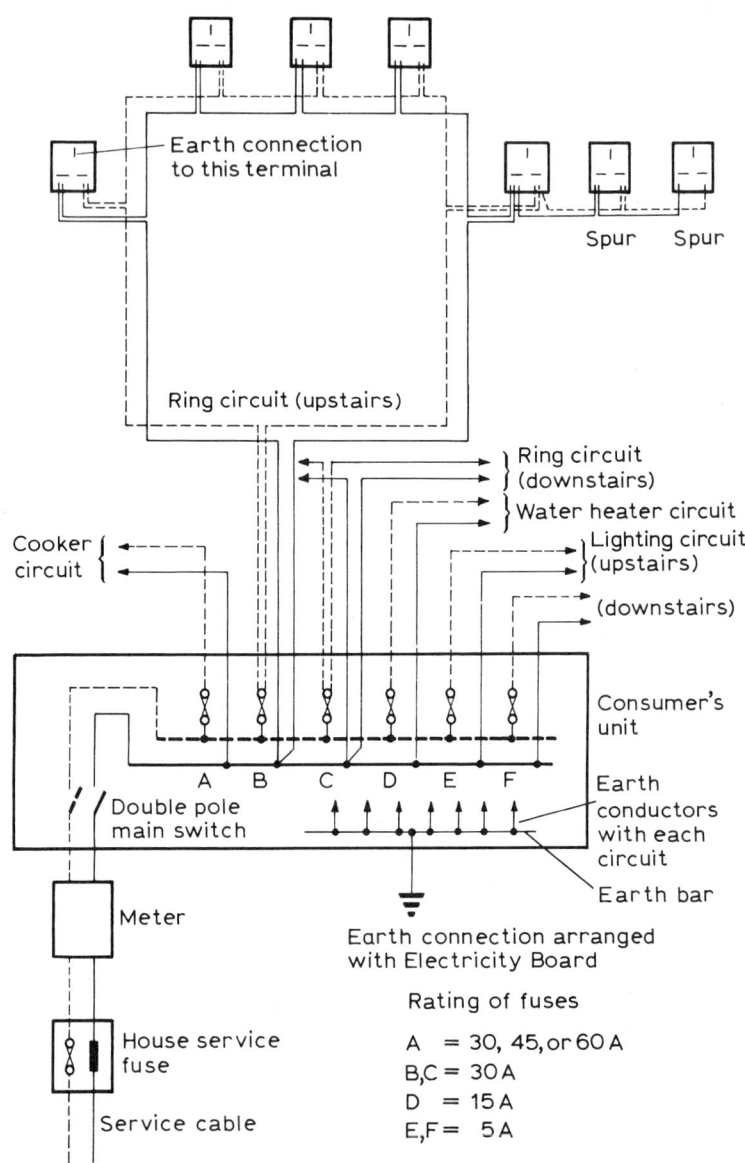

Fig. 9.9 The modern (ring-circuit) wiring system.

DOMESTIC ELECTRICAL INSTALLATION

in the premises would also be live, since they are all connected to the earth wire. However, a fuse would not blow as the earth wire would no longer be connected to earth. The reader should confirm this on fig. 9.5. This would be a highly dangerous condition.

Fig. 9.10 Consumer's unit.

Cooker and water-heating circuits

It will be seen in fig. 9.9 that six circuits are provided from the consumer's unit—cooker, water-heater, two lighting and two ring circuits. The cooker and water-heating circuits are as previously described—a cooker control unit being connected near to the cooker for the cooker circuit, and a spur box with switch, and possibly an indicating light, near to the water heater for the water-heater circuit.

The fuse controlling the cooker circuit will have a rating of 30 A for a small cooker, or 45 A or 60 A for a large cooker.

The fuse controlling the water-heater circuit will have a rating of 15 A.

Lighting circuits

Two lighting circuits are usually provided, one for each floor, as for the traditional system, one of these circuits being shown in fig. 9.11. In the diagram, three lights have been indicated, but often there will be five or six on each circuit. It is obvious that the fewer the number of lights on each circuit the less inconvenience will be caused if a fuse blows. On the other hand, the more lights on one circuit the less wiring will be required.

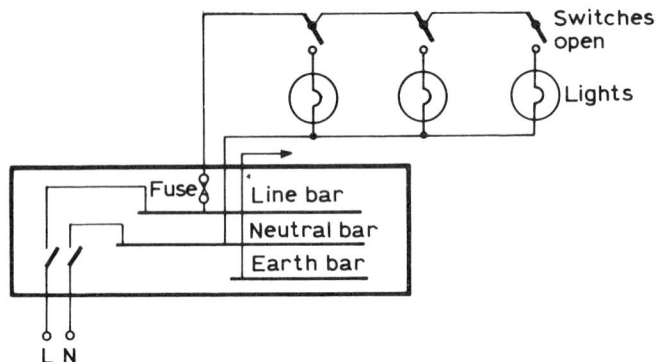

Fig. 9.11 A lighting circuit.

Now, if the reader will start at the fuse—which, it will be seen, is in the line conductor—he will see that it is connected through to one side of each of the three switches. When any one of the switches is 'closed' (or 'put on'), the circuit is completed through the light back to the neutral conductor.

Sometimes it is required to control one light from two positions, e.g. a hall light from switches in both the downstairs hall and the upstairs landing. This arrangement can easily be provided by using two-way switches, as shown in fig. 9.12. A two-way switch has one incoming connection but two outgoing connections, so that the incoming connection can be connected to either of the outgoing connections, as required. A one-way switch has only one outgoing connection, so the switch is either 'on' or 'off'.

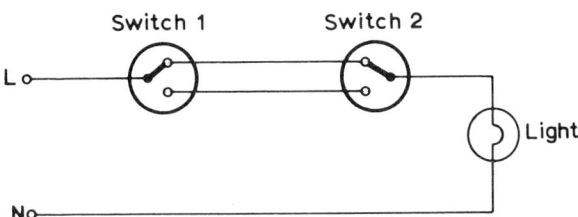

Fig. 9.12 Two-way switching. Diagram showing how a light may be switched on and off from two positions.

The switches are drawn in the 'on' position. If either switch position is altered, however, the light will go off. A further alteration to either switch position will then cause the light to come on again. The reader should draw out the connections for each of the possible conditions.

DOMESTIC ELECTRICAL INSTALLATION

Where necessary, more complicated control may be provided to enable a lamp to be switched on from more than two positions.

The circuit diagrams represent the connections and wiring in the simplest possible way. In practice, however, both line and neutral conductors may be part of the same cable. The necessary joints (e.g. for switch connections) are made in joint boxes or ceiling-outlet positions, and these, of course, are not shown on circuit diagrams.

At the position where the lighting fitting is required, a ceiling rose (fig. 9.13) is often installed—the fitting then being suspended from the rose by a flexible cord connected between the fixed wiring and the lamp holder in the fitting. Where required, a batten holder may be used to give greater headroom (fig. 9.14). In bathrooms and kitchens it is preferable to install a totally enclosed fitting.

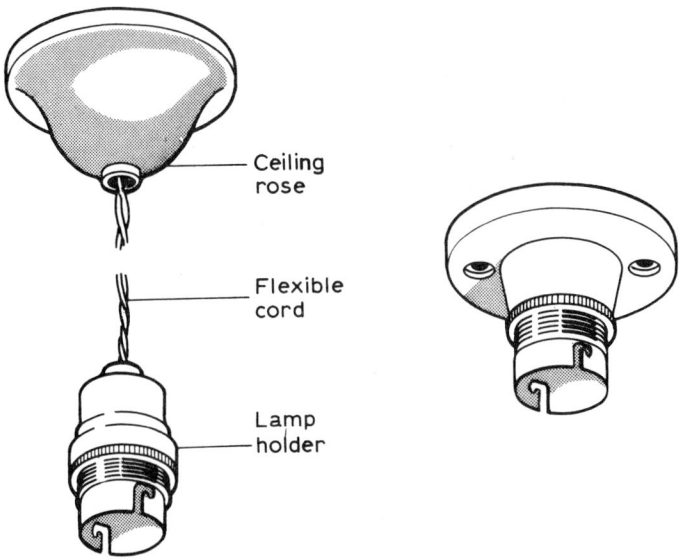

Fig. 9.13 Ceiling rose.   Fig. 9.14 Batten holder.

One important factor, which must be considered by the electrician, is that the heat from the lamp may affect the insulation of the flexible cord, which will often be immediately above the lamp. In these circumstances, as with the connections to storage and immersion heaters, butyl rubber cables are often used. Butyl rubber can withstand a higher temperature than the usual plastic or rubber insulation.

Finally, in bathrooms and similar places where the risk of shock is high, a cord-operated switch, rather than the usual hand-operated type, must be used (fig. 9.15).

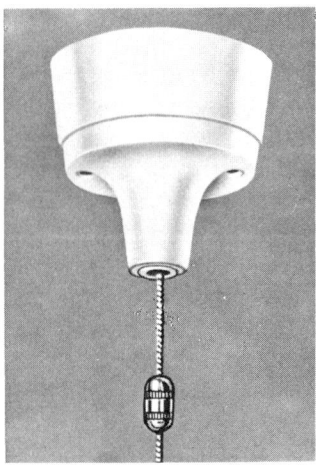

Fig. 9.15 Cord-operated switch for use in bathrooms.

The ring circuit

The main difference between the traditional and the modern systems of wiring domestic premises lies in the method of connecting the socket outlets (fig. 9.9). We saw earlier that, with the traditional system, three sizes of socket outlets are used. With the ring circuit, only a 13 A outlet may be used (fig. 9.16)—the corresponding plug having rectangular pins instead of the round pins used in the traditional system (fig. 9.17).

Fig. 9.16 13 A socket outlet and steel box.

DOMESTIC ELECTRICAL INSTALLATION

Fig. 9.17 13 A fused plug, showing nylon insulating sleeves.

Thus appliances of any rating up to 13 A (3 kW at 240 volts) may be connected to the ring circuit. Plugs and socket outlets must conform to the requirements of BS 1363. The cartridge fuse used in the plug has a rating of 3 A (coloured blue) or 13 A (coloured brown), and, as plugs are normally supplied fitted with a 13 A fuse, it is very important that this fuse should be removed and a 3 A fuse fitted if the appliance to which it is to be connected has a rating of 720 watts or less.

It is a simple matter to replace the fuse in this type of plug. Access to the fuse is only possible when the plug is removed from the socket outlet, and it is, therefore, unnecessary to switch off the supply.

From fig. 9.9 it will be seen that the circuit is arranged in the form of a ring from the consumer's unit—each end of the line conductor being connected to the same 30 A fuse or MCB, each end of the neutral being connected to the neutral bar, and each end of the earth conductor to the earth bar. The size of the cable used is 7/·029 (2·5 mm^2). When the floor area does not exceed 1000 square feet, a domestic consumer may connect as many socket outlets as he wishes to the ring—the wiring being looped in and out at each outlet position. For floor areas in excess of 1000 ft^2, one ring circuit must be provided for each 1000 ft^2, although it is usual practice to provide one ring circuit on each floor of domestic premises.

Furthermore, up to two socket outlets may be provided on each spur connected to the ring, so long as the number of spurs is not greater than the number of socket outlets directly connected to the ring. Each fixed appliance is connected through a fused spur box, incorporating a switch if required (fig. 9.18). Additional socket outlets may easily be added to the ring circuit, the length of wiring required being less than would be the case for a traditional system, where each socket outlet must be connected back to the distribution board.

Fig. 9.18 Fused spur box.

Socket outlets must not be provided in bathrooms, except for electric shavers. In this case a transformer is incorporated with the socket outlet to isolate the socket from the mains supply, and so eliminate the possibility of a shock.

Maintenance of an Installation

As was stated earlier in this chapter, an installation must remain safe at all times, and, in the case of domestic installations, this must be the householder's responsibility. Perhaps the first thing we should say is that, if there is some doubt about the safety of any part of the installation, or any of the appliances, and the householder is not competent to correct the fault, he should immediately obtain the advice of a qualified electrician. There are certain items of maintenance that most householders should be capable of undertaking, however, but before touching any part of the installation, which may be live, the supply must be switched off.

Damage to accessories

Any damage to socket outlets, switches, plugs, etc., should be rectified immediately, and this will normally entail replacement of that item of equipment. Equipment should never be switched on if a cover has been removed. When flexes become frayed they should be replaced—insulating tape should *not* be used (except when a temporary repair is necessary).

Replacement of fuses

Before replacing a fuse, the fault which caused the fuse to blow should be repaired, or, in the case of a faulty appliance, the appliance should be disconnected from the supply. Very occasionally a fuse will blow because it has become 'aged' by continual heating and cooling as loads are switched on and off. Whatever the circumstances, a fuse should never be replaced by one having a higher rating than the safe current for the circuit which is being protected. The screws securing rewireable fuses should be properly tightened, and loose ends of wire should not be left projecting. Finally, if a fuse blows again immediately it has been replaced, an electrician should be called.

Loose connections

Loose connections may occur in most parts of the installation and in most appliances. It would be unwise to suggest that the tightening of screws on appliances or on accessories can be undertaken by anyone. Perhaps loose screws most commonly occur in plugs, and, in this case, anyone who is capable of using a screwdriver should be able to rectify the trouble.

Fitting a new plug

This is a fairly simple job but it is most important to ensure that it is correctly carried out, as follows.
  (i) Ensure that the size of the plug is adequate for the appliance to which it is being connected. Also ensure that the rating of the fuse (where fitted) is correct.
  (ii) Ensure that the appliance is earthed where appropriate.
  (iii) Cut back the outer layer of insulation to expose the required length of conductors.
  (iv) Cut back the insulation on each conductor to expose about $\frac{1}{2}$ inch of wire, taking great care not to cut through any of the strands.
  (v) Twist the strands of each conductor together to ensure that no loose ends project from the terminals. Connect each conductor to the correct terminal as follows (fig. 9.19):

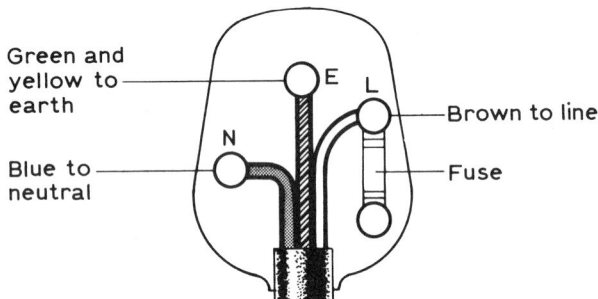

Fig. 9.19 13 A plug, showing fuse and terminals.

(a) BROWN (RED in old flexible cords) to LINE terminal (right-hand terminal connected to fuse),
(b) BLUE (BLACK in old cords) to NEUTRAL terminal (left-hand terminal),
(c) GREEN and YELLOW (GREEN in old cords) to EARTH terminal (top terminal), where required.

It is extremely important that these connections are made correctly. The insulation around each conductor should extend right up to the terminal after the conductor has been connected to the terminal. The appliance will be unsafe and dangerous if a mistake is made.

(vi) Tighten the grip screws around the flexible cord. The whole of the cord should be gripped and not just the conductors.
(vii) Finally, replace the fuse (where fitted), and check all connections. Check that screws have been fully tightened, and that there are no loose strands.

As stated earlier it is most important to ensure that the supply is switched off when repairs are being undertaken to appliances or wiring which may be live.

Meter Reading

There are two types of meter now in common use—the older dial type and the more modern digital type, the white meter (fig. 8.2) being an example of the latter. The digital type is similar to the mileometer on a car, and the reading of this type of meter presents no difficulty.

The dial type, however, is rather more complicated. It is illustrated in fig. 9.20, and the reading is indicated on several dials. It will be seen that, although all the dials are marked with the figures 0–9, the direction in which the figures are shown alternates, so they are clockwise

DOMESTIC ELECTRICAL INSTALLATION

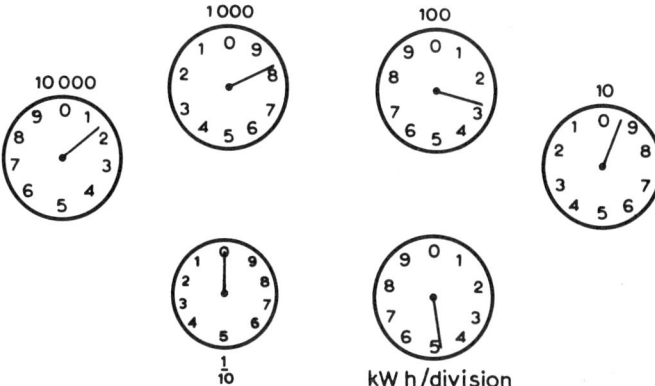

Fig. 9.20 Arrangement of dials on electricity meter. The arrangement is not standard, and variations will sometimes be found.

on the dial on the left, anti-clockwise on the next dial, and so on. The direction of rotation of the hands corresponds to the direction in which the figures are shown.

In reading the meter, the figure that the hand has just passed is noted for each of the dials. Care must be taken when the hand is very close to a figure, for example if the hand on one dial is almost covering 5 we must look at the dial to its immediate right. If the hand on this dial has not yet reached the zero mark, the reading on the first dial should be 4. If the hand has passed the zero mark, the reading will be 5.

The reading on the dials shown is 18295. The reading on the third dial is 2, and not 3, because the hand on the fourth dial has not passed the zero position. The dial marked 1/10th is not used in meter reading—this is used only for checking the meter. When it is required to determine the number of units used over a given period of time, two readings must be taken, one at the start of the period and the other at the end of the period. The first reading is then subtracted from the second.

The meter may be used to check the power consumption of an appliance. A large disc, mounted horizontally, may be seen through the glass at the front of the meter. This disc is connected to the hands on the dials (or the figures, in the digital type) by a series of gear wheels. When current flows through the meter, it causes this disc to rotate, and hence the hands (or the figures) move. It will be seen that the disc is marked with an engraved or painted line, so that the number of revolutions it makes may easily be counted.

It is first necessary to ensure that all other appliances are disconnected from the supply—it will then be seen that the disc remains perfectly stationary. The appliance under test is now connected to the supply, and the number of revolutions made by the disc in one minute, say, is determined (the longer the time interval the more accurate will be the result). It is also necessary to note the meter constant—this is a figure given on the name plate of the meter, showing the number of revolutions made by the disc for each unit of electricity consumed, e.g. 240 revs/kW h. We have seen previously that

$$\text{rating (or power)} = \frac{\text{energy}}{\text{time}}$$

The rating of the appliance will therefore be given by

$$\text{rating} = \frac{\text{no. of revolutions}}{\text{time taken} \times 240}$$

where rating is in kW, time taken is in hours, and the meter constant is 240 revs/kW h.

For example, suppose the disc makes 12 revolutions in one minute. Assuming a meter constant of 240 revs/kW h,

$$\text{rating} = \frac{12}{1/60 \times 240} = 3 \text{ kW.}$$

(Note that 1 minute must be expressed as 1/60 hour.)

Chapter 9—Questions

1 Draw a diagram showing the wiring layout for a domestic installation. Your diagram should indicate the incoming service cable, together with the Electricity Board's apparatus, in addition to circuits for a cooker, lighting, water heating and a 13 A ring circuit. The probable size of all fuses should be indicated.
2 Name and briefly describe three types of cable used in domestic premises, stating the advantages or disadvantages of each type. How does the diversity factor affect the size of cables required for a wiring installation?
3 Make a diagram of a 13 A plug, carefully indicating the markings against each terminal, the colours of the wires connected to each of the terminals, and the precautions to be taken in fitting the wires. State the advantages obtained by using 13 A plugs compared with the older types of round-pin plugs.
4 What is meant by the earthing of electrical appliances? Explain how this is done and how it makes the use of the appliance safer.

5 Write a short note on each of the following:
   (i) why an appliance having a rating of 1 kW should not be connected to a 2 A socket outlet if the supply voltage is 240 volts,
   (ii) the possible effect of using a 13 A fuse in a 13 A plug connected to an appliance which takes a current of 2 A,
   (iii) the effect of putting a 3 A fuse into a 13 A plug connected to an appliance taking a current of 6 A,
   (iv) why an electric cooker should be connected by a separate circuit.
6 Copy and complete the following table by calculating and filling in the missing figures.

	Voltage (volts)	Current (amperes)	Resistance (ohms)	Time (hours)	Power (watts)	Energy (kWh)
(i)	200	5		2		
(ii)		10	10			4
(iii)	240		24	5		
(iv)			20	6	500	
(v)	240				100	1
(vi)	240			2	6000	

7 Make a list showing each of the rooms in a 3-bedroomed house, and indicate for each room the number of socket outlets required for an adequate installation. Include a hall, landing and garage. Outline the advantages of the ring-circuit system compared with the system it replaced.

8 Give reasons for each of the following requirements relating to electrical installations in domestic premises:
   (i) a switch should always be connected in the line conductor,
   (ii) socket outlets must not be installed in bathrooms,
   (iii) electric irons must not be connected to the supply by a two-core flexible cord,
   (iv) an installation must have a main switch.

9 Explain clearly the reasons why the following are important in a modern domestic installation:
   (i) correct fusing,
   (ii) effective earthing,
   (iii) an adequate number of socket outlets,
   (iv) inspection and maintenance of flexible cords.

10 Electric Water Heating

Advantages of Electric Water Heating

Perhaps the most important advantage of electric water heating when compared with other methods of water heating is that it is possible to place the element in the water, so that the efficiency of such a heater approaches 100%. However, there are many other advantages associated with electric water heating.

Unlike other methods, the whole process is completely automatic and requires no regular maintenance. A thermostat automatically disconnects the supply when the required temperature is reached, and also reconnects the supply if the temperature falls for any reason.

The carrying of fuel from a fuel store to the appliance is unnecessary, and no adjustments are required. The process is completely free from noise, dirt and smells, which in turn means that redecoration will not be required as frequently as is the case with other fuels. Furthermore, there is a considerable saving in building costs in new installations, as space and buildings are not required for fuel storage, nor are flues necessary. This involves a saving in the cost of chimney sweeping. It is interesting to reflect that the cost of having a chimney swept would pay for the use of a 1 kW immersion heater for 1 hour per day from the middle of December to the middle of March.

With a correctly installed electrical installation there is no risk of fire or explosion.

Finally, the one disadvantage—that of cost—which was sometimes levelled against electrical heating is no longer valid. Apart from the fact that the initial installation cost will normally be less than for other methods of heating, the running costs will also be low.

By careful selection of the most suitable appliances for given conditions, and by the use of the off-peak tariffs, the running costs of electrical appliances compare very favourably with those for other

ELECTRIC WATER HEATING

fuels, especially when the advantages outlined above are taken into account.

Water-storage principle

Large quantities of water cannot be heated instantaneously by electrical appliances, since the loading required would be too great. It must therefore be heated and stored in a tank until required. The heating can take place at night, when the cost of electricity supplied by the off-peak tariffs is much less than the day-time cost.

Installation Requirements

As with all forms of heating, the most economical running conditions will only be achieved if the installation is carefully planned and installed.

To ensure that the heat losses are as small as possible, it is essential that the storage tank and the pipes carrying hot water are efficiently lagged. The lagging will be included as an essential part of the design of a purpose-made electric water heater, as sold in electricity showrooms. However, where an existing storage tank is modified for electric heating, the lagging must be provided as part of the modification—if the tank was not previously lagged. This may easily be achieved by surrounding it with an insulating material three inches thick, such as fibreglass, polystyrene in slab form, or granulated cork. Alternatively, one of the insulating jackets, which are readily available for this purpose, may be fitted.

It would be very false economy not to lag a hot-water storage tank situated in a linen cupboard, in the belief that this is the best method of airing the clothing or linen. The tank should be properly lagged, and one of the small heaters which are specially designed for use in airing cupboards may be installed if required.

Hot-water pipes should also be lagged by wrapping a suitable insulating material around them, and heat losses are also avoided when the storage tank is near the most frequently used tap, which is usually in the kitchen. This enables the pipes to be kept short.

Another way in which heat may be lost is by what is called 'single-pipe circulation'. This occurs in the draw-off pipe connected to the top of the storage tank. Hot water from the tank will rise inside this pipe and, as it cools, it will return to the storage tank, thus setting up circulating currents within the pipe, as shown in fig. 10.1.

The method of overcoming this heat loss is shown in fig. 10.2. The draw-off pipe must be turned through a right-angle immediately after

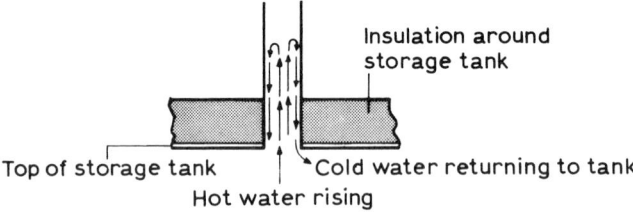

Fig. 10.1 Single-pipe circulation occurs when hot water from the storage tank rises in the outlet (or draw-off) pipe. As it cools, it returns to the tank, setting up circulating currents.

it leaves the top of the storage tank. The connection to the vent pipe must then be not closer than 18 inches to this right-angle bend. The purpose of the various pipes connected to the storage tank are discussed in greater detail later in this chapter.

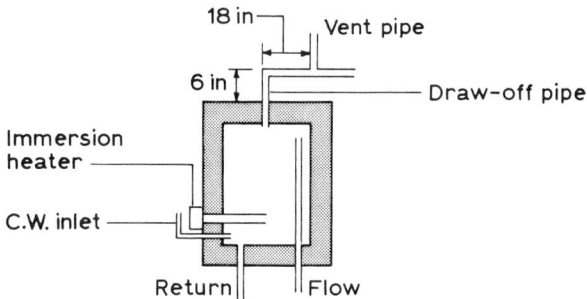

Fig. 10.2 Diagram showing the correct connections to a hot-water tank.

The Immersion Heater

Before discussing the various methods of water heating, we will look at the construction of the immersion heater. The heater may be designed for vertical or horizontal fixing within the storage tank, a typical design being shown in fig. 10.3.

The heater consists essentially of two parts. At the top is a connection plate, on which are situated the terminals for the electrical connections to the heater. Welded to the underside of the plate is a U-shaped tube containing a nickel-chrome wire element, embedded in magnesium oxide. The thermostat, which is connected in series

ELECTRIC WATER HEATING

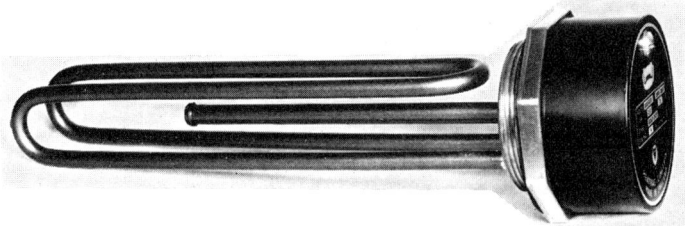

Fig. 10.3 Typical immersion heater. Note the large nut to secure the heater to the side or top of the storage tank; also the thermostat pocket for a stem-type thermostat.

with the element, is also attached to the connection plate. Sometimes two heaters are incorporated in one assembly, which is mounted vertically from the top of the tank. A short element is provided to heat a small amount of water at the top of the storage tank, and a longer element to heat the entire contents of the tank. The larger element is only used when a large amount of water is required, thus giving economy in operation.

The principle of operation of the thermostat is described in Chapter 13.

Methods of Electric Water Heating

Electric water heating may be achieved either by the use of one of the appliances which may be bought as a complete unit, or by the installation of an immersion heater in a storage tank which may also be heated by another method of water heating.

Electric Water Heaters

There are available three basic types of water heater, as follows:
  (i) the free-outlet or non-pressure type,
  (ii) the low-pressure type,
  (iii) the cistern type.

Each type is available in different sizes and consists essentially of a copper storage tank with an immersion heater and thermostat. The tank is surrounded by lagging contained within an outer steel casing, usually finished in white stoved enamel. Provision is made for electrical and water connections, and for floor or wall mounting.

Free-outlet or non-pressure type

This type of heater is used to provide a single outlet, e.g. to supply a sink, wash basin or bath. The outlet, which is usually in the form of a swivel spout, is permanently open, the flow of water through the heater being controlled by a tap on the input side, as shown in fig. 10.4.

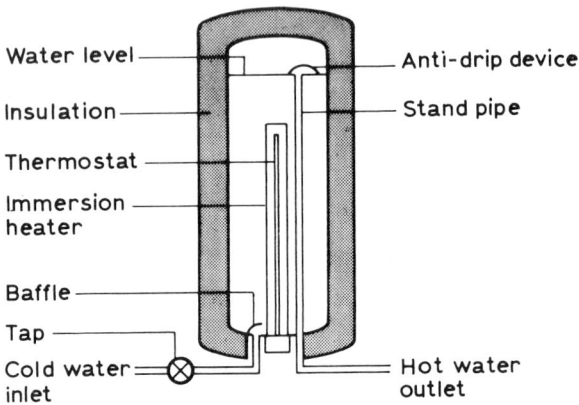

Fig. 10.4 Diagram of free-outlet or non-pressure type of water heater. Water flows out of the outlet when the tap on the inlet is turned on.

The heater may be connected directly to the main water supply or to a cold-water storage tank. When the inlet tap is opened (i.e. turned on), the pressure of the incoming water causes the level of the water in the storage tank to rise above the top of the stand pipe so that hot water flows through the outlet pipe. To prevent the incoming cold water from mixing with the hot water in the tank, a baffle is fitted over the end of the inlet pipe. When the incoming cold water is heated, its volume will increase and give rise to drips from the outlet during the heating period. This may be prevented by the use of an anti-drip device.

Non-pressure type heaters are available in sizes ranging from $1\frac{1}{2}$ gallons to 15 gallons (6·8 litres to 68 litres)—the smaller sizes being suitable for use over domestic sinks whilst the larger size is designed for use with baths. The electrical loading for all sizes of heater is usually 3 kW, to ensure that cold water entering the tank is quickly heated to the required temperature. However, heaters having lower loadings are available.

The non-pressure type of heater is particularly suitable for use where the sink or bath being served is remote from the main hot-water storage tank.

ELECTRIC WATER HEATING

Low-pressure type

Low-pressure type heaters are used to provide a supply to several outlets. They are supplied from a cold-water cistern and are not directly connected to the main water supply. They should be installed at the nearest convenient position to the tap which is in most common use. For this reason, the design is often such that it can be accommodated as a floor-mounted unit under the draining board, thus reducing the heat losses associated with long pipes carrying hot water.

As the outlets with this type of heater are normally closed, it is necessary to provide a vent pipe to allow for the expansion which will occur when the water is heated. This vent pipe is connected from the top of the heater and usually terminates over the top of the cold-water storage tank. As discussed previously, the draw-off pipe must turn through a right-angle bend immediately it leaves the heater, and the vent pipe is connected to this pipe as shown in fig. 10.5.

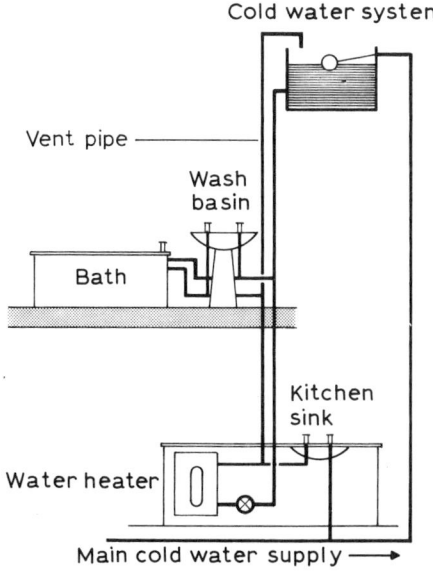

Fig. 10.5 Low-pressure type heater supplying a sink, bath and wash basin. Note also the vent pipe, which must be provided, terminating over the cold-water cistern.

Two immersion heaters are sometimes fitted with this appliance. The heater fitted near the top supplies about 5 gallons (23 litres) of water very rapidly for normal purposes in the kitchen. The heater fitted near the bottom will heat all the water in the appliance for baths or laundry purposes. A changeover switch controls the heaters so that only one heater may be switched on at a time—the rating of the heaters again usually being 3 kW each. It should be appreciated that, as heated water rises, the position of an immersion heater is very important. Water below the level of the immersion heater will not be heated.

The capacity of low-pressure water heaters for domestic purposes varies from about 20 gallons (91 litres) to 50 gallons (228 litres), but much larger sizes are available for commercial and industrial premises. The 50 gallon (228 litres) size is specially designed for use where the off-peak tariff is adopted. With this tariff, the water is heated at night at about half the day-time cost, and it will then supply the requirements of a normal household during the following day. Owing to its large capacity, it cannot be designed for use under the draining board, and it is therefore usually installed in the bathroom.

Cistern type

The cistern type of heater incorporates its own ball-valve cistern, and is used where it is impossible or uneconomical to use the low-pressure type either because there is no available cold-water storage tank in the premises, or because the cost of providing the necessary pipework between the existing storage tank and the water heater would be uneconomical. It must always be fitted above the level of the highest tap in the premises. The construction is shown in fig. 10.6.

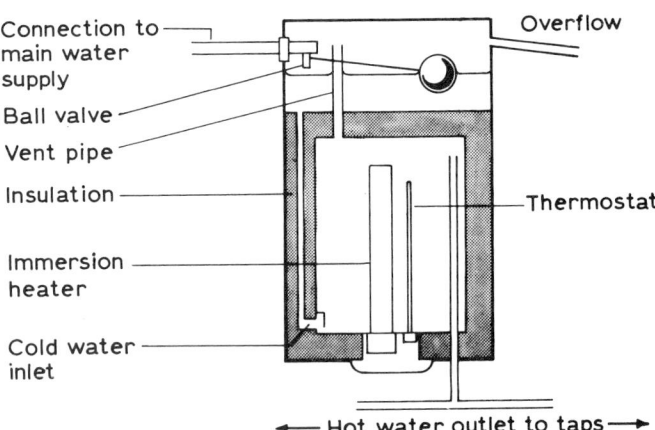

Fig. 10.6 Cistern-type water heater. In this type the cold-water storage tank, and the heater are combined in one unit.

It will be seen that the cistern is situated above the hot-water storage tank, the two being connected by a cold-water inlet pipe discharging

ELECTRIC WATER HEATING

near the bottom of the storage tank, and by a vent pipe from the top of this tank to a point above the water level in the cistern. The capacity of this type of heater may range from 5 gallons (23 litres) to 50 gallons (228 litres), and the loading is usually 3 kW.

Combined System

In many cases where hot water is provided from a solid-fuel or other type of heating appliance it is an advantage to fit an immersion heater in the hot-water storage tank. In this way the immersion heater may provide hot water during the summer, and so the undesirable heat losses which will occur with the heating appliance may be avoided. During the winter, when the solid-fuel appliance is used, the heat losses will be useful in warming the room in which it is situated. When this method is adopted, it is important to ensure that the following requirements are met.

As stated previously, to avoid heat losses the hot-water storage tank should be positioned near to the taps which will be most frequently used. This may involve rather long connections from the storage tank to the heating appliance but, if we remember that this will be used only during the winter months, it follows that the heat losses will usefully contribute towards the general space heating of the premises. The shape of the storage tank is also important. It should be arranged so that its greater dimension is in the vertical position—this dimension being not less than twice the longest horizontal dimension. This will enable a small amount of hot water to be drawn off if required soon after the heater has been switched on. Also, as was discussed earlier, for the most economical operation the storage tank must be properly lagged.

The immersion heater may be positioned either horizontally (in a rectangular tank) or vertically (in a cylindrical tank). In the former case, about two inches clearance should be provided between the heater and the bottom of the tank. This allows for the accumulation of any sludge or scale deposits which will occur in hard-water districts. If the immersion heater is fitted vertically, it must reach nearly to the bottom of the storage tank—otherwise some water in the tank will not be heated. Finally, single-pipe circulation must be avoided.

It is possible to connect a heated towel-rail and radiator to this system, but these appliances should be supplied directly from the solid-fuel appliance, as shown in fig. 10.7, and not from the storage tank.

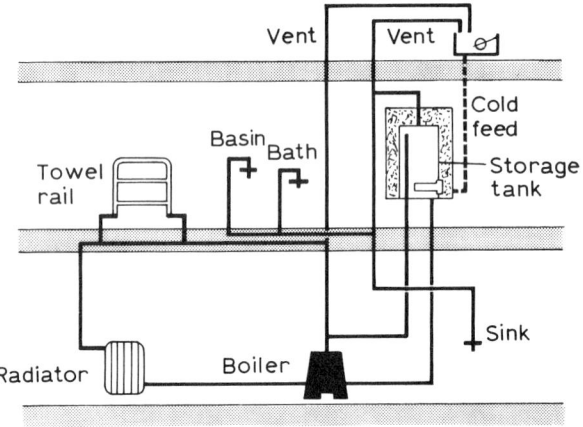

Fig. 10.7 Layout of pipework for use with the combined system.

Indirect System

The indirect system is sometimes used in hard water districts, the arrangement being as shown in fig. 10.8.

It will be seen that the flow and return pipes to the solid-fuel appliance are connected to a cylinder situated inside the hot-water storage tank. (Sometimes a coil through which the water circulates is used instead of a cylinder.) In each case, the water in this circuit is isolated from the hot water outlets, and it will, therefore, be used over and

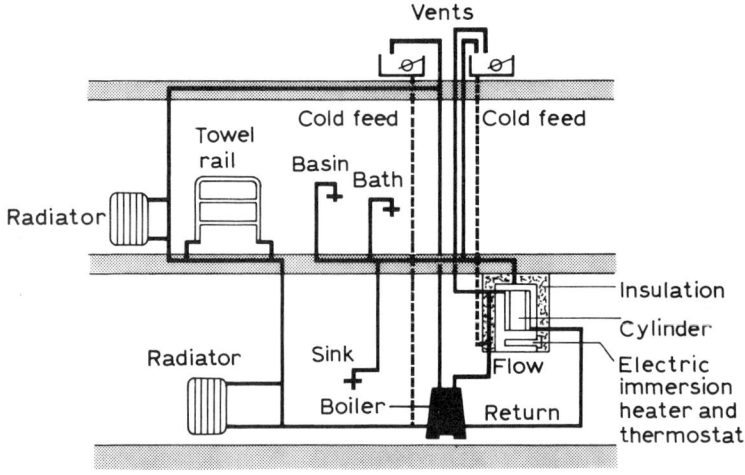

Fig. 10.8 Layout of pipework for use with the indirect system.

ELECTRIC WATER HEATING

over again between the solid fuel appliance and the cylinder. The advantage of this system is that this continually circulating water will deposit hardness salts when it is first heated, but after this there will be no further deposits in subsequent heat cycles. The hard-water deposits in the storage tank will also be slight.

The position of the immersion heater will be as described for the direct system, but care must be taken to ensure that it does not touch the cylinder.

Cost of Electric Water Heating

Even with the introduction of SI units, it is likely to be some time before the gallon, pound, British Thermal Unit, etc. are replaced by their SI equivalent units. It is therefore proposed to perform these calculations separately for each system of units.

The cost of water heating is affected by the tariff employed (see Chapter 8).

Imperial units

The heat unit in the Imperial system is the British Thermal Unit, and it is defined as the quantity of heat required to raise the temperature of one pound of water through one degree Fahrenheit. Since both the British Thermal Unit and the kilowatt hour are units of energy, a relationship exists between them. This relationship has been shown to be

$$1 \text{ kW h} \equiv 3412 \text{ Btu}$$

($\equiv$ means 'is equivalent to').

Now, since 1 gallon of water has a mass of 10 pounds, we can calculate the number of Btu required to heat a given quantity of water as follows.

Heat energy required (Btu) = **quantity of water** (gallons) × **10** × **temperature rise** (°F)

∴ **Electrical energy required**

$$= \frac{\text{quantity of water (gallons)} \times 10 \times \text{temperature rise (°F)}}{3412}$$

Example
Calculate the cost of heating 22 gallons of water from 59°F to 167°F, if electricity costs 0·8p per unit.

$$\text{Electrical energy required} = \frac{22 \times 10 \times (167-59)}{3412} \text{ kW h}$$

$$= 7 \text{ kW h (approx.)}.$$

$$\therefore \text{Cost} = 7 \times 0.8 = 5.6\text{p}.$$

If we wished to calculate the time taken to heat the water in the previous example, we should need to know the rating of the immersion heater. If a 3 kW immersion heater were used, then

$$\text{time taken (hours)} = \frac{\text{energy required (kW h)}}{\text{rating of heater (kW)}}.$$

$$= \frac{7}{3} = 2\tfrac{1}{3} \text{ hours}$$

$$= 2 \text{ hours } 20 \text{ minutes}.$$

SI units

In SI units, the unit of energy is the joule, although the kilowatt hour may be used where it is more practical to do so. Before SI units were introduced, the scientific heat unit was the calorie, which was defined as the heat required to raise the temperature of one gramme of water by one degree Celsius (or Centigrade). It has been shown that the relationship between the joule and the calorie is

$$1 \text{ calorie} \equiv 4.18 \text{ joules}.$$

We could therefore define the joule as the quantity of heat required to raise the temperature of 1/4.18 gramme of water through one degree Celsius. (NOTE—the correct definition of the joule has been given in Appendix B.)

We can calculate the number of joules required to heat a certain quantity of water as follows.

Heat energy required (joules)

= **mass of water** (grammes) × **temperature rise** (°C) × 4.18

= **mass of water** (kilogrammes) × **temperature rise** (°C) × 4.18 × 10^3

Electrical energy required (kW h)

= **quantity of water** (litres) × **temperature rise** (°C) × $\dfrac{4.18 \times 10^3}{3.6 \times 10^6}$

= $\dfrac{\textbf{quantity of water} \text{ (litres)} \times \textbf{temperature rise} \text{ (°C)}}{860}$

Example
Calculate the cost of heating 100 litres of water from 15°C to 75°C, if electricity costs 0·8p per unit.

$$\text{Electrical energy required (kW h)} = \frac{100 \times 60}{860}$$

$$= 7 \text{ kW h (approx.)}.$$

$$\therefore \text{Cost} = 7 \times 0\cdot 8 = 5\cdot 6\text{p}.$$

(NOTE—the reader may have noticed that the quantities expressed in Imperial units in the first example are exactly the same as those expressed in SI units in the second example.)

It should be noted that 100% efficiency has been assumed in both these examples. If, for any of the reasons discussed earlier in this chapter, excessive heat losses occur, the actual cost will be higher than that calculated.

If the efficiency can be estimated, we can obtain the actual electrical input by dividing the 'useful' electrical output by the efficiency.

Example
If in the previous example the efficiency of the heating process is 90%, calculate the actual number of units required.

$$\text{Actual electrical input} = \frac{\text{useful electrical output}}{\text{efficiency}}$$

$$= 7 \times \frac{100}{90}$$

$$= 7\cdot 8 \text{ kW h}.$$

Useful Information Relating to Electric Water Heating

Capacity of cylindrical tanks

If d = diameter in inches,   If d = diameter in millimetres,
  h = height in inches: h = height in millimetres:

$$\text{volume of tank} = \frac{\pi d^2 h}{4} \text{ in}^3 \qquad \text{volume of tank} = \frac{\pi d^2 h}{4} \text{ mm}^3$$

$$= \frac{\pi d^2 h}{4 \times 1728} \text{ ft}^3 \qquad\qquad = \frac{\pi d^2 h}{4 \times 10^3} \text{ cm}^3$$

capacity of tank $= \dfrac{\pi d^2 h \times 6\cdot 25}{4 \times 1728}$

capacity of tank $= \dfrac{\pi d^2 h}{4 \times 10^6}$

$= \dfrac{d^2 h}{353}$ gallons.

$= \dfrac{d^2 h}{1\cdot 28 \times 10^6}$ litres

Example
Calculate the capacity in (i) gallons and (ii) litres of a cylindrical tank having the following dimensions: diameter 15" (380 mm), height 28·5" (720 mm).

$$\text{Capacity of tank (gallons)} = \dfrac{d^2 h}{353}$$

$$= \dfrac{15 \times 15 \times 28\cdot 5}{353}$$

$$= 18\cdot 2 \text{ gallons (approx.)}.$$

$$\text{Capacity of tank (litres)} = \dfrac{d^2 h}{1\cdot 28 \times 10^6}$$

$$= \dfrac{380 \times 380 \times 720}{1\cdot 28 \times 1\,000\,000}$$

$$= 81 \text{ litres (approx.)}.$$

Capacity of rectangular tanks

If l = length in inches,
 w = width in inches,
 h = height in inches:

volume of tank $= lwh$ in^3

$= \dfrac{lwh}{1728}$ ft^3

capacity of tank $= \dfrac{lwh \times 6\cdot 25}{1728}$

$= \dfrac{lwh}{277}$ gallons.

If l = length in millimetres,
 w = width in millimetres,
 h = height in millimetres:

volume of tank $= lwh$ mm^3

$= \dfrac{lwh}{10^3}$ cm^3

capacity of tank $= \dfrac{lwh}{10^6}$ litres.

Temperature conversion
From °C to °F:

$$°F = (°C \times \tfrac{9}{5}) + 32$$

From °F to °C:

$$°C = (°F - 32) \times \tfrac{5}{9}$$

ELECTRIC WATER HEATING

Example
Convert 75°C to °F.

$$°F = (75 \times \tfrac{9}{5}) + 32$$
$$= 167°F.$$

Example
Convert 59°F to °C.

$$°C = (59 - 32) \times \tfrac{5}{9}$$
$$= 15°C.$$

NOTE—if it is required to convert a *temperature change* from °F to °C, we must multiply by $\tfrac{5}{9}$ only. Conversely, if we wish to convert a temperature change from °C to °F, we must multiply by $\tfrac{9}{5}$. In neither case must the constant 32 be used.

Example
What is the temperature rise in °F corresponding to a change from 20°C to 60°C?

$$\text{Temperature change (°F)} = \text{temperature change (°C)} \times \tfrac{9}{5}$$
$$= (60 - 20) \times \tfrac{9}{5}$$
$$= 72°F.$$

Heat loss from hot water cylinder
(30 gallons capacity—air temperature 16°C)

	Granulated cork		kWh lost per week Fibreglass		Uninsulated	
	60°C	70°C	60°C	70°C	60°C	70°C
1″ thick	18·2	22·6	15·8	19·7		
2″ thick	10·0	12·5	8·8	10·8	86	115
3″ thick	6·9	8·6	6·0	7·4		

Example
Calculate the cost of the heat losses from the cylinder referred to above, if it is insulated with (i) 1″ of granulated cork, (ii) 3″ of fibre glass, (iii) no insulation. In each case, take the temperature of the water as 70°C, and the cost of electricity as 0·8p per unit.
 (i) 22·6 kW h, cost = 18·08p. per week.
 (ii) 7·4 kW h, cost = 5·92p. per week.
 (iii) 115 kW h, cost = 92p. per week.
 The electrical energy wasted in the third case would be sufficient to provide between 16 and 20 baths.

Suggested quantities of water required for various purposes
Bath: 25 gallons at 40°C,
Washbasin: 1 gallon at 40°C,

Washing-up: 1–2 gallons at 60°C.
Hot-water requirements for family of four per week have been estimated at 200–250 gallons at 60°C.

Water temperatures
Winter average   4°C
Summer average   10°C
Bath   40°C
Sink   60°C
'Scalding'   66°C
Boiling   100°C.
Recommended storage temperatures:
Hard water   60°C
Soft water   70°C.

Useful relationships
Volume of 1 gallon of water = 277 in^3 = 4540 cm^3.
Mass of 1 gallon of water = 10 pounds = 4·54 kilogrammes.
1 gallon ≡ 4·54 litres.
1 litre ≡ 0·22 gallon.
1 cubic foot of water contains 6·25 gallons.

Chapter 10—Questions

1 Calculate the time taken and the cost of boiling 1 litre of water, given that:
                 original temperature of water = 10°C,
                 loading of kettle   = 1½ kW,
                 1 unit of electricity costs   0·8p.
It may be assumed that one unit of electricity will raise the temperature of 860 litres of water by 1°C.

2 Make a sketch of a free-outlet or non-pressure type of water heater, and label each part of the heater.

3 Explain how a solid-fuel hot-water system can be converted to an electric system.

4 State the reason for fitting two immersion heaters in one hot-water tank, and discuss how this is done. Explain why long pipe runs should be avoided in the installation of hot-water heaters.

5 What are the advantages associated with electric water heating? Describe the construction of an immersion heater and the method of fitting it to a hot-water cylinder.

6 Name the three basic types of electric water heater and describe the principles of operation of any one of the types.

11 Electric Space Heating

Advantages of Electric Space Heating

All the advantages of using electricity for water heating, discussed at the beginning of the previous chapter, apply when electricity is used for the purpose of space heating. They may be summarised as follows:
  (i) it is more efficient than any other method,
  (ii) it may be automatically controlled and requires very little maintenance,
  (iii) it does not involve carrying of fuel from a fuel store,
  (iv) it is free from noise, dirt and smells, and therefore less re-decoration is required,
  (v) the saving in building costs—no chimneys and fuel stores are needed,
  (vi) there is no risk of fire or explosion, provided installation is carried out correctly,
  (vii) the low cost, provided that the most suitable appliances and tariffs are used.

Before considering the various methods of space heating, we will first discuss the three ways in which heat is transferred.

Convection
When air is heated, its volume increases and it therefore becomes less dense. The heated air rises and is replaced by cold air, which in turn is heated and rises. Thus, in a room, circulating air currents are set up which warm the walls and ceiling, and so increase the temperature of the room (fig. 11.1).
The process is a gradual one, and the heater must obviously be placed at low level.

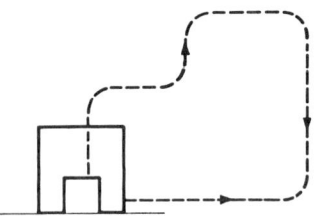

Fig. 11.1 Convection currents set up in a room by a convector heater placed at low level.

Radiation

In this case, heat is transferred from a hot object to a colder one by passing directly between them (fig. 11.2). Thus the 'flow' of heat can be interrupted by placing a solid object between the heat source and the object being heated.

An obvious example of radiation is the way in which heat is transferred from the sun. The heat is not directly transferred to the air, but objects exposed to the sun become heated. Thus we may feel hot when we 'stand in the sun', but much cooler if we sit in the shade of a tree. In time, of course, the sun may heat the ground and buildings so that they in turn heat the air, mainly by convection. We may deduce that radiated heat travels in straight lines.

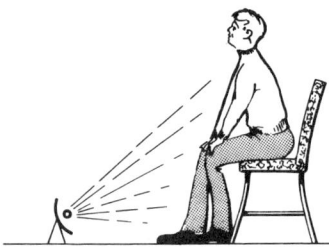

Fig. 11.2 Transference of heat from a radiant heater along a direct path.

Conduction

When heat is transferred by conduction, the heat passes through the object from a hot to a colder region. For example, if a length of wire is heated at one point (fig. 11.3), in time the whole length of wire would become hot. A saucepan placed on the hot-plate of a cooker becomes hot largely due to the heat passing from the hot-plate to the saucepan at the points of contact.

ELECTRIC SPACE HEATING

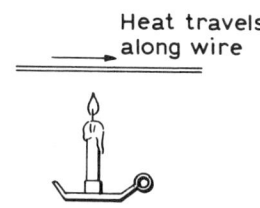

Fig. 11.3 Heat transferred by conduction passes through the object being heated.

The transfer of heat normally involves at least two of the three ways we have discussed, but to all intents and purposes, a particular heat source may transmit most of its heat output by only one way. We will now consider the various methods of electrical heating.

Convector Heaters

As their name suggests, convector heaters supply most of their heat by convection. Basically, the appliance consists of a metal case with openings at the top and bottom. The elements, consisting of long lengths of nichrome wire wound in the form of a spiral and supported on insulators within the case, operate at a comparatively low temperature. When the heater is switched on, warm air passes out through the top opening and is replaced by cold air entering through the bottom opening (fig. 11.4). It is therefore most important that these openings are not restricted by clothing or bedding, etc.

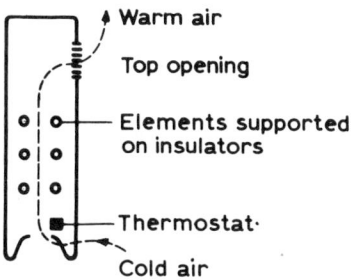

Fig. 11.4 Principle of a convector heater.

Most convector heaters incorporate a thermostat, which is situated near the bottom of the heater and operated by a continuously variable control. When the temperature of the incoming air reaches a predetermined value, dependent upon the setting of the thermostat, the elements are automatically disconnected from the supply. Later, when the temperature falls sufficiently, the thermostat operates to reconnect the elements to the supply. Alternatively, a switch giving several different heat settings (e.g. a quarter, half, three-quarters and full load) may be provided. In addition to the thermostat control or heat-selector switch, a time switch is fitted to some convector heaters so that the heater will switch on automatically at any required time. Thus, for instance, the heater may be used in a bedroom, and set to switch on so that the room will be warm when the occupants wake up. Alternatively, it may be used in a living room and set to switch on, say, in the late afternoon, so that the room is warm when the family returns home.

This type of heater is particularly suitable for background heating anywhere in a house, with additional small radiant fires for local heating if required. It must be remembered, however, that, as they heat the whole of a room, a longer period must be allowed for their effect to be felt, than is the case with radiant heaters.

Convector heaters may be designed to be free-standing (fig. 11.5), so that they may be moved from one position to another as required, or they may be designed for fixing to walls or skirting.

Radiant Heaters

Radiant heaters provide most of their heat output by radiation, and are the most suitable type of heater where local heat is required quickly. There are several types available. In the earlier models the element is set in channels formed in a fireclay block. When the heater is switched on, the element becomes red hot and, after a short time, the fireclay block also becomes very hot. In this type, only a little more than half the heat is provided by radiation, and the remainder is by convection.

In another type, the element is mounted on a fireclay or ceramic rod in front of a polished metal reflector (fig. 11.6). The reflector is designed (rather like the reflectors behind the headlamps of a car) to project the heat forward in a narrow beam. In this case, rather more than 70% of the heat output is provided by radiation, and the remainder is by convection.

In a third and more recent design, the element is enclosed within a silica tube, which is also placed in front of a polished metal reflector. This type provides heat rather more quickly than the two previous types, and it is safer, as the element is enclosed. It also presents a pleasing appearance, and is particularly widely used in kitchens and bathrooms (fig. 11.7).

ELECTRIC SPACE HEATING

Fig. 11.5 A typical convector heater.

Fig. 11.6 A typical radiant heater.

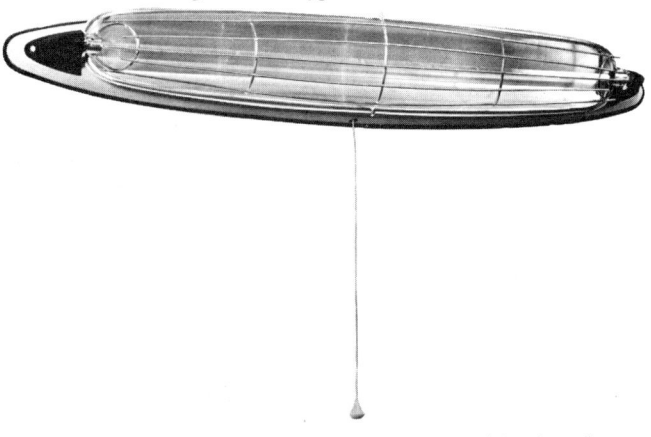

Fig. 11.7 Wall-mounted radiant heater with the element contained in a silica tube.

A very popular design of radiant heater (such as that in fig. 11.6) includes a glowing coal or log effect, so that it may be installed in a fireplace to provide the appearance of a coal fire without the disadvantages of dirt, dust and carrying of coal.

Radiant Convectors

As the name suggests, this type of heater consists of two units, one providing convected heat, and the other radiant heat (fig. 11.8). Thus the advantages of general background heating and rapid heat are obtained from one appliance.

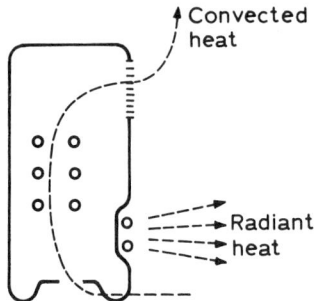

Fig. 11.8 Principle of a radiant convector heater.

The convector is usually thermostatically controlled, as previously described, and two or three heat settings may be available for the radiant section of the appliance, so providing a large range of outputs.

Tubular Heaters

In tubular heaters, the element is mounted on insulated spacers within circular or oval-shaped steel tubes. Most of the heat is dissipated by convection and, like convector heaters, they may be thermostatically controlled.

The tubes are normally positioned on the floor, or secured to the skirting under the windows or near doors. The standard loading is 60 watts per foot length of heater, and they are available in lengths ranging from two to sixteen feet. Where space is restricted, they may be arranged in 'banks' of two or three mounted in vertical formation.

The temperature of the surface of the tube reaches about 80°C in 15 minutes or so, and care must therefore be taken to ensure that they are not accessible to young children.

ELECTRIC SPACE HEATING

They are not suitable for providing the main source of heating in a living room, but they are ideal for providing background heat, especially in halls or bedrooms.

Fan Heaters

Fan heaters are similar to the convector heaters described earlier in that the element is contained within a metal case (fig. 11.9). However, to ensure a quicker circulation of air, a fan is also provided. Separate controls for the fan and for the heater are available, one to control the speed of the fan, and the other to regulate the heat output. The fan may be used without the heater to increase the circulation of air during hot weather. An automatic thermal cut-out is incorporated in this type of heater, so that the supply to the element is cut off if the fan should stop working for any reason. If this were not done, the case of the heater would become excessively hot.

The heater may be floor- or wall-mounted as required.

Fig. 11.9 A typical fan heater.

Oil-filled Radiators

The oil-filled radiator consists of a steel panel within which there are a large number of channels containing oil. An immersion heater is positioned horizontally at the base of the panel so that, when heated,

Fig. 11.10 A typical oil-filled radiator.

hot oil rises through the channels and is replaced by cooler oil. Circulating currents are thus set up within the radiator, and heat is transferred to the air surrounding it. The warm air then gives rise to circulating air currents, and so the heat is transferred to all parts of the room. A thermostat is usually incorporated, and a time-switch control, as described earlier, can also be provided if required.

The radiator is permanently sealed and it is, therefore, never necessary to replace or 'top up' the oil.

Almost all the models described above are available for portable use or for permanent fixing, and for loadings ranging from $\frac{1}{2}$ kW to 3 kW—which is the maximum loading that may be connected to a ring circuit.

There are various other forms of electric heating available, which, by their nature, are not available in portable form. Some of these methods are described below.

Storage Heating

In the chapter on the generation of electricity, it was stated that the demand for electricity at night is small. Therefore electricity may be produced more cheaply then, as the demands may be met by power stations using only the most efficient generators. Electricity cannot be stored in large quantities, but it is possible to overcome this difficulty by storing heat produced from electricity when the generation cost is low, and then using this heat during the day, when the generation cost is higher. The heat may be stored either in water, as described in the previous chapter, or, for space-heating purposes, in specially designed bricks or concrete.

There are two main methods of thermal storage for space-heating purposes, and these are discussed below.

Floor Warming

This is the cheapest form of space heating for new buildings, and is commonly used in new blocks of flats. It is suitable only for 'solid' (i.e. concrete) floors. A special cable is laid in the form of a grid, immediately on top of the concrete floor, as shown in fig. 11.11. The distance between adjacent lengths of cable is about 6 inches, but this distance will vary slightly according to the type of cable used and the heat output required (as a general guide, this should be about 10 to 15 watts per square foot of floor area).

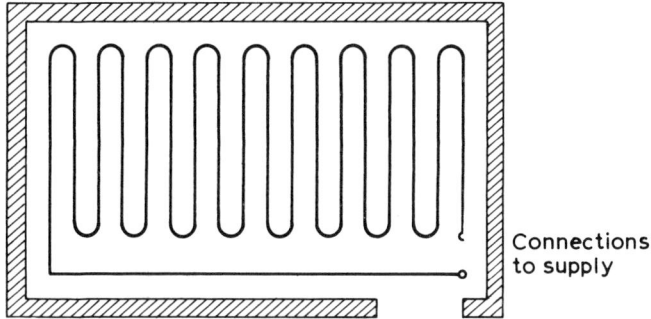

Fig. 11.11 Layout of wires in a concrete floor to provide floor warming. The wires are about 6" (15 cm) apart.

The cable is completely covered by a cement screed about 3 inches thick. It is most important that a sufficient thickness of screed is provided, so that the heat storage capacity of the floor is adequate. The heat losses to the ground under the concrete floor should be as small as possible. A layer of insulation is therefore provided immediately under the concrete, as shown in fig. 11.12. This insulation also extends up the exterior wall to a point above the top of the cement screed.

Wood strips or wood blocks (properly dried before laying), tiles or stone finishes are all suitable for laying on the concrete screed, but mastic (i.e. composition floors) should not be used. Rugs or carpets

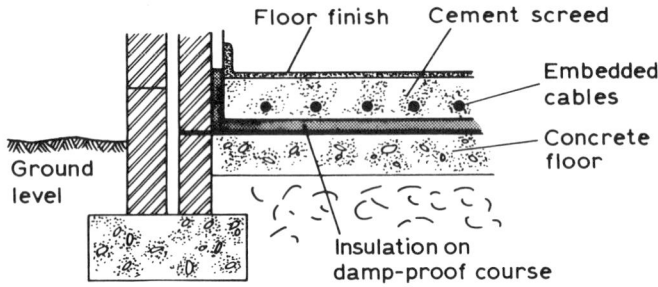

Fig. 11.12 Correct method of installing cables for floor warming. Note the layer of insulation to prevent heat loss downwards.

may be used as desired, although rubber-backed or other solid-backed carpets are not recommended where floor warming is installed.

Floor warming is normally operated in conjunction with an off-peak tariff, so that the floor is heated during the night and the heat stored in the concrete is then given out during the following day. Thermostatic and time-switch control may both be applied to this system, and, where required, circuits for different rooms may be switched independently. Slightly over half of the total heat is dissipated by radiation, the remainder being by convection.

Storage Radiators

Whilst floor warming is ideally suited to new buildings, it cannot be considered for most existing buildings unless large reconstructions are involved. In these circumstances, storage radiators are now the most popular method of providing central heating. Apart from the fact that they are economical in operation, the initial installation costs can be very small, as additions to the number of radiators originally provided can be made later, as required.

Storage radiators consist of a metal case containing a number of bricks of a special material which has a good heat-storage capability. The element which heats these bricks is positioned in channels formed in the bricks, and heat-insulating slabs are placed between the metal case and the heat-storage material, as shown in fig. 11.13.

The early versions of this type of radiator required an 11 hour charge, i.e. they were usually connected to the supply for an 8 hour period during the night, and for a further 3 hour (boost) period during the afternoon. However, improvements in design have made the boost period unnecessary, and the heat-storage requirements can be obtained during the night period only. These more modern radiators are called 'high-capacity storage radiators'. The electricity supply to the radiators is automatically switched on during the off-peak period by a time switch provided and set by the Electricity Board.

A thermostat, or 'charge controller', is incorporated in the radiator, so that the input during the charge period can be regulated. The rate at which the storage radiator dissipates heat is dependent upon the difference between the temperatures of the radiator and the room in which it is situated. Thus, if a radiator receives a full charge during the 8 hour period, it will lose heat more quickly, and therefore maintain a higher room temperature, than it would if it only received a fraction of the full charge. In both cases, however, it will continue to dissipate heat throughout the period until the next charge is due. Furthermore, if the weather suddenly becomes warmer after the radiator has been fully charged, it will dissipate heat at a much slower rate, and will not, therefore, require a full charge during the next charge period.

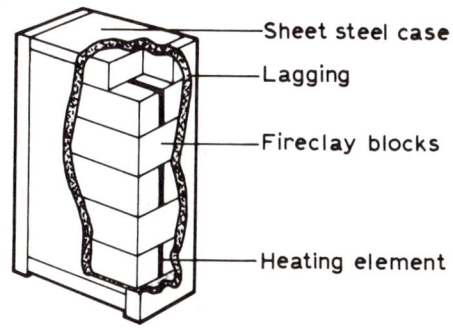

Fig. 11.13 Construction of a storage radiator.

The full charge (or maximum storage capacity) of a storage radiator in kilowatt hours is slightly less than the product of the loading of the radiator in kilowatts and the charging time in hours. Thus a 2·625 kW radiator accepts 20·7 kW h during an 8 hour charging period.

An even greater control of temperature may be obtained by the use of a storage fan-heater. The construction of these heaters is similar to that described above for high-capacity radiators, but the thickness of insulation around the heat-storage material is greater, so that heat is normally dissipated more slowly. However, it may be increased by the use of a fan which is incorporated in the heater. This type may also be thermostatically controlled. Although more expensive than the high-capacity heaters, they are more economical, and provide more flexible control. They would normally be used in rooms where an increase in temperature may be required quickly.

As with convector heaters, it is most important that the inlet and outlet of the radiator are not obstructed by clothing or bedding, etc. placed over the radiator. This might cause serious over-heating, and, to guard against this possibility, a safety device is incorporated to disconnect the supply if the safe working temperature is exceeded. Storage radiators should preferably be positioned at right-angles to windows, rather than immediately under them, so that they radiate across the window.

It is very desirable, when deciding upon the number of storage radiators required for particular premises, to obtain the opinion of the Electricity Board specialist staff, or of a reputable electrical contractor. It will then also be possible to obtain an estimate of the probable running costs. As a very general guide, however, a 3 bedroom house would probably require four high-capacity radiators costing about £150 (including wiring).

With storage radiators, approximately two-thirds of the total heat output is by convection, and the remainder is by radiation.

Electricaire

The principle of Electricaire heating is the same as that of storage radiators but, instead of having separate radiators in each room, one central unit is provided in a convenient position. Warm air is then conveyed by a system of ducts from this position to each room in the house. These ducts are concealed under the floor boards, and two small grilles provide the only visible sign of the heating system in each room. These inlet and return ducts measure about 10 in by 8 in.

The central unit consists of thermal-storage blocks which are heated by elements embedded in them, in the same way as with storage radiators. However, their capacity is larger, ranging from 6 kW to 12 kW, depending on the size of the installation, and a thermostatically controlled fan is provided, so that the output temperature may be maintained at about 60°C. However, the fan speed may be controlled manually, if required, to provide a rapid increase in temperature if for any reason the heating system has been turned off for some time.

This system is naturally restricted to new properties, unless a considerable amount of installation work is acceptable.

Two other types of electric heating are available, although neither is commonly used in domestic premises.

ELECTRIC SPACE HEATING

Panel Heaters

These heaters may operate at either low (about 40°C) or high (about 280°C) surface temperatures, the latter type usually being suspended from the ceiling and not, therefore, suitable for domestic use.

In both cases, resistance wire is embedded in a steel panel, although glass may be used sometimes for the low-temperature type. The loading per square foot is about 40 W for the low-temperature, and 600 W for the high-temperature type. The panels are often permanently fixed to the wall or ceiling, but portable versions of the low-temperature type are available.

About 65% of the heat output of high-temperature heaters, and 30% of that of low-temperature heaters is by radiation, the remainder being by convection.

Ceiling Heating

This is a new system of heating. It is, of course, necessary to ensure that the ceiling is well insulated, to prevent heat losses to the space above the ceiling. As with some of the methods described previously, ceiling heating can conveniently be applied only to new buildings.

Space-heating Calculations

It has already been stated that, for thermal-storage purposes, the electrical loading required may be approximately obtained by allowing 10 to 15 watts per square foot of floor area, corresponding to temperatures of 13°C and 18°C respectively.

Example
Estimate the size of storage radiator required for a room measuring 14 feet by 12 feet 6 inches, to provide a room temperature of (i) 18°C, (ii) 13°C.

$$\text{Floor area} = 14 \times 12 \cdot 5$$
$$= 175 \text{ ft}^2.$$
$$\therefore \text{Loading of radiators} = 175 \times 15$$
$$= 2625 \text{ W}$$
$$= 2 \cdot 625 \text{ kW for room temperature of } 18°C$$

or $\quad 175 \times 10 = 1 \cdot 75$ kW for room temperature of 13°C.

Table 11.1 shows the recommended loadings for background (about 13°C) and comfort (about 18°C) heating.

Rating of radiators (kW)

Room size (ft)	Area (ft²)	Background heating (about 13°C)	Comfort heating (about 19°C)
8 × 9	0– 80	⎱ 2	2
10 × 11	80–120	⎰	2·5
10 × 14	120–160	⎱ 2·5	3·375
12 × 17	160–210	⎰	2·5+2
11 × 21	210–240	3·375	2·5+2·5
16 × 16	240–300	2·5+2	3·375+2·5
15 × 22	300–340	3·375+2	3·375+3·375
19 × 20	340–380	2·5+2·5	3·375+2·5+2
16 × 25	380–410	3·375+2·5	3·375+3·375+2

Table 11.1 Recommended space-heater loadings.

NOTE—it will be seen that, for larger rooms, it is recommended that more than one radiator be provided.

For radiant and convector heaters, the approximate rating of the heater required may be obtained by allowing 1 to $1\frac{1}{2}$ watts per cubic foot of air space to be heated. As with storage heating, these figures correspond to temperatures of 13°C to 18°C respectively.

Example
Calculate the size of convector heater required to maintain a temperature of about 18°C in a room measuring 12 feet by 10 feet by 8 feet high.

$$\text{Volume of air} = 12 \times 10 \times 8$$
$$= 960 \text{ ft}^3.$$
$$\therefore \text{Rating of heater} = 960 \times 1\tfrac{1}{2}$$
$$= 1\cdot44 \text{ kW}.$$

In practice, a 2 kW heater would be used.

Table 11.2 shows at a glance the size of heater required for various room sizes, assuming the room has a height of 8 feet. With larger rooms, two (or more) heaters spaced apart in the room, with a total loading equal to the figure shown, will give a more even temperature distribution. The values given are for living rooms, and may be reduced by about 20% for bedrooms and halls.

ELECTRIC SPACE HEATING

Length of room (ft)	Width of room (ft)					
	6	8	10	12	14	16
8	$\frac{3}{4}$	$\frac{3}{4}$	1	1	2	2
10	$\frac{3}{4}$	1	1	2	2	$2\frac{1}{2}$
12	1	1	2	2	$2\frac{1}{2}$	$2\frac{1}{2}$
14	1	2	2	$2\frac{1}{2}$	$2\frac{1}{2}$	3
16	2	2	$2\frac{1}{2}$	$2\frac{1}{2}$	3	3
18	2	$2\frac{1}{2}$	$2\frac{1}{2}$	3	3	—

Table 11.2 Size of heater (in kW) for various room sizes.

It must be remembered that it will only be necessary for the heater to operate at its full-load rating for about an hour or so, after which the loading may be reduced.

The table is based upon average conditions. If the room has a large window area, the loadings given must be correspondingly increased.

The approximate methods given above will be satisfactory for most domestic applications. In any case, because thermostatic control is available with most types of heater, there are advantages in purchasing a heater with a higher output than those shown in the tables. The fire could then be initially used at full output, so that the room is heated quickly. It could then be switched to a lower output to maintain the required temperature. The cost of a heater is not directly proportional to its loading, e.g. a certain radiant heater is available with both 2 kW and 3 kW outputs. The 2 kW version costs about £9, but the 3 kW version costs only £2 extra.

These approximate methods would not be satisfactory for larger installations. It is then necessary to calculate the required loading more accurately, as follows.

We have seen in the previous chapter that 1 joule is the quantity of heat required to raise the temperature of 1/4·2 gramme of water through 1°C. It has also been shown experimentally that it will raise the temperature of 1 gramme of air through 1°C or

Quantity of heat required (joules)

$\quad$ = **Mass of air** (grammes) × **temperature rise** (°C)

Electrical energy required (kW h)

$$= \frac{\textbf{Volume of air (ft}^3\textbf{)} \times \textbf{36·3} \times \textbf{temperature rise (°C)}}{3·6 \times 10^6}$$

$$= \frac{\textbf{Volume of air (ft}^3\textbf{)} \times \textbf{temperature rise (°C)}}{10^5} \text{ (approx.)}.$$

For comfortable conditions, the air in a room should be changed about every 30 minutes (i.e. two air changes per hour). We may then calculate the loading of the heater required, since

$$\text{power (kW)} = \frac{\text{energy (kW h)}}{\text{time (hours)}}.$$

Example

Calculate the loading of the heater required to maintain the temperature of a room 20°C above that of the incoming air, if the room measures 16 feet by 12 feet by 9 feet high. Allow for two air changes per hour.

Electrical energy required (kW h)

$$= \frac{\text{volume of air (ft}^3\text{)} \times \text{temperature rise (°C)}}{10^5}$$

$$= \frac{16 \times 12 \times 9 \times 20}{10^5}$$

$$= 0{\cdot}346 \text{ kW h.}$$

This amount of heat must be provided every ½ hour, as two air changes are required every hour.

$$\therefore \text{Loading of heater (kW)} = \frac{0{\cdot}346}{0{\cdot}5} = 0{\cdot}69 \text{ kW.}$$

In practice, this size of heater would prove to be inadequate, since, with any type of space heating, considerably more heat must be produced than that required to heat the air. This is because a large part of the heat produced is 'lost' through the walls, ceiling, windows and floor, and more heat is also required to heat these parts of the room and the furniture and fittings in the room. Several factors affect the losses, including the difference between the inside and outside temperatures, the materials of which the walls, floor and ceiling are constructed, the area of the windows and whether double glazing is provided, whether the walls are internal or external, etc. Tables have been drawn up giving the heat losses for different materials at different temperatures, and the losses may be determined reasonably accurately.

As an approximation, we might say that 60% of the heat produced is lost in this way, but it must be remembered that this figure can vary within wide limits depending upon the factors stated above. If 60% of the heat produced is lost, the heating process is only 40% efficient. Thus, if we apply this efficiency to the previous example:

ELECTRIC SPACE HEATING

$$\text{actual electrical energy required (kW h)} = \frac{\text{useful electrical energy}}{\text{efficiency}}$$

$$= \frac{0 \cdot 346}{0 \cdot 4}$$

$$= 0 \cdot 87 \text{ kW h.}$$

The loading of the required heater therefore becomes

$$= \frac{0 \cdot 87}{0 \cdot 5}$$

$$= 1 \cdot 74 \text{ kW}$$

i.e., a 2 kW heater would be necessary.

Guards

The design of electric heaters of all types must ensure that neither the temperature of the case of the heater nor that of the adjacent wall or floor exceeds a safe value. Also, the elements must be suitably guarded. The way in which these requirements must be met is specified in a British Standard (BS 3456, section A2: Electric Room Heaters), and all fires now sold should conform to these recommendations.

It should be emphasised, however, that, although a heater may comply with the requirements of the British Standard, it will not necessarily be safe where children or old people are alone in the room. In these cases, special care must be exercised to ensure that all reasonable precautions are taken to avoid any possible accident.

Chapter 11—Questions

1 Name five different methods of providing electrical space heating in the home. Describe briefly each method and the circumstances for which it would be most suitable.
2 A 3·375 kW electric storage radiator is connected to an off-peak supply. It receives an average charge of 6 hours every 24 hours, the supply voltage being 240 volts.
   (i) What is the average weekly running cost if the cost per unit is 0·32p?
   (ii) What current is taken from the supply when the heater is being charged?
   (iii) What is the apparent resistance of the heater element?
   (iv) Describe briefly the construction of a controlled-output storage radiator.

3 Explain three different methods of heat transmission, and indicate how one of these methods is used in one type of electric heater. Name the three methods of providing electric central heating and describe briefly the essential features of one of these methods.
4 Discuss the factors which should be considered in making a choice between the use of radiant heaters and storage radiators for heating a small house.
5 Explain the advantages of heating a small house by means of block storage heaters. What is the advantage of the fan-assisted type of heater? Explain the purpose of the control fitted to the majority of storage heaters.
6 State, giving reasons for your choice, the type of electric space heater you would recommend for each of the following, assuming that it has been decided not to use storage heaters:
   (i) a child's bedroom,
   (ii) a hallway,
   (iii) a bathroom,
   (iv) a living room,
   (v) a garage.

12 Lighting

Incandescent Electric Lamps

If an electric current is passed through a wire, the wire will become heated. Clearly, the first essential is to find a material which can reach a high temperature without melting, and Sir Joseph Swan's first lamp (1878) contained a carbon filament having an extremely high melting-point. But, since heated carbon combines very readily with any oxygen present and rapidly burns away, the filament had to be enclosed in a glass bulb from which all the air had been removed. Nowadays only a few lamps, mainly the tubular and candle types, have vacuum bulbs.

Though the filament of this 'vacuum' lamp did not burn away, it evaporated, leading to progressive thinning and eventual breakage of the filament. Also, the evaporated carbon adhered to the inside of the bulb, and formed a dark layer which prevented much of the light from emerging. In the early 1900's, a search was made for other filament materials which would not evaporate so readily, and in about 1909 it became clear that tungsten would be the most satisfactory material.

Gas-filled Lamps

If an inert gas, such as argon, is introduced into the bulb, the evaporation is slowed down, and it is possible to make the filament hotter (and therefore give more light) without early breakage. On the other hand, the gas circulates around inside the bulb and cools the filament, so more power is required to keep it hot. This cooling effect is reduced by coiling the filament into a very tight spiral (fig. 12.1), but, even so, the efficacy of the lamp (i.e. the 'light output' per watt) is a compromise between the two effects of:

(i) increased efficiency due to the higher temperature,
(ii) reduced efficiency due to the cooling effect of the gas.

In the case of the larger gas-filled lamps, the effect of the first far outweighs that of the second, and a more efficient lamp is the result. Except for a few special cases, all ordinary pear-shaped lamps for general lighting service (GLS) are gas-filled, in sizes from 40 watts upwards.

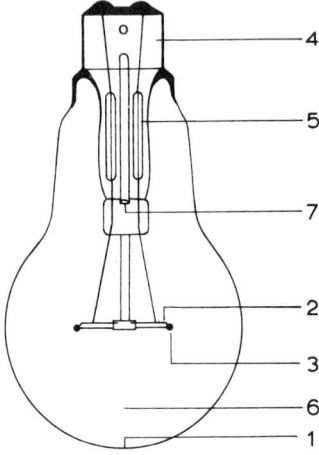

Fig. 12.1 Gas-filled lamp.

1—Inside of glass bulb clear or frosted; 2—Support wires with closed loops; 3—Coiled tungsten filament; 4—Bayonet cap; 5—Fuse; 6—Inert gas; 7—Exhaust tube

Coiled-coil lamps
In these lamps, the spiralled filament (fig. 12.2) is again coiled upon itself, with the aim of further reducing the cooling effect of the gas. The result is a considerable gain in efficiency (from 20 per cent in the 40 watt size to 10 per cent in the 100 watt size), and a corresponding increase of light from a given power, with no loss of life of the lamp.

Bulb finish
Lamps with clear bulbs give a hard light and sharp shadows, and are not generally suitable for domestic use. Pearl lamps are identical, except that they have the inner surface of the bulb roughened, to provide some diffusion with negligible loss of light. They are less glaring, owing to the concealment of the brilliant filament, and cast softer shadows. White lamps are identical with pearl lamps, but, with the addition of a white powder inside the bulb, these provide even

LIGHTING

Fig. 12.2 Filament of a coiled-coil lamp.

softer lighting and less shadow. The loss of light compared with the pearl or clear lamps is approximately 10 per cent. As a general rule in domestic premises, pearl lamps should be used in enclosed fittings and silica lamps in open types of shade. Lamps with pink glazed bulbs are extremely flattering to the complexion, but, as the effect is obtained by absorbing most of the blue rays from the filament, there is an appreciable loss of light compared with ordinary lamps.

Watts	Type	Standard cap	Approx. hours burning per unit of electricity consumed	Average lumen output through life (240 volts)	Average lumen output through life (coiled-coil— 240 volts)
25	P	BC	40	200	—
40	P	BC	25	325	390
60	P	BC	17	575	665
100	P	BC	10	1160	1260
150	P, C	BC	7	1960	—
200	P, C	ES	5	2720	—
300	C	GES	$3\frac{1}{2}$	4300	—
500	C	GES	2	7700	—
750	C	GES	$1\frac{1}{3}$	12400	—
1000	C	GES	1	17300	—
1500	C	GES	40 min	27500	—

P = Pearl. C = Clear, BC = Bayonet cap, ES = Edison screw, GES = Goliath Edison screw.
40, 60, 100, 150 and 200 W silica-coated lamps are available, having a light output about 10% less than the corresponding lamps above. Also, lamps with pink silica-coated or enamel-glazed bulbs in 60, 100 and 150 W ratings may be obtained.

Table 12.1 Standard pearl and clear lamps.

Lamps for special purposes

Apart from 'general lighting service' lamps, there are a number of other types of filament lamps suitable for domestic and general use.

Tubular lamps have a cap at one or both ends, and a clear or white bulb, making them suitable for lighting cornices, mirrors, and showcases where space is limited.

Architectural lamps are straight or curved, permitting lamps to be butted together to form a continuous line of light.

Reflector lamps, incorporating their own internal mirror, give a concentrated beam of light. These are also available coloured red, yellow, green and blue. The smallest reflector lamps, used for shop window displays, require a low-voltage transformer.

Candle and decorative lamps in a variety of bulb shapes and finishes are available for decorative lighting from multi-arm brackets, etc.

There are several thousand different types and sizes of lamp, and from this variety it is possible to find one to suit any purpose.

Operating characteristics of tungsten-filament lamps

All the lamps mentioned above are designed to have an average life of at least 1000 hours when burned at their rated voltage. Some individual lamps fail earlier than 1000 hours, and some last longer, but, with the best makers, the great majority will have a life close to 1000 hours.

The applied voltage, however, has a great effect on lamp performance. If a filament lamp is over-run by 5 per cent, e.g. if a lamp rated for 230 V is run at 242 V, its life will be approximately halved, and its light output increased by about 20 per cent. Conversely, if it is under-run by 5 per cent (rated 240 V but run at 228 V) its life will be prolonged, but it will only give some 82 per cent of its normal light output whilst still consuming some 92 per cent of its normal power. Thus, in the former case one has to renew lamps frequently, whereas in the latter case electricity is being wasted. Lamps should, therefore, always be matched to the voltage at which they are to be run.

All types of vacuum lamps can be burned in any position without any change in their performance. Pear-shaped GLS lamps are normally burned cap-up; in other positions there may be a slight loss of life (in domestic sizes), especially if there is vibration present. The light output will be slightly reduced towards the end of the life by blackening of the bulb due to the evaporated particles of filament which adhere to the part of the bulb immediately above it, being carried there by the flow of hot gas in the bulb. Neither of these effects is normally serious, and, if it is considered desirable to use lamps up to 150 W size in sideways or upside-down positions, there are no valid objections, provided that the above points are recognised.

Quartz-halogen lamps
The addition of iodine or bromine to a gas-filled lamp has the effect of returning evaporated tungsten to the filament. The tungsten-halogen cycle requires a high bulb temperature, and the envelope of these lamps is smaller and made of fused silica (quartz). Heat losses by convection in the gas are reduced, and the lamp life and the luminous efficacy can be increased compared with conventional lamps. These lamps are very suitable for floodlights, projectors and car headlights.

Electric Discharge Lamps

If a high voltage is applied to the terminals, or *electrodes*, of a glass tube containing a gas or metallic vapour, the gas or vapour produces light directly, without anything having to be heated to incandescence. The colour of light produced depends on the gas or vapour used. Neon gives a red light, xenon—white, mercury—bluish-white, sodium—yellow, etc. Neon-filled tubes are very widely used for advertising signs, but they—and indeed every form of discharge lamp—must have in the circuit some kind of device to limit the current to an appropriate value, as otherwise, once started, it will rise to destructive values instantaneously. Tubes of the kind described also require a high voltage, up to 10 000 volts, and this must be provided by a transformer from the a.c. mains. On account of the high voltage, the Institution of Electrical Engineers and many local authorities have special regulations covering the installation of neon signs.

Hot-Cathode Discharge Lamps

One of the reasons why a simple neon tube requires such a high voltage is that much of it is required to force the current to leave the cold metallic electrode and enter the gas. The voltage necessary is very much reduced if the electrode is heated and coated with an electron-emitting material. Development of coated hot electrodes has enabled discharge lamps to be made which can be operated from ordinary mains-voltage supplies, and which give useful quantities of light at much higher efficacy than do ordinary filament lamps. Mercury and sodium are the two vapours most commonly used in discharge lamps, the former giving a bluish-white light at about three times the efficacy of filament lamps, and the latter a yellow-orange light at up to ten times the efficacy of filament lamps. In the case of the mercury lamp, current limitation is provided by a choke in series with the lamp, and for the sodium lamp a leakage transformer is used. Both require a capacitor across the mains, to raise the power factor of the circuit, which is lowered by the control gear.

A filament lamp gives all colours of light mixed together, the result being a yellowish-white, since there is more energy emitted in the yellow and red parts of the spectrum than in the others. In the case of discharge lamps, however, only certain colours of light are present: sodium lamps give out only yellow light, with no blue, red or green, and some mercury lamps give only a yellow, a green, a violet-blue and perhaps a very little red, other colours being missing. Thus the colour effect of these lamps is unusual—though familiar enough in street lighting, where colour is relatively unimportant—and they are not suitable for ordinary domestic and commercial use.

Fluorescent Mercury Lamps (MBF)

Besides generating visible light, a mercury discharge also generates ultra-violet radiation which is invisible and therefore seems useless. Materials have been developed, however, which have the remarkable property of fluorescence, that is they can absorb the invisible ultra-violet energy and give it back in the form of visible light of a colour dependent on the material used. Fluorescent powder of this type can be coated on to the inner surface of the outer bulb of a mercury lamp, and can be so chosen to fluoresce with a reddish colour which supplies some of the colour deficiencies of the mercury discharge itself. Thus the light output of the lamp as a whole is a blend of the colours from the discharge and the powder, and is good enough for many industrial and commercial purposes.

Mercury-Tungsten (Blended Light) Lamps (MBT)

Another way of improving the colour of mercury lamps is to use them in conjunction with filament lamps, the latter being strong generators of the red radiations which are notably weak in mercury lamps. In the blended-light lamp, a tungsten filament is incorporated in the same outer bulb as the mercury discharge tube, and is connected in series with it, so that it limits the current in the circuit, and no exterior control gear is necessary. Due to the high efficacy of the mercury component, the overall efficacy of this type of lamp is a little higher than that of ordinary filament lamps, and the colour and life are comparable with that of the fluorescent mercury lamps referred to above.

Metal Halide Mercury Lamps (MBI)

To improve the colour of high-pressure mercury discharge lamps, other metals can be added to the discharge. Sodium iodide is one suitable compound, although the halides of other metals may be introduced. The colour and brightness of a 400 watt version of this lamp make it suitable for projecting colour transparencies.

High-Pressure Sodium Lamps

This lamp is similar to the high-pressure mercury discharge lamp, but uses sodium instead of mercury vapour. This was made possible only by the invention of a translucent ceramic tubing (synthetic sapphire) which withstands hot sodium vapour. The colour and the luminous efficacy are good.

Ultra-Violet Lamps

Various types of mercury discharge lamp are made to generate short-wave ultra-violet radiations which can be used for medical, therapeutical and sterilising purposes, but, as these short-wave radiations are potentially dangerous to the eyes and skin, exposure to them should be made only under expert advice, and then for very limited periods. Long-wave ultra-violet radiations, however, are not harmful, and a special 'black' lamp is available for producing them. This is an ordinary 125 watt mercury lamp, but with a special deep blue-violet bulb ('Wood's Glass') which absorbs all the visible light generated by the discharge, and all the short-wave ultra-violet, but lets the long-wave ultra-violet emerge to stimulate anything in the vicinity which fluoresces naturally or has been specially prepared to do so. Special fluorescent tubes have been produced to give a similar effect. These objects then become self-luminous, and, as a very wide range of strong fluorescent colours is available, some most spectacular effects are possible, as has been shown many times on the stage and elsewhere. Small amounts of ordinary light, however, are quite likely to swamp the effect, which should therefore be attempted only in an otherwise fairly dark room. Neither of the colour-modified mercury lamps previously referred to gives a colour of light generally acceptable for domestic purposes. A large proportion of the total light is provided by the discharge itself, which radiates with a discontinuous spectrum, i.e. light is emitted in a small number of sharply defined colours only. Not all colours of light are present, as when it is produced by incandescence, e.g. by the sun, a candle, or an ordinary lamp filament.

If fluorescence is to be used to produce a really good colour of light, it follows that a mercury lamp must be used which generates very little visible radiation (because this would be of a colour-distorting nature), but a great deal of ultra-violet, which can subsequently be converted into light of a suitable colour by means of fluorescent powder. In practice, this requires a fairly long tube filled with mercury vapour at very low pressure, and with the fluorescent powder coated on its inside surface. At each end of the tube, an electrode is required. This consists of a coil of tungsten wire coated with electron-emitting material, the two ends of each electrode normally being connected to a two-pin cap.

Tubular Fluorescent Lamps (MCF)

Fluorescent lamp characteristics

The lighting design value of light output, associated with a life of 5000–7000 hours, is given in table 12.2. For the first 100 hours or so of life, the light output may be in excess of the figures shown, but after 100 hours it will have settled down to a value slightly above the 'average' figure, declining gradually throughout life. The light output of the various standard colours of lamp is different, as shown in the table and the main colours are as follows.

White and Warm White: of exceptionally high efficiency and creamy appearance. The colour-rendering of these lamps is adequate, but red colours will not show in their proper strength, and they are therefore of doubtful value when used alone for domestic purposes, though ideal for many industrial and commercial applications.

Daylight: nearly as efficient as the above, but whiter in appearance, blending well with natural daylight. Colour-rendering and applications are similar to the above.

Natural: with rather better colour-rendering than either of the above, but not quite so efficient. Has a whitish appearance and is a very good lamp for general purposes where high efficiency and good colour are both important, but neither is paramount. Often used in shops, offices, etc.

Northlight or Colour-matching: with colour rendering very similar to that of natural daylight without sun. The effect produced may appear cold at low levels of illumination, but the coldness disappears when a fair quantity of light is used. Ideal for all purposes where true colour rendering is required, and used in furriers', drapers' shops, and wherever industrial colour matching is carried out.

Deluxe Warm White: having both colour appearance and colour rendering very similar to ordinary filament lamps. Both types can

Nominal watts	Nominal length (*diameter of circular lamps) (m)	(in)	Nominal tube diameter (mm)	Approx. total circuit* (watts)	Lighting design lumens Warm White or White	Caps
15	0·45	18	25	40**	680	2-pin
15	0·45	18	38	40**	650	2-pin
20	0·6	24	38	30	1050	2-pin
30	0·9	36	25	40	1750	2-pin
30	0·9	36	38	40	1700	2-pin
40	0·6	24	38	95**	1550	2-pin
40	1·2	48	38	50	2650	2-pin
50	1·5	60	25	70	3100	2-pin
65	1·5	60	38	80	4400	2-pin
80	1·5	60	38	95	4850	2-pin or BC
85	1·8	72	38	95	5550	2-pin
85	2·4	96	38	100	6400	2-pin
125	2·4	96	38	140	8300	2-pin or BC or RDC
22	0·21*	8¼*	29	31	850	4-pin
32	0·305*	12*	32	41	1500	4-pin
40	0·406*	16*	32	50	2150	4-pin

*The total circuit power is quoted for switch-start circuits.
**For two lamps in series on 200/250 V.
A range of four miniature fluorescent lamps rated at 4–13 watts is available. Strongly coloured lamps in red, green, blue, pink, peach, gold and yellow are also made in certain sizes.
Relative light output when White and Warm White are taken as 100%: Daylight—95%; Natural—75%; Warm tone—70%; Colour-Matching (Northlight), Deluxe Warm White, Colour 32, Kolorite, Colour 34—65%; Softone 27, Trucolor 37, Deluxe Natural—55%; Artificial Daylight—40%.

Table 12.2 Tubular fluorescent lamps
(NOTE—38 mm = 1½″, 25 mm = 1″).

therefore be used in the same room without any colour change being obvious. The Deluxe lamp is mainly intended for social purposes, e.g. homes, hotels, restaurants, and the like, but has also become popular in shops. This is only one of a range of lamps designed for similar purposes.

Deluxe Natural, Kolorite, Colour 37: very good colour and fair efficiency. Suitable for departmental stores or supermarkets, and particularly for food displays.

Artificial Daylight: simulates average daylight without sun, for accurate colour matching. It provides an improvement on the Northlight or colour-matching types.

Colour rendering	Colour appearance	Suitable lamp types	Relative lamp efficiency
Some colour distortion, especially of reds and purples	Cool Intermediate Warm	DAYLIGHT, Cool White 33 WHITE WARM WHITE	95–100%
Good, suitable for shops, home, hotels, restaurants, etc.	Cool Intermediate Warm	NORTHLIGHT, COLOUR-MATCHING NATURAL, Colour 34 Deluxe Warm White, Warm-tone, Colour 32 Soft-tone 27	65–75%
Enhances the appearance of the human complexion and of foodstuffs	Intermediate	Deluxe Natural, Trucolor 37, Kolor-rite	50–65%
Excellent, used for clinical examinations	Intermediate	Trucolor 37, Kolor-rite	50–65%
For accurate colour matching (900 lux)	Cool	Artificial Daylight	40–45%

(i) The lamp names in capitals are the standard designations, as in BS 1853.
(ii) When fluorescent lamps are used to supplement daylight, the choice of lamp colour must be made with care.
(iii) Normally the same colour of lamp should be used throughout an interior.

Table 12.3 Colour appearance and colour-rendering properties of fluorescent lamps (adapted from IES *Code of Recommendations for Lighting Building Interiors,* 1968).

Fluorescent Lamp Circuits

The essentials of a fluorescent lamp circuit are:
  (i) the lamp,
  (ii) a choke to control the current in the lamp,
  (iii) a capacitor to correct the power factor of the circuit,
  (iv) either a starter-switch or a transformer, to provide the necessary conditions to enable the lamp to start.

If the lamp were to be started instantaneously from cold, the action of the discharge would tend to tear away the active electron-emitting coating on the electrodes. This would shorten the life of the lamp since, when all the active material had disappeared, the lamp would fail to start. To prolong the lamp life, arrangements are normally made to heat the electrodes to the correct operating temperature before the lamp is started, and this is achieved by 'switch-start', 'transformer-start' or other circuits.

Starter-switch circuit

When the lamp (fig. 12.3) is first switched on, current flows through the choke, through both lamp electrodes, E (warming them to operating temperature), and through the starter contacts, S, which are closed. These contacts are mounted on bimetallic strips, one of which is warmed until it bends away from the other, thus breaking the whole circuit. This sudden break induces a momentary high voltage in the choke, the voltage appearing across the break at S, and therefore also across the lamp. The discharge then starts, and is kept running by normal mains voltage applied through the choke.

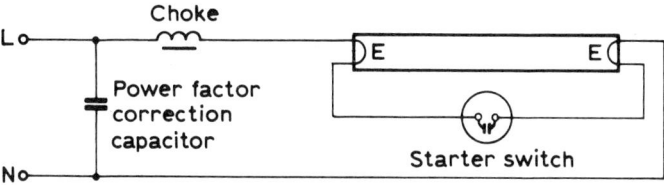

Fig. 12.3   Switch-start circuit.

The capacitor shown connected across the mains is to correct the power factor of the circuit, which would otherwise be unacceptably low, on account of the necessary inclusion of the choke. The capacitor connected across the switch contacts is mainly for the purpose of suppressing radio interference which might be generated within the lamp.

Transformer-start circuit

In this circuit (fig. 12.4), a transformer replaces the starter-switch. It is so arranged that, when the circuit is first switched on, the end windings of the transformer pass heating current to the lamp electrodes, E, and, as soon as they have become sufficiently hot, the voltage between them is sufficient to start and maintain the discharge. Starting is therefore not strictly instantaneous, but usually occurs within a small fraction of a second. An essential requirement is that the lamp must either be fitted with a metallic strip along the outside of the glass, connecting the caps, and this strip must be earthed by some convenient means, or the tube surface must have a water-repellant (silicone) coating, and there must be earthed metal (perhaps part of the fitting) close to the whole length of the lamp. Most present-day lamps have the strip or coating already applied. The transformer is initially more expensive than the starter used for the circuits already mentioned, but, once installed, there are no replacements to make,

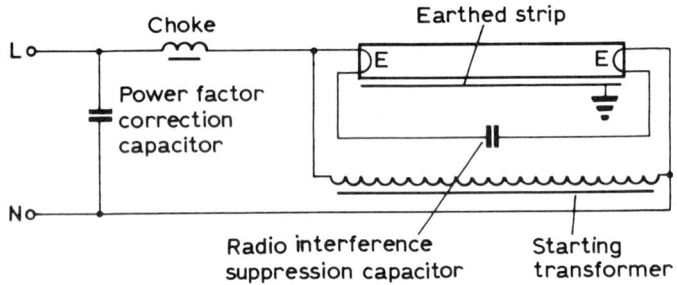

Fig. 12.4 Transformer-start circuit

and in the long run it may work out the cheapest and most convenient system.

Resonant-start circuit
This circuit (fig. 12.5) ensures equal heating of both lamp electrodes, E, since initially they are connected in series. The choke carries two windings, each having an approximately equal number of turns, but wound in opposite directions, L_1 and L_2.

When the mains is applied, the choke has a low inductance and impedance. The pre-heating current flows through both its windings, the capacitor and both lamp electrodes. The voltage across the lamp increases as the capacitor charges up, and unequal currents flow through the windings when the lamp 'strikes'.

The lamp and the capacitor are then in parallel, and a good power factor is obtained.

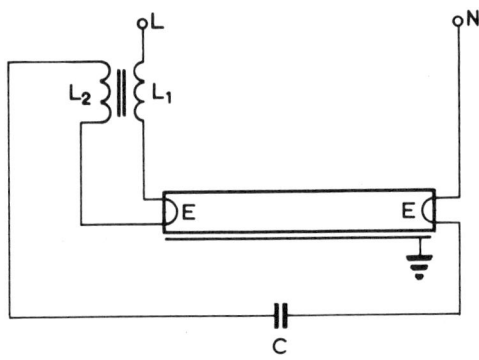

Fig. 12.5 Resonant-start circuit.

Lighting Quantities

The nature of light
Light is an electromagnetic radiation similar to radio waves or X-rays, except in wavelength, and travelling at the same velocity (300 million metres per second). The wavelength of visible light is about the same size as a particle of talcum powder. (See also Appendices 1 and 2.)

Luminous flux
The luminous flux is a measure of the rate of passage of this visible electromagnetic radiation (taken to be radiation having wavelengths between 380 and 760 nanometres, one nanometre (1 nm) being 10^{-9} metres, or one thousand millionth part of a metre.

This flux is measured in lumens (lm), the definition of a lumen being given in Appendix 2, and the light output of lamps may be compared by considering their luminous fluxes: for instance a 100 watt incandescent tungsten lamp gives about 1260 lumens.

Luminous efficacy (η) (previously luminous efficiency)
The luminous flux (lumens) divided by the power consumed (watts) give the luminous efficacy. Thus the luminous efficacy of a 100 watt tungsten lamp is about 12·6 lumens per watt (lm/W).

If a source of light could completely convert the power it consumed into greenish-yellow light at a wavelength of 555 nm—the wavelength of light to which the average eye is most sensitive—its luminous efficacy would be approximately 685 lm/W.

The yellow low-pressure sodium lamp used for street-lighting concentrates its light output at 589·3 nm, for which the relative spectral sensitivity of the eye $= 0·765$, and its theoretical maximum luminous efficacy is $0·765 \times 685 = 525$ lm/W. Practical sodium lamps give 100–150 lm/W. 'White' lamps have lower luminous efficacies, since red, green and blue light is also present, e.g. fluorescent lamps have a luminous efficacy of 30–70 lm/W, depending on their colour and their length (fig. 12.6).

Luminous intensity (I)
Luminous intensity is a measure of the intensity with which light is emitted in a particular direction, but not of its light output, e.g. a parabolic mirror reflector behind a motor-car bulb will not increase the light output of the bulb, but will enormously increase the intensity of light in the forward direction.

Its unit, the candela (cd), can be reproduced as a primary standard

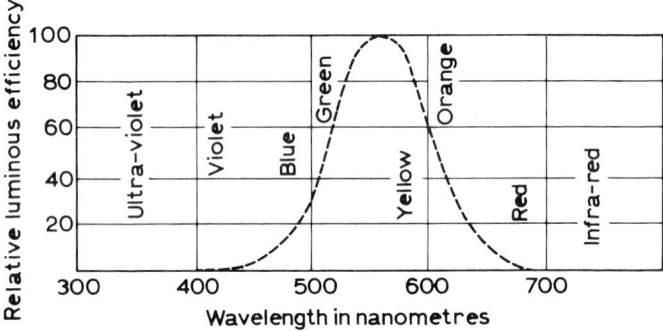

Fig. 12.6 Relative sensitivity of the average human eye to different wavelengths of light.

by the National Physical Laboratory, Teddington, and other national laboratories abroad. A 'uniform' source has the same value of luminous intensity in all directions. For a practical light source, such as a lighting fitting, the variation of its luminous intensity with angle can be plotted on graph paper.

Illumination (illuminance) (E)

Illumination is the amount of light falling on unit area of a surface per second. If one lumen of luminous flux is spread evenly over an area of 1 square foot the illumination is said to be 1 lumen per square foot (lm/ft^2), sometimes called one foot-candle.

The SI unit of illumination is the lux (one lumen per square metre). 10·76 lux = 1 lm/ft^2. 1 lux = 0·093 lumens/ft^2. 1000 lumens spread evenly over an area 10 ft × 12 ft (120 ft^2 or 11·2 m^2) would give an illumination of 1000/120 = 8·3 lm/ft^2 or 1000/11·2 = 90 lux.

Suppose a piece of paper is held 2 ft from a small source of light, such as a 100 watt bulb. If then the paper is moved to twice the distance, or 4 ft from the lamp, it will have to be made twice as long and twice as wide to intercept the same beam of light. In other words, the same light flux now covers four times the area, so that the illumination is a quarter of its previous value. This is the 'Inverse Square Law', which states that the illumination varies inversely as the square of the distance from the source.

Thus, in this example, the illumination would fall from 100/4 = 25 lm/ft^2 (270 lux) to 100/16 = 6·3 lm/ft^2 (68 lux). The law holds true only for 'point' sources, and when no inter-reflection of light occurs from the ceiling and walls.

In practice, most light sources are 'linear' or 'area', but they may be treated as 'point sources' so long as their maximum dimension is less than a fifth of the distance from the source to the measurement point. Much of the illumination received at a working plane is usually by reflection from walls and ceiling. There are usually several sources in a room, and the change in illumination when lighting fittings are raised or lowered is considerably less than that indicated by the above law, particularly where fluorescent lamps are used.

The illumination of a surface also depends on the angle between the direction of the source and the plane of the surface. If a surface is tilted, the amount of luminous flux which it intercepts decreases (fig. 12.7).

Fig. 12.7 Illumination of a surface.

The value of the luminous intensity to be used in these calculations can be found from the distribution curve of luminous intensity, available from the manufacturer for most types of light fittings.

Illumination meters

One cannot rely on one's eyes to tell how much light is falling on a surface, and a 'lightmeter' is necessary (fig. 12.8). This will indicate whether a recommended value is being attained, or whether light fittings or windows require cleaning to avoid excessive light losses. A

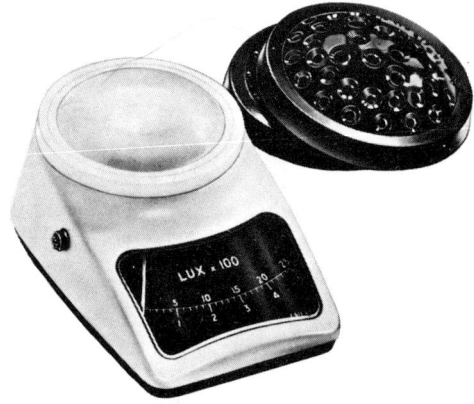

Fig. 12.8 Lightmeter.

simple pocket-type lightmeter costs about ten or fifteen pounds, though more accurate and expensive instruments are available. The instrument contains a photoelectric cell which generates an electric current when light falls on it and moves a needle over a graduated scale. The photocell must be placed parallel to the surface on which the illumination is required, and this is not necessarily horizontal.

If the lightmeter is placed, say, on a kitchen table, and there is a large fall in the reading when the housewife stands in front of it, it indicates that she is casting a heavy shadow, and that the lighting is unsuitable for this particular task. A fluorescent fitting mounted parallel to and vertically above the front edge of the sink and working surface would improve this situation. The photocell will not respond exactly as the human eye does to different colours of light, unless a correction filter is fitted. Factors (obtainable from the manufacturer of the lightmeter, or stated on it) may have to be applied when the light is not from incandescent lamps.

A lightmeter may also give a lower reading than the true value when the light is from an oblique angle.

Brightness
When the brightness (or brilliance) of a light source or of an illuminated surface is measured, the quantity is called 'luminance', symbol L. Clear, pearl and opal lamps differ in their luminance, rather than in their intensity or luminous flux output.

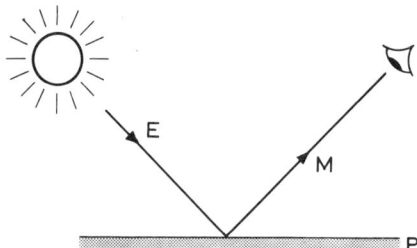

Fig. 12.9 Brightness of a surface.

Luminance is defined as luminous intensity per unit projected area of surface (the area as seen at right-angles to the line of sight), and is usually measured in candelas per square metre. When one object or surface appears brighter than another, as judged by the eye, it is said to have greater 'luminosity'. Luminosity, or apparent brightness, depends on the observer and his subjective judgement. The luminosity of an object also depends partly on other brightnesses in the field of view.

LIGHTING

A wall bracket with a translucent shade, for instance, looks less bright when seen against a light coloured wall than when against a darker colour: wall lights may easily appear uncomfortably bright.

Luminous emittance (M)

An illuminated surface (e.g. wall-paper, a desk top, etc.) appears bright or not according to the illumination which falls on it, and on its ability to reflect light. It is often more convenient to measure the brightness of surfaces in units which depend on the properties of a perfect diffuser. This appears equally bright no matter at what angle it is viewed, blotting paper and matt white paint being practical examples.

Luminous emittance is measured in lumens per square foot or lumens per square metre (lux).

For these units $M = \rho \times E$, where ρ is the reflection factor of the surface, and E the illumination in the appropriate units.

If the illumination on a lightly coloured surface is 200 lumens/metre^2 (lux) and it reflects 75 per cent of the light it receives, its luminous emittance will be $200 \times 75/100 = 150$ lux.

The Eye and Vision

No light source in common use, when correctly used, has any harmful effect on the eyes, but glare from any source, including natural daylight, may cause noticeable discomfort, or even reduce the ability to see.

In many respects the eye is similar to a camera. More light allows:
 (i) a shorter exposure time (say $\frac{1}{200}$th instead of $\frac{1}{25}$th second), i.e. seeing is more rapid,
 (ii) the lens aperture (iris diaphragm) to be reduced in size (say from f5·6 to f11), giving a sharper picture and better depth of focus. Thus an object, such as a book, can be held at a greater distance so that the eyes do not have to turn inwards so much to focus on it, and the lens of the eye is in a more relaxed condition. This relieves the eye muscles of strain.

The natural deterioration of the eyes with age means that older people need more light.

There is justification for advocating high levels of illumination, especially where the objects looked at are dark in colour (e.g. in sewing dark cloth). We cannot reach daylight levels—around 10000 lux on an overcast day—but electric lighting can economically provide levels one-tenth of this.

The high illumination necessary for difficult visual tasks can be provided by additional local lighting, which makes the work brighter than its surroundings.

For work places, it is desirable to provide moderate illumination as an amenity. As a rule, this should not be less than 200 lux (25 lm/ft^2). Recommended minimum values of illumination for a large number of visual tasks are given in the Illuminating Engineering Society's *Code of recommendations for lighting building interiors.*

A given level of illumination will only be fully effective if it is not accompanied by glare.

Glare

There are two main kinds of glare.

'Disability glare' has a measurable effect on visual performance, and makes seeing difficult. It is mainly caused by intense light sources such as the sun at a low angle, bare lamps or car headlights near to the line of sight, and to excessive contrast between them and the general surroundings. It may also be due to highlights seen by reflection in a glossy surface.

'Discomfort glare' causes a feeling of distraction and irritation. Sometimes light fittings or windows are too bright and too large in relation to other parts of the field of view.

While excessive contrasts in luminance must be avoided, diffused lighting may make the environment appear uninteresting. The distribution of light should have a directional quality, to reveal the detail and shape of objects.

Lighting Design

Illumination

The illumination required to perform a visual task satisfactorily depends mainly on the visual angle, S, subtended by the critical detail, and on the contrast. For very severe tasks, such as dressmaking and mending, daylight illumination levels of the order of tens of thousand of lux are required. (However, it may be better to increase the apparent angular size of the task by providing illuminated magnifiers, or to enhance the contrast in the task, rather than to provide very high illumination.)

Recommended values of illumination for various visual tasks are published by the Illuminating Engineering Society in *Recommendations for good interior lighting* and in the handbook *Interior Lighting Design* published by the Electricity Council.

LIGHTING

The recommended minimum illumination level should be increased by 50–100% where:
  (i) the reflectance and contrast are very low,
  (ii) mistakes are costly or dangerous,
  (iii) protective goggles are worn,
  (iv) the average age exceeds 40,
  (v) the interior has no natural lighting.

The 1941 *Factory Act* gives the legal minimum illumination as 65 lux (6 lm/ft^2) in working areas, and 5 lux (0·5 lm/ft^2) in storage areas and corridors. The *Shops, Offices and Railway Premises Act* (1963) says 'sufficient and suitable' lighting shall be provided. There are also recommendations specifically for schools and hospitals.

Discomfort glare

The IES/BRS Glare Index system allows the degree of glare discomfort to be pre-determined for an interior. A simplified method of calculation is given in *Interior Lighting Design*.

Light Fittings

Fittings can be placed in three categories of light distribution: direct, general diffusing, and indirect (fig. 12.10).

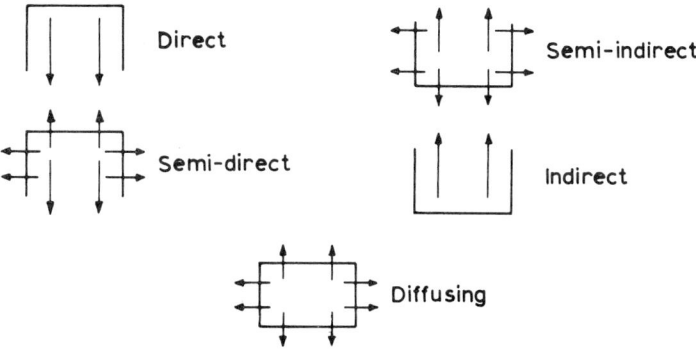

Fig. 12.10 Light distribution.

Direct

These fittings emit all, or nearly all, of their light downwards. They tend to give rise to hard shadows and a dark ceiling. They can cause glare by direct view of the lamp or by reflection in polished surfaces, such as table tops.

General diffusing
This category includes fittings which give light in all directions, as well as those with opaque sides which allow approximately equal light both up and down. Although their lighting effects are similar, their appearance is very different. These are some of the most useful fittings for general lighting, if the brightness of the sides is limited to prevent glare.

Indirect
These fittings give all, or nearly all, of their light upwards, and are a relatively inefficient method of producing a given illumination, especially if the ceiling is not very light in colour. Shadows are softened almost to vanishing point. These fittings are unlikely to be glaring, although the ceiling may become uncomfortably bright if high levels of illumination are attempted.

Maintenance
The slow accumulation of dust and dirt on lamps and fittings can easily account for a loss of one-third of the light without the dirt becoming noticeable, especially with indirect types of fitting. Regular cleaning is therefore essential. Lamps should be removed from the fitting, and wiped with a damp cloth wrung out in a solution of a soapless detergent, the caps being kept dry.

Shades, etc. should be dealt with according to the material of which they are made. Plastic diffusers, louvres and shades should be rinsed in a solution of detergent and allowed to dry naturally. If rubbed dry with a cloth, the surface will acquire a static electric charge which will rapidly attract dust; there are proprietary cleaning fluids which prevent this.

Filament lamps which have been used on their sides should be replaced in the same holders, and in the same positions as before, i.e. with the darkened part of the bulb upwards.

In the original design of installations of several fittings, an allowance of about 20% is often made for the loss of light which inevitably occurs in service, due to dirt on light fittings and room surfaces, even with reasonably frequent maintenance (say every three months).

Spacing
Where a substantially even distribution of light is required over an area, say an office, a number of fittings will be required, and these must not be spaced too far apart from each other or from the walls. Nearly even illumination is obtained with most types of fittings used

for general lighting when the spacing does not much exceed their height above the working plane, e.g. desk and bench tops, etc. This allows overlapping of the light from each fitting, and applies to fluorescent lamps, whichever direction they are lying in, as well as to filament lamps (fig. 12.11). Fluorescent lamps are often mounted in continuous lines for lighting shop windows and supermarkets, and in industry, where a high level of illumination is required.

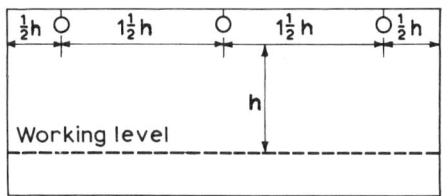

Fig. 12.11 Relation between mounting height and maximum spacing of lighting fittings.

The lumen method of design

The method is fully described, with worked examples and tables, in *Interior Lighting Design*, published in metric and imperial editions by the Electricity Council.

For an open area, such as a school classroom, the lighting system is designed in the following steps.

(i) Decide how much illumination is required. This may be settled by considering the visual task, and using the value recommended by the Illuminating Engineering Society or required by regulations. The statutory minimum average is 10 lumens per square foot (108 lux), but a minimum service value of 300 lux is recommended by the Illuminating Engineering Society.

(ii) Decide what type of fitting to use. In a school, economy in capital cost and running cost is important, and a direct or general-diffusing fitting will probably be chosen. Within these categories, ease of cleaning and satisfactory appearance (on or off) will influence the choice of style. Lighting fittings used in schools should comply with the Ministry of Education standards of maximum brightness, etc. (Unless the school is used for evening activities, fluorescent lighting may not be justified.)

(iii) Decide on the spacing of the fittings. For example, if the ceiling is 3 metres high, the centres of the fittings will be about 2 metres above desk level, and they can therefore be spaced up to $1\frac{1}{2} \times 2 = 3$ metres apart, with half this spacing between the end fittings and the wall. Thus, a room of this height, 8 metres wide, could not be covered by two lines of fittings, as they would have to be about 4 metres apart and the illumination would be patchy. Three lines would be needed, about 3 metres apart. Similarly, the spacing in the other direction, to cover the desk area from front to back, would be worked out, and the total number of fittings required would then be known.

(iv) Find what size of lamp each fitting requires. Allowance has to be made for:
 (a) some reduction from the initial efficiency of the installation, owing to normal soiling of the lamps and fittings, and deterioration of the room decorations. (This is called the maintenance factor, and is often assumed to be 0·8.)
 (b) the fact that some of the light output of the lamps is absorbed in the fitting itself, and some by absorption by the ceilings, walls and furnishings.

The proportion of the original light from the lamps that eventually falls on the working plane can be found by reference to tables of utilisation factors.

The total installed luminous flux required is, therefore,

$$\frac{\text{illumination (lux)} \times \text{area (square metres)}}{\text{utilisation factor} \times \text{maintenance factor}}.$$

Reference to tables—or catalogues—will give the appropriate lamps to use, and the total number of lamps and fittings required. Directional lighting for the chalk-boards should also be provided.

Home Lighting

No domestic lighting installation can be satisfactory unless it obeys the lighting rules previously discussed, which can be broadly summarised as the avoidance of
 (i) gloom,
 (ii) glare,
 (iii) shadow.

Home lighting is so much a matter of personal taste that there can be no hard and fast rules beyond these, but the following notes, and the books listed at the end of this chapter, may be a useful guide.

NOTE—all wattages given are for filament lamps, and do not include any provision for lighting effects mainly intended as decorative features. If fluorescent lamps are used, the wattage can be reduced to one-third, of the figures given, but the correct choice of lamp colour is important, as discussed earlier. It is easier to mix fluorescent light with daylight than with tungsten light.

Lounge

The lighting must be adaptable for various purposes: rest, recreation, or work. A ceiling light, or (particularly with a low ceiling) wall brackets or pelmet lighting (fig. 12.12) should be switched from the door. For these, allow at least two to three watts per square foot, or 25 watts per square metre of floor area.

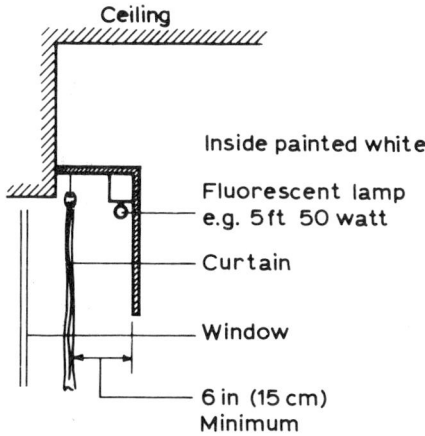

Fig. 12.12   Pelmet lighting.

Sewing, darning and other difficult visual tasks require local lighting by movable lighting fittings—preferably with white diffusing bulbs: 100 or 150 watts for table lamps and 150 or 200 watts for floor standards, discussed later under 'Portable lamps'. The whole appearance of the room can be changed by moving these around. Wall brackets and pelmet lighting tend to make the room look larger.

For viewing television, there should be some light in the room. An effective way of producing a dimly lit background, without reflections in the screen, is to have a lamp behind the T.V. set.

Dining or breakfast room

A light, which could be adjustable in height, is required over the table. If it is a multi-purpose room it requires similar treatment to the lounge.

Kitchen

Above all, have the lights where they are required, to avoid casting shadows. Even though it may not be the choice elsewhere, this is the room where fluorescent lighting is suitable. The ceiling-mounted fittings should be parallel to the edge of the main working surface, whether this is a cooker, a sink, or a food preparation counter. A 5 ft 65 watt or 80 watt fluorescent lamp, or two 4 ft 40 watt lamps, generally provides adequate lighting in an average size of kitchen.

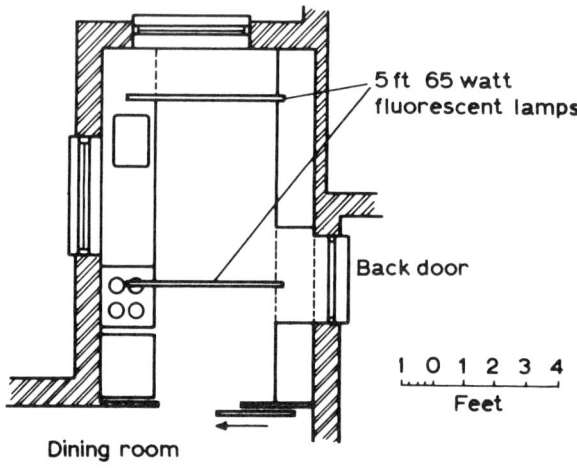

Fig. 12.13 Fluorescent lighting in the kitchen.

Even a small kitchen should have not less than 200 watts of tungsten lighting, and one fitting alone is seldom enough. The lighting fittings should be enclosed in a diffuser, to keep out grease and steam, and to protect the lamp holders and wiring.

A larder or storage cupboard requires a small light, say 40 watts, which can be controlled by an automatic door switch.

Bedroom

Here, a central light of about 100 watts, switched from the door and preferably also from the bedhead, is needed for general purposes.

For reading, provide an individual bedside table lamp or bedhead light, preferably fixed to the wall rather than to the bedhead, where it is generally too low. Lighting is essential at the dressing table, and here the aim is to light the face, not the mirror. This can be done by tubular lamps mounted on both sides of the mirror, or by two small lamp standards on the dressing table. Overhead lighting tends to cast shadows under the nose and chin.

For the nursery, a low-wattage neon lamp makes an effective nightlight.

Fluorescent lamps underneath wall-mounted cupboards will throw light on to working surfaces below.

LIGHTING

Bathroom
A totally enclosed 100 watt lamp should be placed so as to light the interior of the bath and basin. Shaving mirrors can be self-illuminated or there are light fittings, especially designed for use in a bathroom, which also have a safety socket for an electric shaver.

Stairs
Stairs are the danger point of the home. Usually the hall light (100 watts) can be arranged to light the lower half of the stairs also, and the landing light the upper half. Both should be switched by two-way switches from the top and bottom.

Care should be taken in the choice and positioning of the lighting fittings, so that no one is partially blinded by an over bright lamp. Dense confusing shadows should be avoided.

Exterior
There should be a light, 60 or 100 watts, to illuminate both the front and side entrances. If exposed, they should be of a weatherproof type. The diffusing glass can carry the house number as an aid to identifying the house by night or day.

Such lighting is a cheap form of insurance against burglary if left on when the house is empty: a 60 watt lamp switched on during the hours of darkness throughout the year would cost only 50 pence.

To save the inconvenience of frequent lamp replacement, lamps rated at ten volts higher than the mains supply voltage, or miniature discharge or fluorescent lamps, can be used.

Fluorescent lighting is suitable in a garage or workshop.

Portable lamps
Although decorative, portable lamps are not a useful means of illumination unless the standard is of reasonable height (say 5 feet—1·5 metres), and the shade is sufficiently wide at the bottom to allow a spread of light.

To get the maximum downward light, the shade should either be a light colour or have a white interior-lining. For decoration, and to match other furniture, loose covers can be made for portable lamps. Portable lamps should have a substantial base so that there is no likelihood of their being knocked over. If metal lampholders are used, they should be earthed. A special opal bulb and lampholder, which can be switched to 60, 100 or 160 watts, is available from one manufacturer.

To avoid undue contrast in the room when there is no general lighting on in the room, shades with open or translucent tops are recommended.

Commercial Lighting

The majority of industrial and commercial premises are lit by general lighting; where this proves inadequate for specific tasks, a local light should be provided. Fluorescent tubes are suitable for both general and local lighting from fixed points. Flexible arm brackets or portable lamps frequently have tungsten lamps, which for industrial safety should be at low voltage.

General offices are often lighted by a symmetrical arrangement of fluorescent fittings, which may be recessed into the ceiling or suspended from it, allowing the layout of desks to be altered. Diffusing light fittings are a common cause of the discomfort glare prevalent in offices. Private offices are often furnished and lit in a modern and semi-domestic style.

Shop Lighting

Windows

A well-lit shop window attracts attention, and displays the goods to advantage. The vertical illumination should be high, and one background light coloured, to achieve brightness and drama without glare.

Tungsten lamps are still the preferred source where a warm colour is required (foodstuffs) or a degree of sparkle (jewellery and glass). Fluorescent lamps provide light at a high efficacy and without the heat associated with tungsten lamps, but, without additional spot or flood lamps, the display tends to look flat. Pelmets or louvres should be used to hide the lamps from the normal view of passers-by.

Interiors

The lighting should be free from glare and harsh shadows. The counter, and goods in display cases, should be separately lit. Illumination levels of 1000 lux are common, implying a lighting load of 30–50 watts per square metre, approximately half of which will be for high-lighting displays.

Self-service shops, for economy, are frequently lit by long lines of bare fluorescent lamps. Domestic types of lighting may be suitable for fashion and furnishing shops. The choice of light should suit the merchandise. Tungsten and Deluxe Natural, or Colour 32 fluorescent lamps, enhance the colour of meat. A sunlight effect for selling fashions and fabrics can be obtained with 'Kolorite' or Colour 34 tubes.

Where the colour rendering is not important, e.g. for ironmongery, White or Warm White tubes are more efficient.

Further Reading

Lighting: Derek Phillips. The Design Centre, 1966.
Interior Lighting Design: Lighting Industry Federation and The Electricity Council, 1969.
Lighting Your Home: Lighting Industry Federation and The Electricity Council, 1969.
Lamps and Lighting: H. Hewitt and A. S. Vause. Arnold, 1966.
Lighting: D. C. Pritchard. Longmans Green, 1969.
The Provision of Electric Lighting in Dwellings: British Standards Institution.
Lighting for Shops, Stores and Showrooms: Lighting Industry Federation and the Electricity Council, 1969.
Plan Your Home Lighting: R. T. O. Freeth. Studio Vista Press, 1970.

Chapter 12—Questions

1 Outline the principles involved in the production of light in (i) a gas-filled tungsten lamp, (ii) a tubular fluorescent lamp. Explain the reasons for chokes, and capacitors being used with discharge lamps.

2 Describe the construction and operation of a gas-filled tungsten lamp. Describe the type of bulb-finish available, and suggest places in a house for which each is suitable, giving your reasons.

3 Discuss the choice of lighting fittings in a kitchen. Why are fluorescent lamps often more suitable than tungsten lamps in this situation?

4 Describe the main features of a 5 ft 65 watt fluorescent lamp, and a 100 watt tungsten lamp. What would be the approximate cost of using each light source for 100 hours if electricity costs 0·8p per unit?

5 Describe two applications where you consider special attention should be paid to the colour quality of the light, and suggest suitable light sources for the situations you have chosen.

6 Define and differentiate between disability glare and discomfort glare, and show how they can be reduced or avoided in interior lighting. Consider both daylight and electric light in your answer.

7 What advice would you give on lighting a lounge 6 metres by 4 metres and 3 metres high?
 (i) Sketch the position of the light fittings.
 (ii) Give the type and ratings of the lamp(s) you would use in each position.

8 Describe briefly the operation of a lightmeter, and explain some of its uses.

Distinguish between luminous flux and illumination, and give the units of each.
9 What is meant by the terms coefficient of utilisation (utilisation factor) and maintenance factor, as applied to lighting design. Quote typical figures you might use in lighting a large office.
10 A school classroom measures 10 metres × 7 metres × 4 metres high. Plan an artificial lighting scheme, suggesting the average illumination to be provided, and the precautions to be taken to avoid glare.

13 Domestic Cookers and Small Cooking Appliances

In cooking with electricity, heat without smoke, fumes or dust is under the control of the cook. By manipulating a switch, safe clean and hygienic heat may be regulated to any desired temperature. In order to achieve the best results, it is necessary to study the manufacturer's instructions, together with the cooker. This chapter seeks to give some idea of the construction and function of electric cooking appliances, and to give suggestions about the selection of apparatus, and methods of use, and general hints on the care and control of electric cookers and cooking appliances.

Fig. 13.1 Cooker main control panel with socket for 13 A fused plug.

Cooker Main Control

A control with a double-pole main switch and possibly a signal should be fitted for each cooker installation. This control (fig. 13.1) is usually attached to the wall in a convenient position near the cooker.

The main switch should be turned off when the cooker is cleaned, when the hob is raised, and when the cooker is not in use (unless the cooker is an automatic one, and it is desired to use the clock).

Many control panels are fitted with a socket outlet, so that a kettle or other small appliance may be used from the same panel. Other controls are situated on a panel at hob level, on the front of the eye-level grill compartment, or on the back splash plate. The back panel of the splash plate is removable for ease of access by the service engineer.

Domestic Cookers

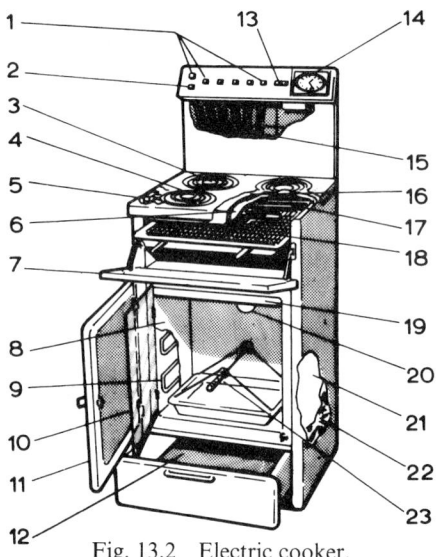

Fig. 13.2   Electric cooker.

1—Variable heat control for plates and grill; 2—Oven thermostat control; 3—Thermostatic contact disc; 4—Boiling plates (4); 5—Hinged plate contact assembly; 6—Grill deflector; 7—Grill compartment door; 8—Removable oven sides; 9—Oven element; 10—Inner glass door; 11—Oven door; 12—Storage drawer; 13—Warming drawer and spit switches; 14—Automatic timer; 15—Internal wiring; 16—Spillage tray; 17—Grill element; 18—Grill pan with food support; 19—Removable oven roof; 20—Oven light; 21—Fibreglass insulation; 22—Aluminium foil insulation; 23—Spit and handle.

DOMESTIC COOKERS AND SMALL COOKING APPLIANCES

The modern electric cooker is made of pressed steel, and most of the surface is usually finished all over in vitreous enamel. The copper wiring from switch to elements is supported on clips called *harness*, and is covered with a form of glass fibre. Table 13.1 gives a short list of domestic cookers of various sizes and designs, which may be installed for different requirements.

Total loading	Boiling plates	Grill	Oven	Table model or floor standing
3 kW Cookers to run from 15 A or 13 A socket		1500 W (grill boiler)	600 W	table
		2000 W (grill boiler)	1200 W	table
	2000 W	2000 W	1800 W	*floor standing
	1000 W	(grill only)		
8 kW	2 × 2000 W	1500 W	2500 W	floor standing
9·8 kW	3 × 2000 W	2000 W	1800 W	floor standing
12·6 kW	4 × 2000 W	2200 W	2400 W	floor standing or split level
13·3 kW Cooker with secondary slow oven	4 × 2000 W	2000 W	2500 W **800 W	floor standing or split level
16·0 kW Cooker with 2 full size ovens (includes heated cupboards and lights)	4 × 2000 W	2200 W	2600 W 2600 W	floor standing or split level

*Current restricted to a maximum of 3 kW by special switch.
**When secondary oven thermostatically controlled, loading may be 2000 W.

Table 13.1 Loading of representative types of domestic cookers.

There are many variations on cookers, and to list them all would be confusing and not helpful. The following are the main characteristics to be found in family cookers.

Hob, with 3 or 4 boiling plates, one of which may have a loading higher than that of the others for quick boiling.

Grill, which is usually under the hob, or at eye-level.

Grill compartment, which may have an additional 800 watt element in the base, in order that it may serve as a second oven which may also be thermostatically controlled.

Drawer below the oven, heated by a 200–400 watt element. The drawer is usually absent where the grill compartment below the hob serves as a second oven.

Oven A rotary spit may be situated in the oven or in an eye-level grill compartment.

Split-level cookers have the hob separated from the remainder of the cooker, so that both parts of the cooker may be mounted at the most suitable height, and in different parts of the kitchen if necessary. The hob is usually let into the top of a kitchen unit, with easy access to the sink, and the oven and grill are at waist height, near to the place where items for baking are prepared.

Sizes of Cookers

In order that cookers may fit into the space available in the kitchen, the hob is usually only about 18" or 21" wide, and in this small space cookers possess all the modern attributes of a family cooker. Even the table-standing cooker, with an overall size of a cubic foot, will perform all cooking functions. The hob of the traditionally shaped cooker can be up to 24" wide, although where the four boiling plates are placed side by side, instead of two and two, the cooker may be 40" wide.

The hob is 34"–36" from the ground, and a plinth is sometimes provided for the cooker to stand on, to bring the lower hob level up to the height of adjacent work surfaces.

In general, a connection cable capable of carrying 30–45 amperes is necessary for full sized cookers, and the current-carrying capacity of the cable is decided in relation to the diversity in use of the various parts of the cooker.

Table-standing cookers and griller-boilers (sometimes known as breakfast cookers) may be connected to a 13 A or 15 A socket outlet.

The Oven

A good oven is always constructed with door, walls, top and base well lagged with insulating material, which is frequently glass-fibre wool enclosed in aluminium foil, to reduce heat loss by conduction to the outside air (fig. 13.3).

Oven elements may be arranged so that the heat comes from the sides of the oven, from the sides and bottom, or from the top and bottom.

Ventilation may be at the top or bottom of the door, through a permanent shaft opening in the hob, or behind the cooker.

Fig. 13.3 Cooker, with the sides and back panel removed to show wiring.

Automatic Control of Temperature in Electric Ovens

The oven is maintained at a pre-determined temperature by a *thermostat*.

The control dial of the thermostat has numbers corresponding approximately to thermometer readings. When it is set at a selected marking, current flows until this oven temperature is attained. When the oven has reached the selected temperature, the current is switched off automatically, and the pilot light goes out. When the oven temperature has dropped by a small amount, the mechanism again operates causing the current to flow. The oven is thus kept at a temperature varying from the selected temperature by only a small amount which, for the purpose of cooking, may be considered negligible (fig. 13.4). A typical thermostat time cycle, necessary to maintain an oven at a moderate temperature (about 350°F, 177°C) is in the nature of 50 seconds ON and $2\frac{3}{4}$ minutes OFF. Naturally, the loading of the oven heating elements, the type of thermostat used, and the oven contents would cause these figures to vary.

THE EAW ELECTRICAL HANDBOOK

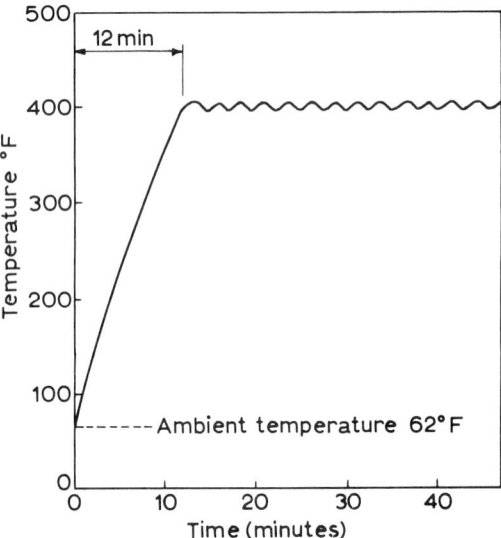

Fig. 13.4 Graph showing variations in oven temperature during operation of the thermostat, with the oven door closed.

Among thermostats used in connection with electric oven control, two of the main principles are:
(i) expansion and contraction of a metal tube used in conjunction with a rod of a special alloy,
(ii) expansion and contraction of a liquid or vapour in a tube, acting as bellows.

The rod type uses the property of a metal alloy, which, over a certain temperature range, has a negligible coefficient of expansion. The sensitive element consists of a fixed brass tube surrounding such a rod, which is anchored to the tube at the end remote from the control head. The other end of the rod advances or is withdrawn, following the contractions or expansions of the brass tube, and is mechanically coupled to a switch mechanism, or to a mercury tube switch.

In the vapour-tension, or hydraulic, type a rigid phial, filled with a volatile liquid, is fixed in the oven, and is connected by means of a capillary tube to a flexible metal bellows situated inside the thermostat. When heat is applied to the bulb, the fluid in the unit expands or vaporises, and causes the bellows to increase in length. This acts directly on an insulated member which, in turn, depresses the switch arms. These arms are provided with substantial tips of fine silver, and are part of the current-carrying system. Expansion of the bellows causes the silver contacts to separate and so break the circuit.

When the circuit is so broken, the oven slowly loses heat, and a reversal of the above operation takes place.

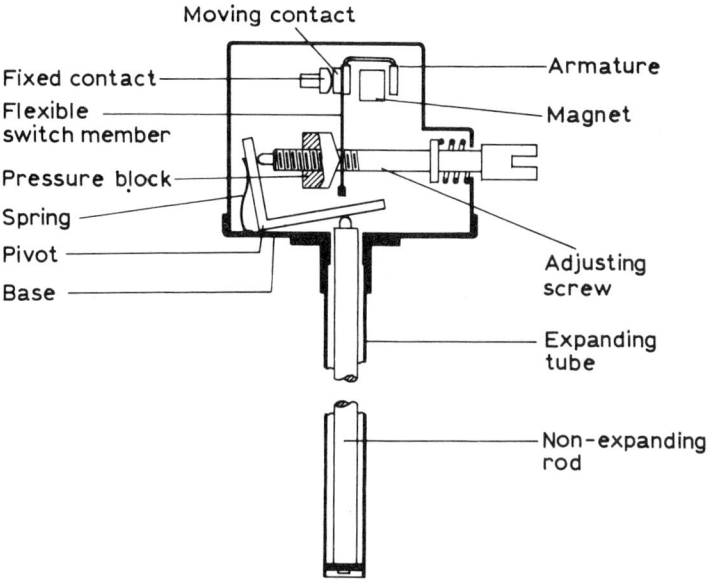

Fig. 13.5 Interior of a rod-type thermostat.

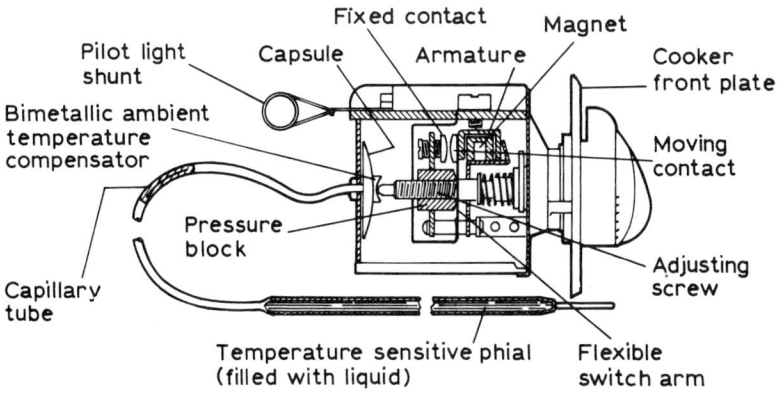

Fig. 13.6 Oven thermostat—vapour-tension (hydraulic) type.

The advantages of thermostatic control are briefly:
(i) a steady temperature is maintained in the oven,
(ii) no attention is required, and no change in switching, as the oven temperature is regulated automatically,
(iii) uniformity of cooking on different days, independent of voltage variation, atmospheric conditions, etc.

Oven temperatures

By about 1973, metric markings will be used for oven thermostats. The comparative oven temperature table below gives an early indication of how the electric oven controls will be marked, so that temperature comparisons can be made with existing markings.

Suggested °C scale	*Present electric scale*
110°C	225°F
130°C	250°F
140°C	275°F
150°C	300°F
160°C	325°F
180°C	350°F
190°C	375°F
200°C	400°F
220°C	425°F
230°C	450°F
240°C	475°F

Automatic Time Control in Electric Ovens

Most cookers now have oven-time control. The food may be placed in the oven, and, when the desired oven-thermostat setting has been selected, the time at which the food is to start cooking, and the duration of the cooking period are registered by adjusting dials. The current will be automatically switched on at the desired time, and automatically switched off when the cooking time has expired.

Self-cleaning and Easy-clean Ovens

A self-cleaning oven is usually the same size as that in the normal family cooker, but the external measurements may be greater, because of increased lagging around the oven. In addition to the controls for normal cooking, there are special controls for the cleaning cycle, and, in addition, there are sometimes special elements.

During the cleaning cycle, the oven interior attains a temperature of about 900°F (482°C). Food soil and dirt are broken down into fine ash by the effect of heat. The smoke and fumes created during this breaking down process are prevented from reaching the atmosphere, being rendered virtually odourless by passing through an eliminator— a heated catalytic oxidisation unit mounted in the oven roof. All that remains in the oven is a little powder.

Another type of cooker stays clean because fats of all kinds, deposited on the oven interior during cooking, are cleaned away by oxidation when they come into contact with the special coating on the vitreous enamel finish, and the oxygen contained in the oven. The floor panel is coated with non-stick 'Fluon', so that 'boil-overs' on the oven floor will not smother the coating and prevent the oxygen making contact.

Some ovens, although not self-cleaning, have an easy-clean surface to the oven linings. A coating of aluminium is applied to both sides of the basic mild-steel pressing which forms the interior of the oven. The top surface is coated with a layer of stainless steel, to the roughened surface of which is bonded a non-stick surface of polytetrafluoroethylene (PTFE). The stainless steel adds extra strength to the PTFE coating, and gives greater resistance to abrasion.

Control of Boiling Plates

Three-heat switches
These switches provide three different heat outputs from one element. The element is made in two sections, so that the sections may be switched in series or in parallel across the supply, as shown in fig. 13.7.

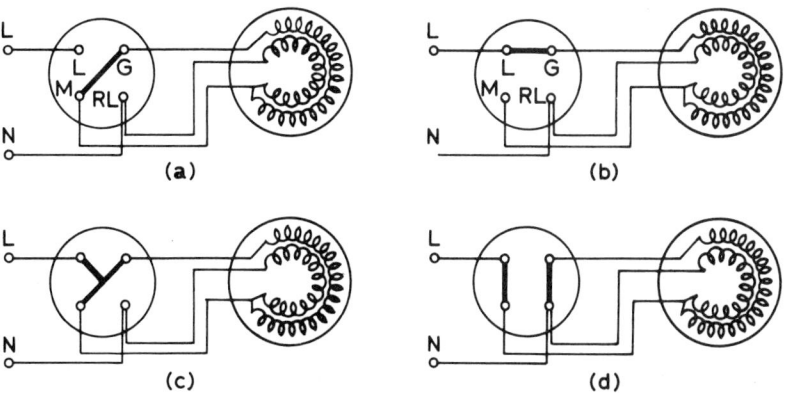

Fig. 13.7 Three-heat switches.

In fig. 13.7a, the switch is in the OFF position, so that the supply is disconnected from both the inner and outer sections of the element.

In fig. 13.7b, it will be seen that the two sections are connected in series across the supply (the circuit is from the L terminal of the supply, to L on the switch, to G, through the outer section of the element, through the inner section to RL on the switch, to the N terminal of the supply).

If each section has a resistance of 120Ω, and the supply voltage is 240 V, the current taken from the supply will be

$$I_L = \frac{V}{R} = \frac{240}{120+120} = 1 \text{ A},$$

and the power output

$$P_L = I_L^2 R = 1^2 \times 240 = 240 \text{ W}.$$

In fig. 13.7c, only one section is connected across the supply (the inner section).

The current taken from the supply will be

$$I_M = \frac{V}{R} = \frac{240}{120} = 2 \text{ A},$$

and the power output

$$P_M = I_M^2 R = 2^2 \times 120 = 480 \text{ W}.$$

In fig. 13.7d, the two sections are connected in parallel across the supply. The power taken will therefore be twice that for the previous case, i.e.

$$P_H = 2 \times 480 = 960 \text{ W}.$$

The three positions, therefore, give quarter, half and full heat output.

The three-heat switch was very satisfactory in domestic use for boiling plates of about 1000 W. At 'low' or quarter heat, the input of heat into a pan was sufficient to maintain simmering. In recent years, the rating of boiling plates has been increased so that the contents of the pan may be raised to the boil more quickly. It will be seen that for, say, a 2800 W boiling plate, low or quarter heat is too great for easy achievement of simmering. More flexible controls, such as the energy regulator, have therefore been developed.

The energy regulator

The energy regulator (fig. 13.8) consists basically of a bimetal strip carrying a heater winding which, when energised, opens and closes a snap-action switch in the boiling-plate circuit at short definite intervals, roughly once a minute when simmering. After the heater has been energised for some time, the bimetal strip bends sufficiently to open

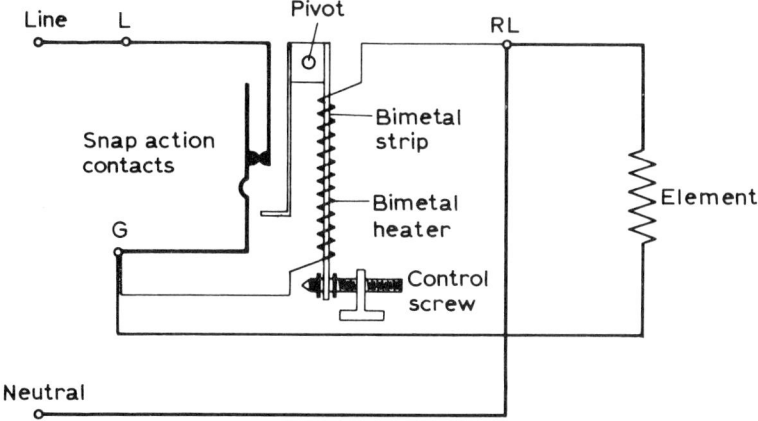

Fig. 13.8 Energy regulator.

the switch, which opens the circuit of the heater and of the boiling plate which it controls. The bimetal strip then cools and allows the switch to close again, thus repeating the cycle.

The energy regulator does not control temperature, but varies the energy input to the boiling plate. The time on, or energy input, is varied by turning the knob, which is connected to a cam. This action changes the position of the bimetal strip relative to the switch. More or less time is then necessary for the strip to reach the switch-off point, thus an infinitely variable output from OFF to FULL is available. The knob markings are nominal, to enable the user to repeat a setting.

The energy regulator may be fitted to any solid or radiant boiling plate, to a grill, or to a 13 or 15 A socket outlet, so that the input of electricity to the appliance connected may be exactly controlled, and current consumption reduced to a minimum. It is compensated for changes in ambient temperature and voltage, and normally has a voltage range of 220/250 volts.

Thermostatic control

The sensing head of one type of boiling-plate thermostatic control is a spring-loaded oil-filled disc in the centre of the radiant boiling plate, which makes good contact with the pan. A capillary tube connects the sensing head to a flexible diaphragm which is situated in the control head, the latter being placed alongside the other cooker controls.

The rise in temperature makes the oil increase in volume, and this, in turn, causes the diaphragm to expand. The latter pushes the switch into the OFF position by means of a rod, so that the supply to the boiling plate is interrupted. It is switched on again as the temperature falls. The intermediate rod is in the form of a proportioning tube, which prevents the temperature from over-shooting at the first cycle.

Another method of thermostatic control is operated by 6-heat controls which give six levels of heat from SIMMER to FULL.

Construction of Boiling Plates

Radiant or sheathed-wire-element boiling plates (1000–2600 W)

In this type of boiling plate, a spiral element is drawn inside a metal tube and packed around by insulating material. The surface of the tube is usually flattened, to ensure better contact with the base of the pan. Any type of pan may be used, but, as with all kinds of cooking, best results are obtained with a good-quality pan with a level base. The boiling plate becomes red hot when switched to top setting.

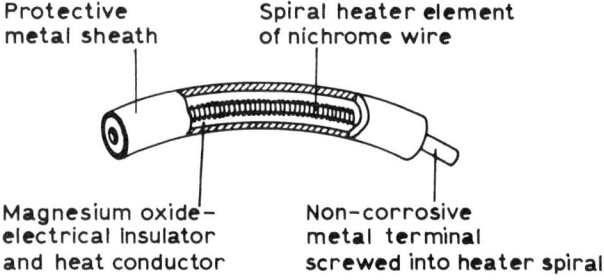

Fig. 13.9 Small section of sheathed-wire element.

Two-in-one boiling plates have two completely independent element tubes which are coiled concentrically, so that one lies within the other. The control circuiting is arranged so that by turning the knob in one direction the inner coil is energised, whilst rotating in the opposite direction causes both circuits to be energised. The control operates similarly to that for a normal boiling plate, in that infinitely variable outputs up to full power can be controlled in either operation.

Totally enclosed boiling plates (1000–2500 W)

The earlier types of totally enclosed or solid plates weighed about 11 lb (4·4 kg) and had a loading of 1000–1800 W. The heating element, enclosed in a special cement, was encased in the plate, which required some time to heat up, and retained heat for a corresponding period when cooling down. In order to give good contact with the boiling-plate surface, utensils with a ground base $\frac{1}{4}''$ (6 mm) thick were necessary. This type of boiling plate is rarely used now.

DOMESTIC COOKERS AND SMALL COOKING APPLIANCES

An improved type of boiling plate (fig. 13.10), which was continental in origin, is used on some cookers, and for individual boiling plates let into a working surface. The plates weigh about 7 lb (3·2 kg), and have a loading of 2500 W. The underside of the metal plate is grooved to accommodate the element spirals, so that there is quick transfer of heat. Any level pan may be used.

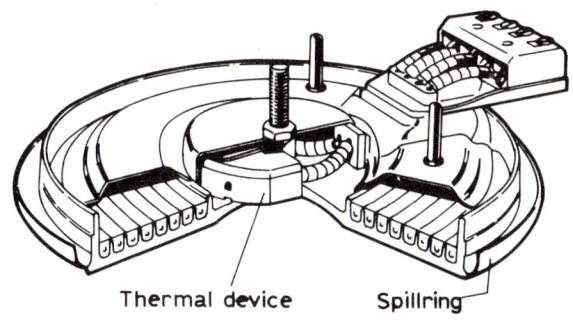

Fig. 13.10 Underneath view of 7·1″ 2400 watt speed-ring plate with thermal device. Stainless steel spillring for hob mounting.

The plates are controlled by an energy regulator which ensures that, according to which regulator is fitted, the full current flows in it for 45 seconds or for 3 minutes after switching on, to give an initial boost.

Open-type boiling plate (1200 W)
In this type, the element is partially or entirely exposed, and radiant heat is obtained. Any type of utensil, preferably with a dull base, can be used, since contact with the boiling plate is not relied upon for heat. It is not considered so durable as other types, and is used for some free-standing boiling plates.

The Grill (2000–3300 W)

The grill element is usually tubular, and it may be controlled by an energy regulator or a single heat switch. In the latter case, the amount of heat reaching the food is varied by adjusting the distance of the food from the heat. The grill may be under the hob, in a compartment which may also serve as a second oven, or it may be raised to eye-level, above the hob. In some grills, the element is divided into two sections, so that only one half need be used at one time.

The Griller-Boiler

The griller-boiler, at one time used on all electric cookers, is now found mainly on small cookers operating from a 13 A or 15 A socket outlet. It is a double-purpose plate let into the hob, and may be used for boiling at the same time as grilling is carried out below. The top surface may resemble a solid boiling plate, or it may be of the radiant tubular type. A rustless deflector plate is provided to fit below the griller, for use when boiling only is required. This, as its name implies sends the major part of the heat upwards.

Care of Cooker

Daily clean
Switch off at the cooker control panel. Wipe over the inside of the oven, including the top, with a damp cloth whilst the oven is still warm after use. Wipe the hob and floor of the grill compartment with a damp cloth.

Weekly clean
Switch off at the cooker control panel. Wipe over the hob and hot cupboard with a cloth wrung out of hot soapy water: use a cleaning agent if necessary. Remove the spillage trays from under the hob and above the grill. Remove the oven shelves.
    The oven interior may be cleaned in one of the following ways.
- (i) Remove the oven lining sections, and wash with fine steel wool and soap or fine abrasive. Ovens with special easy-clean surfaces may also be cleaned in this way.
- (ii) Leave the oven interior in position, and use one of the modern aerosol cleaners, following carefully the instruction on the tin.
- (iii) For self-cleaning ovens, set the appropriate switches which will automatically control the cleaning cycle.

To keep the oven as clean as possible, avoid unnecessarily high temperatures, use the minimum of fat, use a roasting tin only large enough to take the joint, stand pies on a baking tray, and cover food liable to splash.

Points for consideration when choosing an Electric Cooker

It is very difficult to make accurate comparisons between the relative costs of cooking by electricity and other forms of fuel, owing to variations in the thermal efficiency of the apparatus, and also to

DOMESTIC COOKERS AND SMALL COOKING APPLIANCES

variations in the economy-efficiency of cooks. When cooking by electricity, allow about 1 unit per person per day, but rather more per head for the very small family.

The size of cooker needed for the household depends entirely on whether plain or elaborate cooking is undertaken, and on the space available (see p. 198).

An electric oven is larger than it appears to be because, owing to the absence of flame, the entire space is available for cooking. Only $\frac{1}{2}''$ (12 mm) clearance is necessary between the sides of the oven and the cooking tin. Where there is only side heat, the base of the oven may also be used for cooking.

Special saucepans are not needed for modern boiling plates, but they should be solid and even-based.

The service cable should be large enough to carry the current required for the cooker. If only power cable for heating has been installed, special wiring will be necessary for a standard domestic cooker. Expert advice should be obtained.

An electric kettle is invaluable. It is quicker and more economical for boiling water than is the boiling plate.

Small Appliances

The following small appliances all contain their own heating elements. They can all be operated from a 13 or 15 A socket outlet.

Kettles

All BEAB approved kettles are now fitted with safety devices which cut off the current before the kettle boils dry. The safety device acts when the temperature of the kettle begins to rise, as happens when there is too little water to carry off the heat. The safety device may cut the current off in one of two ways:
 (i) by a switch which is thermostatically controlled,
 (ii) by releasing a spring plunger which ejects the connector from the kettle.

In some kettles, the vapour from the boiling water causes the current to be automatically switched off.

Kettles are filled either through a removable lid or through the spout. In use, they should always contain sufficient water to cover the element, and, when not in use, they should be left empty. There is a mark inside all BEAB approved kettles, showing the maximum filling level.

One spout-filling kettle has an indicator gauge on the inside, operated by the weight of water. It shows how much water is in the kettle.

THE EAW ELECTRICAL HANDBOOK

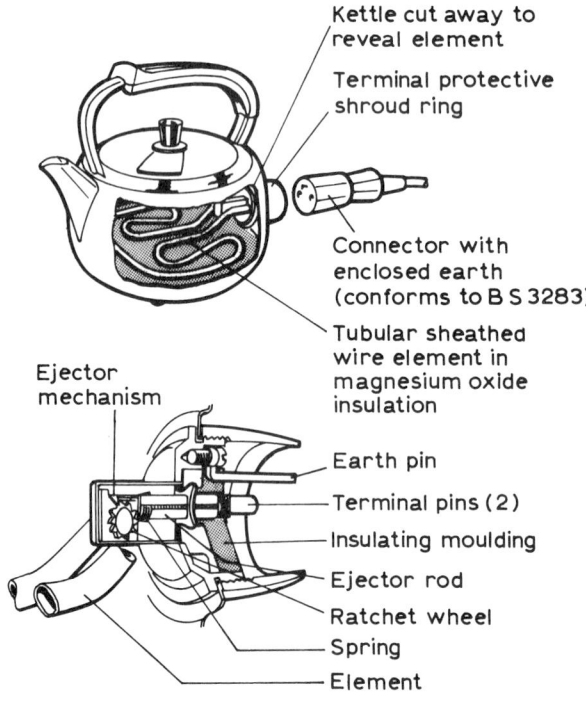

Fig. 13.11 Electric kettle.

Wall kettles are water heaters which fill from a cold tap, and which will boil anything from 1 pint to 7 pints of water at a time. They have a 2½–3 kW heater.

Percolators, milk warmers and coffee makers
Many coffee percolators are fitted with a device similar to that in a kettle, to prevent damage due to boiling dry. The current may also be cut off by the melting of a fuse embodied in the percolator.

Milk warmers in ceramic, to match the percolators, are thermostatically controlled, and prevent the milk from boiling over.

Coffee makers, in heat-resisting glass, are used on separate specially-designed boiling plates, with a loading of 400 watts approximately. A larger urn-shaped coffee maker (chromium-plated) is thermostatically controlled, and will make up to 40 cups of coffee. There is a separate compartment at the top, with a separate element and control, for heating milk.

Boiling rings and warming plates

Boiling rings may be obtained individually, or two may be mounted on a small stand.

Warming plates are designed for use on a table or sideboard. They maintain a steady temperature with a small consumption of energy, just sufficient to keep plates, dishes, coffee, etc. hot.

Toasters and waffle irons

The type of automatic toaster in common use holds 2 slices of bread, and toasts both sides of each slice simultaneously. A dial is set to determine the length of time the current is switched on, and, when the current is automatically switched off, the toast springs up. In the older type of toaster, which is not automatic, the toast is turned by lowering the door. Since the toaster does its work so quickly, it is the most economical way of making toast, especially when only 1 or 2 slices are needed.

Waffle irons are fitted with a light signal which goes out when the baking temperature is reached. It comes on again when the batter is poured in and goes out when the waffle is cooked.

Infra-red grills. Frypans and spits

Infra-red grills cook at 'black' heat, in the same way as the solid boiling plate. The grill has an upper and a lower plate, both heated, and the food may either be in direct contact with them, or placed in

Appliance	*Loading*	*Capacity/size*
boiling ring	750–2000 W	
bottle warmer	150–180 W	
coffee percolator	400–800 W	1–3 pts ($\frac{1}{2}$–1$\frac{1}{2}$ litres)
coffee maker	380–1200 W	1–10 pts ($\frac{1}{2}$–5 litres)
deep fat fryer	1600–1850 W	4$\frac{1}{2}$–8 pts (2$\frac{1}{2}$–4 litres)
frypan	1060–1250 W	
hostess food trolley	200–460 W	
infra-red grill	1500–3000 W	
jug	600 W	1$\frac{1}{2}$ pts ($\frac{3}{4}$ litre)
kettle	1000–3000 W	2–6 pts (1$\frac{1}{4}$–3$\frac{1}{2}$ litres)
plate warmer	175–800 W	
rotary spit	650–2115 W	
teamaker	560–750 W	1–2 pts ($\frac{1}{2}$–1$\frac{1}{4}$ litres)
toaster	400–600 W	
toaster (automatic)	650–1380 W	
urn	3000 W	1$\frac{1}{4}$–6 gals (5$\frac{1}{2}$–27 litres)
waffle iron	750–1100 W	

Table 13.2 Loading of small domestic appliances.

special cooking trays which stand on the lower plate. To get the maximum benefit of speed, the chops, etc. should be evenly cut, so that both the top and bottom surfaces are in contact with the heated grill plates.

Electric frypans have an element sealed into the base, so that they may be immersed in water for washing. A variable thermostat in the handle automatically maintains the temperature selected. The frypan may have a detachable control.

Independent, free standing and wall-mounted rotary spits will cook joints, chickens, small cuts of meat and fish, and skewers of kebabs.

Table 13.2 gives a list of the various types of small appliances, with approximate loading and capacities.

Chapter 13—Questions

1 Give a list of the controls you would expect to find on a modern electric cooker.
   Explain one of them in detail, and indicate which part of the cooker it controls, and the way in which the housewife can make best use of it. (Exclude the hob light.)

2 Describe the action of either the rod-type thermostat or the hydraulic-type thermostat.

3 What is the main difference in the principle of operation of the thermostat and the energy regulator?

4 What is the difference between the radiant or sheathed-wire-element boiling plate, and the open-type boiling plate? Comment on their respective usefulness.

5 What is the difference between a grill and a griller-boiler? Where would you expect to find them?

6 Describe three types of ovens which are either self-cleaning, or easy to clean.

7 Give hints on keeping the oven clean to someone whose oven has no self-cleaning cycle or easy-to-clean surface.

8 Describe, with the aid of sketches, a suitable cooker, complete with timer, for a family of six. List the features which make the cooker efficient and popular, and give the ratings of the oven, boiling plates and grill.

9 (i) Discuss briefly the advantages of an auto-controlled electric cooker.

   (ii) Give a suitable menu for a three-course meal to be served at 7 p.m., describing the regulation of the oven controls, the arrangement of dishes in the oven, and the timing of the meal.

DOMESTIC COOKERS AND SMALL COOKING APPLIANCES

10 An electric kettle is found not to be working. Enumerate the various faults which may give rise to this, and indicate how you would locate any two such faults.

11 (i) Give a brief description of an electric kettle, illustrating your answer with appropriate sketches.
   (ii) (a) How is the user protected from shock?
   (b) How is the element protected against burning out due to the kettle boiling dry?

12 What type of cooking appliance would you recommend for the following persons:
   (i) a woman in a wheelchair,
   (ii) a person with disabled hands (poor grip),
   (iii) someone who could not bend?
   Explain why your recommendations are suitable.

13 A thermostat is a switch actuated by changes of ....

14 The thermostat time cycle in the oven varies according to the following:

   (i) .... (ii) .... (iii) ....

15 An energy regulator is a device that closes and opens a circuit with changes of ....

16 The suggested amount of electricity per head per day when a family of 4 are cooking by that means is ....

17 The operation of an electric cooker depends on the .... effect of electric current.

18 An oven is usually lagged with ....

19 Show, by a sketch, how heat is conveyed from the elements to the food in the domestic electric oven.

20 Complete the following information about oven temperatures:

F	C	
......	135	SLOW
350	......	MODERATE
500	260	....

21 A typical electrical loading for a modern domestic electric kettle is ....

22 An appliance rated at 400 watts, if switched on for five hours, would use .... kW h.

23 Which two small appliances do you think would be most useful in a flatlet with no room for a cooker?

24 Which small appliances would be most useful to a hostess who wished to serve in the dining room without returning to the kitchen?

14 Motor-driven Appliances for Domestic Use

Vacuum or Suction Cleaners

Cleaning by the vacuum method is effected by the suction of air either through the material to be cleaned or across its surface, thus removing all accumulated dust and dirt. This is deposited in a canvas or paper bag fitted to the apparatus.

In addition, for cleaning carpets and heavy materials, a revolving brush giving a beating action, which loosens mud and grit embedded in the pile, is sometimes fitted.

The suction is produced by a fan revolved at high speed by a small electric motor (fig. 14.1). The motor, fan and brush are housed in a case (usually plastic) on runners or wheels, and the apparatus is easily pushed over the carpet by means of a handle. The fan can also be used for blowing instead of suction. When removing dust from cornices, picture rails, book shelves or carved surfaces, special accessories provided for this purpose are connected to the machine by flexible tubing.

Some vacuum cleaners have the dustbag enclosed in a container which remains stationary, cleaning operations being carried out by means of a number of adjustable tools attached to a flexible hose through which air is drawn (fig. 14.2).

A smaller form of vacuum cleaner, known as a dusting cleaner, is now in general use for lighter work, e.g. upholstered furniture, cars and anything within easy reach, as the whole apparatus is carried in the hand. A light-weight cleaner, with the dust container half-way up the handle, is useful for stairs, etc., or where storage space is limited.

The vacuum-cleaner motor is controlled by a switch which is usually foot operated, the connection to the electric supply being made by the usual flexible conductor. The motors used for vacuum cleaners are of the universal type already described, with a loading usually between 450 and 750 watts.

MOTOR-DRIVEN APPLIANCES FOR DOMESTIC USE

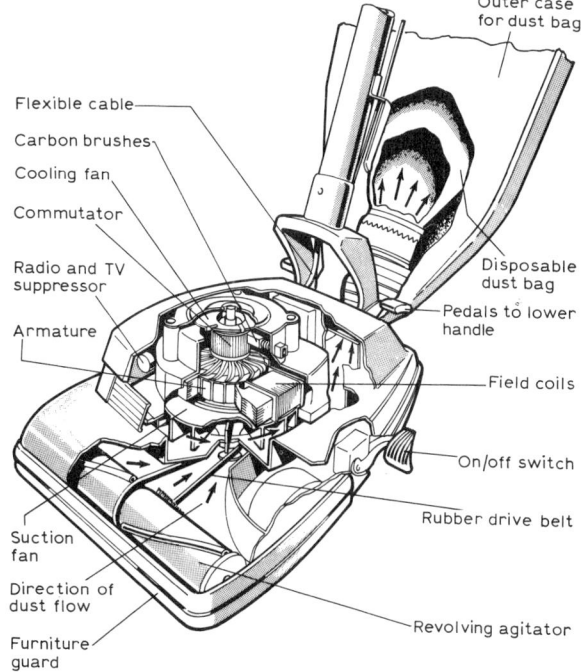

Fig. 14.1 Suction cleaner (upright type).

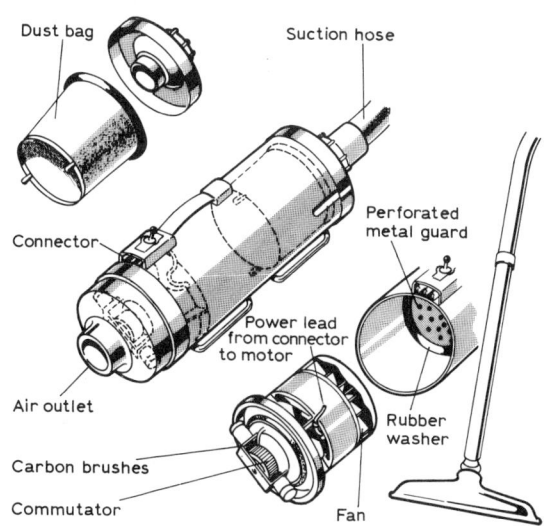

Fig. 14.2 Electric suction cleaner.

In order to get the best results from using the cleaner, it should be moved only slowly over the surface to be cleaned. Where the air has to pass through accumulated dust, the dustbag should be emptied frequently, so that it is never more than one-third full. There are some variations in the details of the dust bag: in addition to the cloth dust bag there may be an inner disposable paper bag, and there may be an inner tube which continuously conveys the dust away from its point of entry into the bag, so that the force of suction is not reduced by accumulated dust.

The upright cleaner does not have such a strong suction as the cylinder type, since it employs a beater and brushes in addition to suction.

Floor Polishers

The electric polisher consists of a small motor mounted vertically, and geared to one or more brushes of horsehair or other suitable material. The brushes revolve in contact with the surface to be polished, the latter having previously been prepared with wax, and when there are two or more brushes in the apparatus they generally revolve in opposite directions. These appliances are usually made without any speed regulation and are controlled by a switch in the handle. Universal motors are fitted and the loading is from 300 watts to 450 watts.

One polisher incorporates suction, and one cylinder-type vacuum cleaner may have a polishing attachment quickly fitted to it.

A combined floor polisher and carpet shampooer has special brushes, and a separate container for carpet-cleaning detergent. Carpet shampooers disperse and brush detergent evenly all over the carpet, which is allowed to dry before being vacuumed.

Floor scrubber and polisher

This machine cleans, waxes and polishes all types of floors, and the respective brushes can be changed in a few seconds. The loading is 300/450 watts.

Fans

Domestic fans may be divided into two groups, viz. extractor fans and cooling fans.

Extractor fans are used to increase the natural ventilation rate in a number of situations. They are especially useful in the kitchen and dining room for removing cooking odours, food smells and cigarette smoke. Some designs are equipped for speed control and reverse operation, the latter allowing direct intake of fresh air. The fans, which are generally variations of a simple propeller fan, are directly driven by small shaded-pole or capacitor motors, both of which require the minimum of maintenance. Models are available for both wall and window fixing, and incorporate either hand-operated or automatic draught-excluding louvres.

Cooling fans are used to produce air movement either locally, by 'personal' or desk fans, or generally, by ceiling mounted or oscillating fans.

The 'personal' fan is usually driven by a single speed shaded-pole motor, and generally utilises a moulded plastic or rubber-blade propeller fan (although one design uses a small centrifugal fan).

Ceiling and oscillating fans use metal blade propellers which, in the latter case, are guarded. Shaded pole motors for a.c. supply, and series-wound motors for d.c. supply are invariably provided with speed-control chokes or rheostats.

Cooker Hoods

Ducted hoods

A powerful fan in the cooker hood draws up cooking fumes and steam before they can circulate around the kitchen, and passes them through a duct to the outside atmosphere, so that there is a complete air change in the kitchen. Grease and dust are trapped in the hood, and must periodically be cleaned away.

The installation of this type of hood involves structural alterations, but it is especially efficient in situations where condensation is a problem.

Ductless hoods

These hoods are completely self-contained, and recirculate the air, rather than effecting a complete air change, as is done by the ducted hoods.

The cooking fumes and steam are drawn up by a fan, and they then usually pass through two filters, one of a fine mesh, such as aluminium, which traps grease and dust, the other of activated charcoal, which removes the cooking odours. The purified air is then passed back into the kitchen. This type of hood prevents heat loss, and enables the cooker to be placed on an inside wall.

The carbon filters need replacing at regular intervals, according to the manufacturers' instructions. The grease filter can be washed in soapy water.

THE EAW ELECTRICAL HANDBOOK

The size of the hood depends on the width of the cooker, as it should give adequate cover to the hob. The hood should be positioned between 1' 10" (560 mm) and 2' 6" (760 mm) above the hob of most cookers. If there is an eye-level grill, the hood should be 15" (380 mm) above this. Most hoods are fitted with a built-in light to illuminate the hob.

To use them to their best advantage, hoods should be switched on a few minutes before cooking begins, and left on for a short while afterwards.

Food Mixers

Household food mixers have a universal motor and vary in loading from less than 100 watts to 450 watts. They can all be used for whisking, and the great majority can be used to cream fat and sugar for cake making. The more powerful mixers will cream up to 1 lb ($\frac{1}{2}$ kg) each of fat and sugar, and, in addition, will complete the making of a rich fruit cake. They may also be used for kneading bread dough.

Users may be interested not only in the work that the mixers undertake but also in the 'weight' of hand-held mixers. They weigh from $2\frac{1}{4}$ lb (1 kg) upwards). The mixer may operate at only one speed, or there may be a choice of 3 speeds, or the speed may be infinitely variable from its starting speed to its top speed.

The parts which come into contact with food are removable, and only these should be taken to the sink for washing. Attachments for a variety of operations may be fitted to some mixers. The most commonly used attachment is the liquidiser, although this also exists as an independent appliance. It has a goblet with, at the base, knives which rotate very quickly.

Hair Dryers

Hair dryers incorporate an electrically heated element over which air is blown by a motor-driven fan. Two types are in common use, the hand-held dryer, which discharges a stream of warm air from a nozzle, and allows hand manipulation during drying, and the hood type which, as the name suggests, utilises a hood through which warm air is discharged at low speed, and which partly envelops the head.

Hand-held dryers are invariably of all-insulated construction, their casings being made of moulded plastics. The loading is usually in the order of 300–400 watts, and two 'dolly-operated' switches in the handle control the fan and heater.

Hood dryers are usually double insulated and the loading is of the order of 500–800 watts. Some models incorporate heat control.
Hand-held dryers are available with table stands, and may have accessories such as 'bag' hoods and extension hoses and manicure aids.
Hood dryers have either table-clamp or free-standing floor stands.

Heated Rollers

Although not a motor-driven appliance, this hair-dressing aid may be considered here.
A base unit (500 watts) supports between 5 and 20 rods which become hot when the base is switched on. Sealed rollers, which may contain wax to help retain the heat, are fitted on to the rods, and so become hot. A red spot at the base of each curler darkens in colour when they are hot enough for use.

Sewing Machines

Nearly all currently available domestic sewing machines are power-driven by small fractional horse-power variable-speed electric motors. The only exceptions are hand- and treadle-operated machines, which are used where electricity is not available. Older machines of this type are easily converted to electric drive.
Sewing speed is regulated by speed control of the motor, achieved by incorporating a variable resistance (rheostat) in the motor circuit. The rheostat can be incorporated in the machine itself, or in a separate box. In the former case, control is usually by a knee-operated extension lever, and, in the latter, by toe or heel-and-toe foot-actuated treadle. Bedplate-illuminating lamps are invariably provided, both in self-contained and converted machines.

Clocks

Mains-operated domestic electric clocks, including the oven timers in cookers, are driven by miniature synchronous motors. These motors, which are suitable for a.c. supplies only, operate at a constant speed determined by the frequency of the electricity supply. It is not possible for the clock to 'gain' or 'lose' unless the supply frequency is varied. As the supply frequency is carefully controlled within close limits, it will be seen that the electric clock is extremely accurate, and its simple construction ensures reliability.

Most clocks are self-starting, although hand-started clocks are still available. Battery-operated clocks, which run for about a year with one set of batteries, usually incorporate a conventional mechanical-escapement mechanism, and hence do not possess the time-keeping properties of the mains-operated clocks.

Shavers

Electric dry shavers can be classified into two groups, viz. the 'clipper-head' and the 'foil-head' types. In the case of the 'clipper', a multiple-edged cutter blade is located behind and in contact with a slotted grille, which is pressed against the skin. Hairs project into the slots, where they are trapped and sheared by the blade. The motion of the blade may be reciprocating, in which case the drive is obtained from an eccentric and a simple motor, or it may be rotary, when it is driven via gears by a miniature series motor. Shavers of this type are usually suitable for both a.c. and d.c. supplies.

In the foil-head shaver, the slotted grille is replaced by a very thin perforated metal foil, which is held against a multi-blade cutter. In this design, the drive is usually from a mains-frequency vibrator-motor, which is suitable for use on a.c. supplies only. One particular design with a foil head is driven by a miniature series motor, and is thus suitable for a.c. or d.c. operation.

All mains-operated shavers are of double-insulation construction, and some are available as 'multi-volt' models, which makes them suitable for travelling.

Shavers of both types are available in battery-operated versions which may be fitted with either replaceable or rechargeable batteries. Shavers of the latter type either incorporate the necessary components for battery recharging by connecting the appliance to the supply in the normal way, or are provided with an auxiliary charging unit, through which the shaver is connected to the supply for recharging.

'Ladies' shavers, of more compact design, based on the above principles are also available.

When shavers are used in bathrooms, they must be operated from a special socket outlet and not by means of a normal plug and socket outlet. The shaver socket outlet incorporates a double-wound transformer to isolate the shaver from the mains, and a safety cut-out in order to protect the transformer from overloading. In this way, the user is completely protected from shocks to earthed metal in what may be a 'wet' situation.

Dishwashing Machines

Dishwashing machines will wash, rinse and dry crockery and cutlery. They will handle such items from a complete dinner for about 5–15 people. In some cases they will wash some of the cooking utensils.

The machines may be classified according to the way in which the water is directed onto the dishes. In any dishwasher, a water pattern is set up to ensure that the water reaches the dishes and all parts of the cabinet.

Jet type

Water under pressure from a pump is forced through holes and/or slits in one or more arms. These may be located near the bottom, centre or top. The water pressure causes the arms to rotate. Where there is only one arm there may be additional sprays at the top of the cabinet. In some machines the crockery basket(s) are also rotated.

Impeller type

A motor-driven impeller, which may have fan-shaped blades, is located at the base of the cabinet. The machine automatically draws in a regulated quantity of water (approximately $1\frac{1}{2}$ gal—7 litres), and, when the impeller is energised and starts to rotate, the water circulates in the cabinet (fig. 14.3).

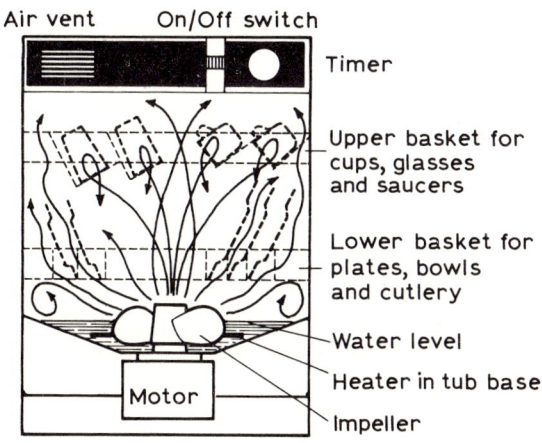

Fig. 14.3 Jet-type dishwasher.

Heaters are usually included, whether the machine fills with hot or cold water, to ensure that the water attains the correct washing temperature, and to provide a heat source during drying. The best results are obtained when:
   (i) the crockery and cutlery are positioned according to the manufacturers' instructions, i.e. so that they are at the correct angle to ensure that (a) the water currents hit the dirty surfaces, and (b) to facilitate drying,
  (ii) the correct quantity of detergent is used. Most manufacturers recommend suitable detergent(s) and the quantity to be used. The latter will vary depending upon the water hardness and whether or not the machine is fitted with a water softener,
 (iii) the rinse aid is at the correct level. All automatic machines dispense a rinse-aid, usually into the final rinse water, to ensure that water runs readily off the surface of the crockery. In the absence of a rinse aid, the speed of draining is decreased, and drops of water remain on the surface of the crockery and cutlery, causing spotting.

The majority of machines are suitable for 'building in' and connecting permanently to the plumbing. The transportable machines may be fitted with castors, and some are compact enough to be used on a draining board or working surface. Such machines are connected to the cold or hot water during the washing programme, and discharge waste water into the sink by means of a hose.

Most machines are completely automatic in operation, and there may be one or more wash programmes. In some machines, the detergent is added manually after loading the dishwasher. In other machines, the detergent is automatically dispensed at the commencement of either the wash cycle or the pre-wash and wash cycles. A programme may be comprised as follows.

Cycle	*Number*	*Water*
Prewash	One or more	Cold
Wash	One. Duration and intensity of spray may be varied.	Hot
Rinse	One or more	Cold, warm or hot
Rinse	One or more	Hot
Dry		

Waste Disposers

Waste-disposal units are fitted underneath the sink drain outlet, and it is essential that the outlet hole should measure at least $3\frac{1}{2}''$ (90 mm) in diameter. Sinks made of stainless steel, enamelled steel or earthenware are all obtainable with holes of this size.

It is not satisfactory to cut a hole in an existing sink, since the machine flange will then be slightly higher than the sink surface, and water will not drain away properly.

The domestic waste disposer is powered by a $\frac{1}{4}-\frac{1}{3}$ h.p. motor. The shaft is coupled directly to the cutter blade, which rotates at high speed (about 1425 rev/min), forcing the waste material against the serrated shredding ring. The steel blade and shredding ring are located in a grinding chamber, the upper end of which is open and connects directly with the sink. All have an overload cut-out, which is automatically reset on batch-feed types, and manually reset on continuous-feed types.

While the machine is in operation, water is allowed to flow through the chamber to wash away the ground waste. Most units are of the continuous-feed type, in which waste is fed into the machine while it is in operation. In the batch-feed type, the machine has to be loaded, and the chamber closed by means of a magnetic stopper which completes the circuit, before grinding can commence.

In both types, waste material is disposed of very rapidly, although no attempt should be made to deal with such items as cans, bottles, tough card containers or string. Reversing switches can be fitted to some machines, so that the cutting blades revolve in alternate directions to equalise wear. They also help to prevent the cutters from jamming.

Refrigerators

In most refrigerators, the food-storage compartment is finished in vitreous porcelain enamel or has a plastic interior lining. It is heat-insulated with mineral wool or plastic foam, and has an insulated door. Inside this food-storage compartment is located the evaporator, or frozen-food storage compartment, which is maintained at a low temperature, and so cools the storage compartment. In some refrigerators, the frozen-food storage compartment is completely separated from the main storage compartment.

Compressor type

The diagram of the compressor-type refrigerating system (fig. 14.4) shows the details of the evaporator and the condensing unit, which are connected together by two copper tubes. The complete refrigerating system is hermetically sealed, after it has been charged with a lifetime's supply of refrigerant and oil.

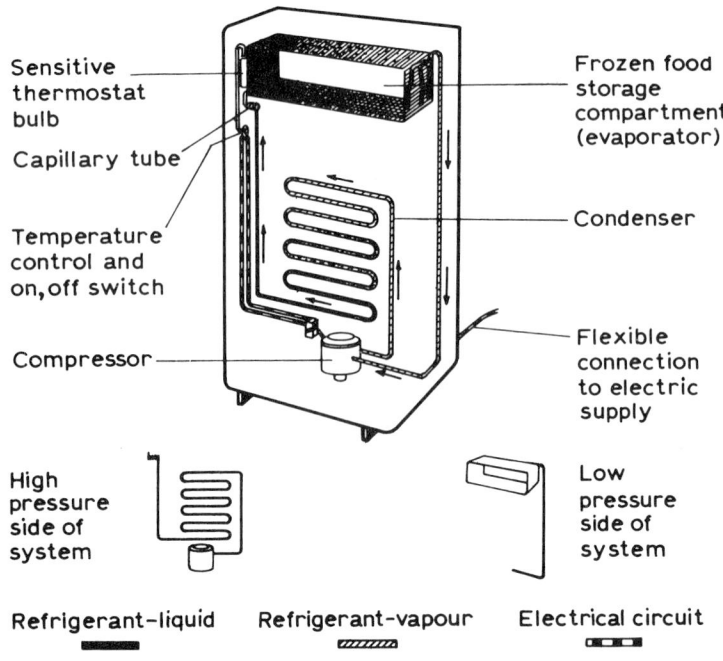

Fig. 14.4 Compressor-type refrigerator cycle.

The refrigerant is a chemical liquid which will 'boil' (that is turn from a liquid to a vapour, when heat is applied) at a low temperature. During this process of boiling in the evaporator, the refrigerant absorbs heat from the food in the storage compartment. The heat-laden vapour is exhausted from the evaporator by the operation of the compressor, a form of pump driven by the electric motor. The compressor forces the heat-laden vapour into the condenser, making it hotter and hotter. When it becomes hotter than room temperature, heat passes out into the room through the walls of the condenser. As a result of this heat extraction, the vapour is converted back to liquid while under pressure in the condenser. This liquid returns to the evaporator, circulating and extracting heat in this way in the period when the compressor is running.

The running of the compressor is governed by an automatic switch in the electric-motor circuit. The switch or thermostat is controlled by the temperature, either in the food-storage compartment or in the evaporator. When the temperature rises above a certain level, the switch closes, starting the compressor. As the compressor runs, the temperature in the food-storage compartment gradually falls until the

MOTOR-DRIVEN APPLIANCES FOR DOMESTIC USE

Liquid and suction lines passing to evaporator

Filter drier

Relay and overload protector within terminal housing

Motor compressor

Fig. 14.5 Rear view of compressor-type refrigerator.

desired low level is reached. The thermostatic switch then opens automatically, stopping the compressor. This switch is usually provided with an adjustable knob, so that the temperature in the refrigerator can be controlled by the housewife to suit her own requirements.

The refrigerant usually used in modern automatic electric refrigerators is known as 'Freon-12' or 'Arcton-6', is non-toxic and non-inflammable, and has a boiling point of about $-21°F$ ($-29°C$).

The electricity consumption of this type of refrigerator, with a $\frac{1}{12}$–$\frac{1}{8}$ h.p. motor, is from about $\frac{1}{2}$ unit per day, depending on the size of the refrigerator.

Absorption-type refrigerator
This type of apparatus is hermetically sealed, and has no moving parts. The refrigerant, ammonia gas in aqueous solution, is in a boiler to which gentle heat is applied from a small heater, liberating ammonia gas from the solution, which remains in the boiler in a weakened form. The ammonia vapour is then conveyed to the condenser, which is cooled by natural air circulation, the ammonia thus being liquefied.

The liquefied ammonia flows into the evaporator, which is also supplied with a circulation of hydrogen, making up the bulk of the pressure, and causing the ammonia to evaporate. In so doing, it absorbs heat from the food-storage compartment, in which the evaporator is fitted. The mixture of ammonia and hydrogen gases then flows out of the evaporator to an air-cooled absorber where the ammonia is washed out of the mixture by weak aqueous solution flowing from the boiler. The hydrogen gas rises back to the evaporator, while the aqueous solution containing the ammonia returns to the boiler to repeat the cycle (fig. 14.6). The heating unit, loading from 85 to 125 watts, depending on the size of the refrigerator, is controlled by a thermostat, which ensures automatic maintenance of steady temperatures in the food-storage compartment.

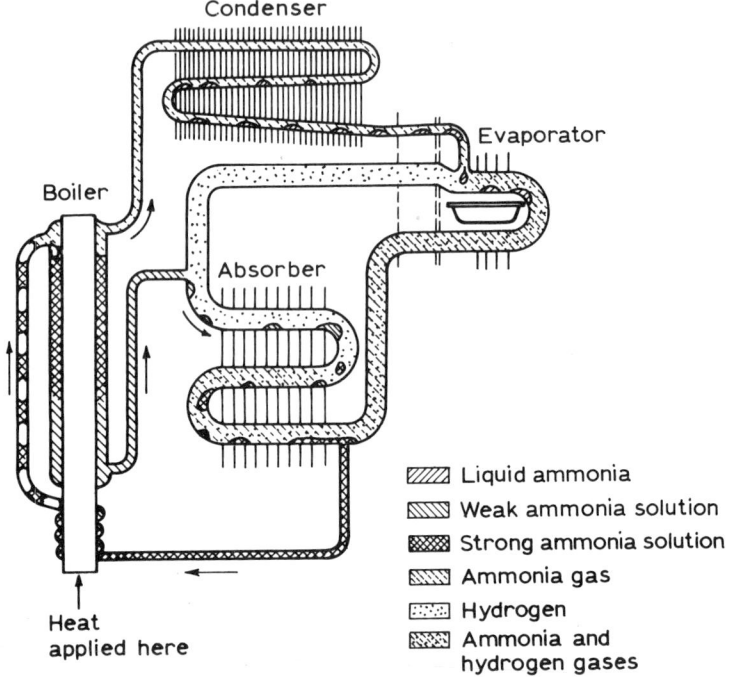

Fig. 14.6 Diagram of an absorption-type refrigerator cycle.

This type of refrigerator will operate on an a.c. or d.c. supply, and, having no motor or compressor, it works in complete silence.

The electricity consumption of this type of refrigerator, with an 85–125 watt heater, is from $1\frac{1}{4}$ units per day, depending on the size of the refrigerator.

Hints on the use of a refrigerator

Food should be arranged so that air can circulate all round it, because the contents of the cabinet are cooled by the circulation of cold air from the evaporating unit.

All foods, especially milk, should be covered, to prevent flavour absorption, drying, etc. Plastic containers, moisture-proof bags, and aluminium foil are suitable.

All foods should be at room temperature before being placed in the refrigerator.

In older-type refrigerators, the air immediately around the evaporator is usually coolest. In modern refrigerators there is often little, if any, variation of temperature in the main part of the cabinet.

See that the door of the cabinet is closed tightly. Do not open the door more often than is necessary.

To clean the refrigerator, wash it with a weak lukewarm solution of odourless soapless detergent.

Take care to keep the deposit of frost on the evaporator to an absolute minimum, since it affects the correct operation of the machine. When frost is deposited to a depth of about $\frac{1}{4}''$, either switch off for a short time, until it melts, or turn the switch to the defrosting position incorporated in the control of certain machines. Where there is automatic defrosting, the cycle is self-operating.

Where there is no automatic defrost, a convenient method of quick defrosting (which, unless manufacturers' instructions advise differently, should always be used when frozen foods are being stored) can be carried out as follows:

(i) make sure the drip-tray is empty and in position beneath the evaporator,

(ii) turn the cold control to OFF,

(iii) remove everything from the evaporator; wrap frozen foods in several thicknesses of clean paper and place them on one of the shelves in the refrigerator; take out, empty and clean the ice trays,

(iv) fill a shallow pan or baking dish with hot water, and place it on the bottom shelf inside the evaporator.

Using this method, the defrosting should be easy, and the frozen foods will not thaw out if well wrapped. After defrosting, the evaporator should be wiped clean and dry, the refrigerator switched on again, the ice trays refilled with clean cold water, and the frozen food unwrapped and replaced.

Storing frozen foods

The evaporator, or frozen-food storage compartment, has trays for making ice cubes, and, according to the size of the refrigerator, it provides space for storing 7–50 lb (3–22 kg) of frozen food. Temperatures of evaporators vary considerably from one make and size of refrigerator to another, and the possible storage times of frozen food therefore varies from 7 days to 3 months. In refrigerators made to the BEAB standard (see British Standard 3739: 1964), the frozen-food storage compartment is marked with one, two or three stars, according to whether the temperature is $-6°C$ (21°F), $-12°C$ (10°F) or $-18°C$ (0°F), indicating that ready-frozen foods may be kept in the freezer up to 1 week, 1 month or 3 months respectively. Food in the food compartment, for day to day use, is maintained at a temperature between 32° and 47°F (0° to 8°C).

Frozen foods are prepared and frozen at a very low temperature, $-20°F$ ($-29°C$). The lower the storage temperature the longer the food can be kept stored and remain nearly perfect in flavour, colour and food value. The frozen-food display cabinets and conservators in shops are kept at 0°F ($-18°C$).

Home (or Domestic) Freezing Units

There are two main types of domestic freezers, the top-opening or chest type and a front-opening cabinet type, as well as the combined refrigerator-freezer. It is recommended that manufacturers' instructions are read carefully and followed in all circumstances relating to the care and use of the freezer.

The thickness of the insulation has now been nearly halved, and the weight reduced, by the use of polyurethane foam insulation.

The majority of freezing cabinets have controls called 'fast-freeze switches', which can be operated during the freezing process. These controls, when operated, ensure continuous running of the unit. This helps to limit the rise in temperature of frozen foods already stored in the cabinet, when fresh unfrozen foods are added, and also speeds up the process of freezing the food.

It is important not to overload the cabinet with too much food to be frozen at any one time. Satisfactory freezing can be expected if fresh unfrozen food can be reduced to 0°F ($-18°C$) and the temperature of the cabinet restored to this level in not more than 18 hours. There should be no excessive rise in temperature when unfrozen foods are first added.

If a mains power failure occurs, it is unlikely to last long enough to affect the safety of the food, provided thawing has not taken place.

MOTOR-DRIVEN APPLIANCES FOR DOMESTIC USE

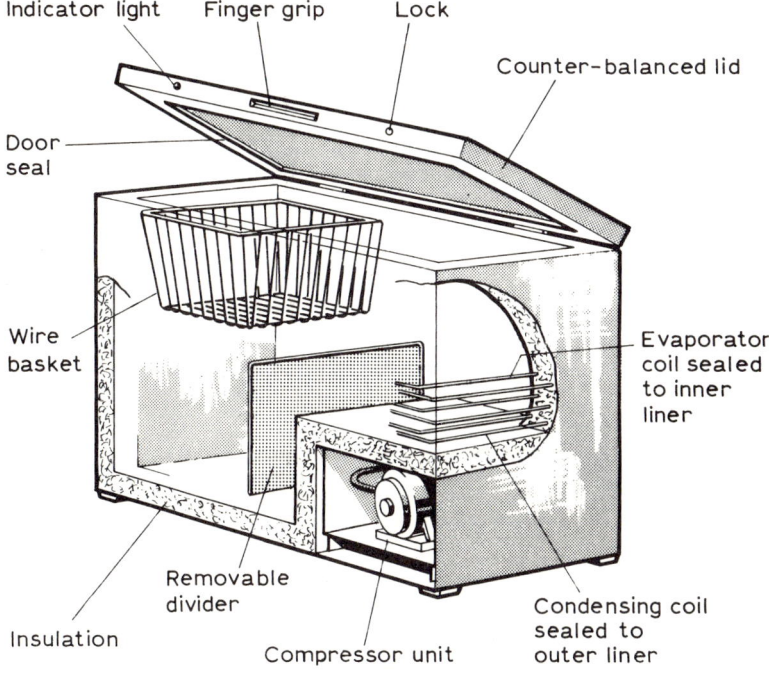

Fig. 14.7 Home freezer.

Keep the door or lid closed. Some cabinets are now fitted with warning signals which operate if the temperature rises more than about 10°F (5·5°C).

Cleaning the cabinet
If the freezer is used carefully, frequent defrosting is not necessary. This can usually be done when the stock of food is at its lowest. The current should be switched off, and the food placed in a refrigerator. Alternatively, packages may be wrapped in flannel or several sheets of newspaper and left in a cool place.

Remove the frost as rapidly as possible with a plastic scraper, which may be provided with the freezer. Wash the interior, and, if it is necessary to use any form of cleaner, see that it is odourless and non-abrasive. Rinse and dry. Switch on the current and replace the packages.

Fresh food for freezing should not be added until the cabinet temperature has once more stabilised at 0°F (−18°C).

Preparation of foods for freezing

Quick-frozen foods are nutritionally the equivalent of fresh foods. The following notes are a general guide to preparing food for freezing. Detailed information on food freezing may be obtained from one of the specialist books available, but it is important also to read the individual manufacturers' instructions, since times and quantities vary somewhat according to the freezer.

All produce must be at its prime: over-ripe or starchy fruit and vegetables, or old tough poultry and meat will not be rejuvenated in the freezer.

If the best results are to be obtained, the produce should be prepared for freezing immediately, but if this is not possible, it may be kept in a refrigerator for up to 24 hours.

Keep food chilled while working on it.

Blanch vegetables.

Package all food in moisture-proof containers.

Keep packages as small as possible, i.e. 1 lb or 2 lb in mass.

Avoid placing packages of fresh food in direct contact with already frozen packages.

Packages should be placed in the freezer as soon as possible: the more perishable the food the more important this is.

Do not freeze at one time more than is recommended for the size of the freezer. It is generally recommended that the amount of fresh unfrozen food added to the freezer at any one time should not exceed 10% of the total freezer capacity.

General storage temperatures must be maintained not higher than $0°F$ ($-18°C$). Running costs vary between 1·5p and 2p per cubic foot per week.

Defrosting times for foods

The length of storage time for home-frozen foods may be obtained from a specialist text-book, but it is not possible to state definite defrosting times, as conditions vary widely between different foods.

As a general guide, packets of commercially frozen food stored in the freezer should be used in accordance with the instructions printed on the packets for storage in '3-star' refrigerators. In many cases, satisfactory storage for considerably longer periods can be achieved in a freezer.

All foods which have been defrosted should be consumed immediately, and no remains should be refrozen.

Appliance	Appropriate loading (watts)
clocks	negligible
combined scrubber and polisher	300–450 W
dishwasher	up to 3 kW (with heater)
fans	25–120 W
floor polishers	300–450 W
food mixers	100–450 W
hair driers	350–600 W
portable motor-operated tools	210–360 W
refrigeration	
compressor	100–175 W
absorption (no motor)	85–115 W
home freezers	100–250 W
rotary ironers	1200–3000 W
sewing machines	75 W
spin driers	100–320 W
tumble driers	2750 W
vacuum cleaners	220–750 W
dusting cleaner	from 150 W
washing machines	up to 3 kW (with heater)

Table 14.1 Loading of motor-driven appliances.

Chapter 14—Questions

1 Outline the main features of construction and the principle of operation of a compressor-type refrigerator. List the advantages and disadvantages of compressor- and absorption-type refrigerators.

2 What advice would you give a housewife about putting food into the refrigerator, and keeping the refrigerator in good condition?

3 (i) What is the fundamental difference between an electric refrigerator and a home freezer unit?
 (ii) Give notes on how you would advise a customer to prepare foods for home freezing.

4 A prospective customer is contemplating the purchase of a domestic dishwasher. Describe which points you would explain to the customer, and the advice you would give about using it. Explain the rating and type of socket outlet to which the machine should be connected.

5 A domestic electric food mixer of the standard type, i.e. not a hand-held model, is supplied with a number of accessories.
 (i) Describe, as if giving a demonstration, the use of this type of appliance.
 (ii) Answer the following questions which might have been asked in such a demonstration.
  (a) What is the approximate cost of running the mixer if electricity is 0·8p a unit?

(b) Why are some mixers unearthed, even though they are of metal construction?
(c) Why do the manufacturers' instructions frequently state that some mixers should be used for only a limited time without switching off?

6 Explain the difference in the work for which the following may be used:
 (i) a small hand-held mixer,
 (ii) a large mixer where the motor and stand cannot be separated.

7 Heated hair rollers are earthed, but food mixers are double insulated. Why is this?

8 A refrigerant frequently used in a modern refrigerator is ....

9 The type of refrigerator which does not have a motor is known as the .... type.

10 The freezing compartment of a domestic refrigerator is now marked with 1, 2 or 3 stars to indicate its ability to ....
 The temperatures indicated by the stars are as follows:
 *
 **
 ***

11 'Frozen food display cabinets and conservators are unsuitable for efficient freezing.'
 True ....   False ....

12 Dishwashers may be classified according to their water action. They are of the following types:
 (i)   (ii)

13 The 2 types of waste disposal unit are:
 (i)   (ii)

14 As a safety measure the case of a hand hairdryer is made of ....

15 The accuracy of an electric clock connected to the house supply is dependent upon the .... of the electricity supply.

16 A vacuum cleaner rated at 500 watts would operate for .... hours on one unit.

17 It is possible to scrub, wax and polish the floor with the same electrical appliance by ....

18 Say where you would expect to find the following, and what function would you expect them to fulfil:
 (i) an aluminium mesh filter,
 (ii) an activated-charcoal filter.

19 In an electric sewing machine, sewing speed is regulated by .... which is achieved by incorporating a ....

15 Electric Home Laundry

About 64% of the households in this country have washing machines. The most popular form of washing machine is the twin-tub, but sales of automatic washing machines are mounting. Single-tub washing machines with wringers are still sold. An immersion type of heater is normally fitted as standard in all machines. For the safe and efficient use of a washing machine, it should be used from a correctly installed (earthed) 13 or 15 A socket. For a non-automatic type of machine, an adequate supply of hot water is necessary for rinsing.

Home Laundering Consultative Council
As a result of discussion and co-operation, the manufacturers of electrical home-laundry appliances, textiles, garments and washing powders employ instructions and markings which incorporate common wording and symbols. Some or all of the symbols below can be found on washing machines (or in their instructions), washable garments and washing powders.

The instructions should be carefully followed, particularly with an appliance as complex in construction and controls as an automatic washing machine.

Preparation
Unless a biological washing powder is used, it is unnecessary to soak articles before washing, but stains should be treated, zip fasteners closed, and trailing ribbons loosely knotted.

Water
Some automatic machines take in only cold water; others are connected to both hot- and cold-water supplies, and the machine fills with either hot, cold, or both hot and cold water simultaneously, which cuts down the duration of the washing cycle. In the case of automatic machines, the water is heated to the correct temperature

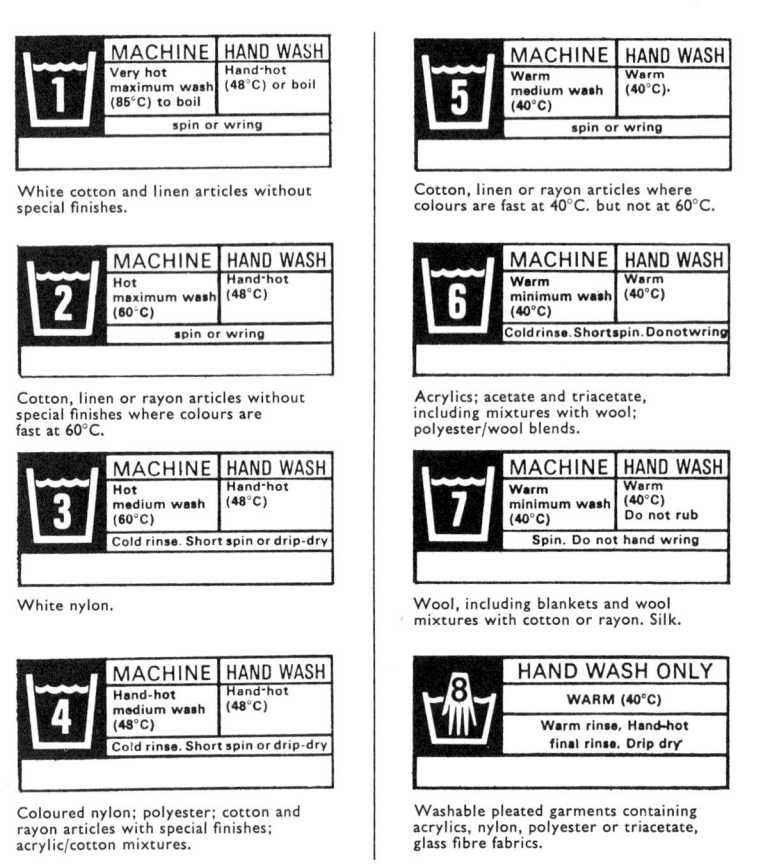

Fig. 15.1 Home Laundering Consultative Council markings.

before washing commences. In other machines, the temperature of the water may be boosted by switching on the heating element in the machines. Where a softening agent is used, such as dissolved soda (2 oz to 10 gal—57 g to 46 litres) or a sodium sesquicarbonate preparation (4 oz to 10 gal—340 g to 46 litres), it should be added while the tub is filling.

Washing powders
Modern washing powders are based on soap or a soapless detergent. In either case they contain other substances, such as bleach (perborate),

ELECTRIC HOME LAUNDRY

fluorescers and fillers. Both types of washing powder are made in normal-lather, and a low-lather version, the latter being particularly suitable for the machines with a horizontal drum, which are sensitive to excessive lather as too much lather prevents the clothes from tumbling about freely, and so they do not become clean.

In addition to the components of a normal washing powder, biological washing powders contain small amounts of enzymes, which promote specific chemical reactions to digest stains of animal and plant origin. Biological washing powders are not recommended for use in machines with a horizontal drum, due to the amount of lather which they produce.

Rinsing

Where the washing cycle is under the control of the user, three rinses are advisable, and these may be done in the spin dryer, the tub or the sink. The more expensive types of spin dryer maintain a continuous flow of clean rinsing water by means of a hose which feeds water into a special opening in the back of the machine.

Types and Use of Washing Machines

The most usual types of washing action are produced by the pulsator, agitator and horizontal drum. The latter may revolve always in the same direction, or it may revolve in alternate directions, with a stationary period in between.

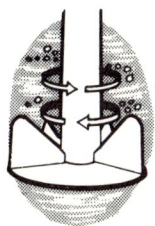 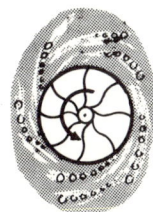 

| The agitator makes 60 or more alternate $\frac{1}{2}$–$\frac{3}{4}$ turns per minute to left and right. This causes water currents which move the clothes back and forth and over and over in the water. | The small disc set in the side or in the base of a washer revolves in the same direction 600 times a minute. This pushes the water round the tub causing the clothes to revolve in the water. | The horizontal perforated drum revolves about 60 times per minute, in some cases in the same direction, in others back and forth. The clothes are lifted on the baffles and tumbled back into the water. |

Fig. 15.2 Mechanical washing actions (from EAW chart).

One-tub washing machine with wringer
This is the simplest type of washing machine. There is a pulsator or an agitator, the wringer is usually power-operated, and there is a pump for emptying the tub. The length of the cycles and the water temperature are controlled by the user.

Twin-tub washing machine
The washing tub and the spin dryer are side by side in the same unit. There is a pulsator or an agitator, and usually two motors to control the washing action, the spin dryer and the extract pump. Water from the spin dryer may, at will, be returned to the wash-tub. There may be dials for controlling the temperature of the water, and the duration of the washing and spinning cycles.

Automatic washing machines
These are one-tub machines containing a perforated drum, which may be horizontal or upright. In the former, the washing action is produced by the rotation of the drum, which may be continuous in the same direction, or reciprocating. In the upright drum, the washing action is produced by an agitator.

There are two methods of selecting the programme.
  (i) The sequence of cycles in each programme is decided by the manufacturer, and the timing and water temperature are automatically controlled. The user selects the programme appropriate to the fabrics to be washed.
  (ii) Before the cycle begins, the user selects the temperature and quantity of water, and the duration of respective parts of the washing cycle. Once the dials are set, the desired programme is automatically completed.

Some automatic washing machines contain a separate heater, to aid the tumble drying of the clothes after the washing programme is finished.

Washing machines are usually driven by a $\frac{1}{6}$–$\frac{1}{4}$ h.p. motor. The motor is not of the universal type, and both voltage and frequency, in the case of alternating current supply, should be ascertained. The clothes capacity of the machine is usually stated as being equivalent to a certain number of sheets, shirts, etc., or the mass of dry clothes.

Approximate masses of a few articles usually included in the wash are as follows.

single sheet	12 oz (340 g)	cotton pyjamas	14 oz (400 g)
double sheet	$2\frac{1}{2}$ lb ($1\frac{1}{4}$ kg)	man's cotton vest	6 oz (170 g)
pillow case	4 oz (115 g)	man's shirt	8 oz (230 g)

bath towel	1 lb (450 g)	overall	9 oz (250 g)
hand towel	7 oz (200 g)	boy's shirt	6 oz (170 g)
table cloth	12 oz (340 g)	child's dress	4 oz (115 g)

One-tub Machine with Wringer

The water line is marked on the tub of the machine, or on the centre agitator post, and, when a full load of washing is being carried, the importance of having the correct amount of water cannot be too greatly emphasised.

Power-driven wringers vary in construction, but the general principles are as follows. There are two rollers made of rubber, in some cases one being hard and the other soft: the tension is automatic, or there may be an adjusting screw. All are equipped with a safety release. The rollers may be made to rotate in either direction. Some wringers can be swung round into any one of five positions, thereby facilitating the direction of rinsing.

A finished load of mixed clothing retains about 100% of its own dry mass of water after passing through the wringer.

Pulsator type

The pulsator is situated in the side of the machine or in the base, and revolves rapidly in one direction when the current is switched on.

After the water softener and detergent have been added to the water and dissolved by the action of the pulsator, the current is switched off, and the clothes are fed in at one side of the washer, so as to avoid splashing and the trapping of air. When all the clothes are in the tub, the machine is again switched on, and the movement of the water caused by the pulsator, in conjunction with the special shaping of the tub, makes the clothes turn in all directions.

Agitator type

The agitator is in the centre of the tub, and is constructed to oscillate in half turns, averaging from fifty to eighty turns per minute.

Twin-tub Washer

A washer, either with a pulsator or with an agitator, is mounted in the same cabinet as an independent spin dryer. The spin dryer only operates when the lid is shut, and revolves at a speed up to 2800 rev/min.

A finished load of mixed clothing will contain about 40–50% water, expressed as a percentage of its dry mass.

Automatic Washing Machines

Automatic washing machines are no longer bolted to the floor. Some are connected to the water supply by hoses, and discharge water into the sink by the same method; others are permanently connected to the water supply and the house drainage system. The latter method involves some expense, but is more convenient in use.

The machines wash (and sometimes pre-wash as well), rinse several times and then spin dry the clothes. The length of the cycle varies according to whether only cold water is drawn into the tub, or whether both hot and cold water are drawn in, and according to the programme selected.

The standard cotton load is usually 9 lb (4 kg). In the upright drum, the amount of water is determined by the selector switch, which is set before the cycle begins. The inner perforated drum revolves at between 750 and 1100 rev/min, to remove the water, and between 55% and 65% water remains in the clothes, expressed as a percentage of the dry mass of clothing. In the horizontal drum, the ratio of water to weight of clothes is automatically adjusted during the cycle, and is determined by the absorbency of the load. The drum revolves at 600–750 rev/min to remove the water, and between 64% and 80% water remains in the clothes, expressed as a percentage of the dry mass of clothing.

Cleaning

The washing tubs of simple washers and twin-tub washers should be wiped out after use. In the case of the agitator washer, the agitator should be lifted out, and both it and the tub should be thoroughly wiped.

Automatic washers do not need wiping out, but there may be a drain screen to be cleared of scraps of lint.

Solid-state Control

The most modern type of control in the washing machine is solid-state control, which has no moving parts. Although the external control knob looks the same as the standard type of control knob, the control is effected by means of electronic components similar to those in transistor radios. A solid-state control can provide a type of heat control similar to that provided by an energy regulator, or thermostat. It can also control the speed of electric motors, and the power supply to an item such as a lighting fitting. In the domestic field, the controls are still being developed, and so far have been used in washing machines, electric drills, blankets and light-dimming switches.

Methods of Drying

Drying cabinets may be 36 in to 70 in high. The heating elements (1–3 kW) are in the base of the cabinet, and there is ventilation at the top. The racks on which the clothes are hung are movable. Smaller portable models may be stored in a limited space, and are often more suited to airing than drying.

The spin dryer (up to 320 W) whirls out the water by centrifugal force, at a speed of up to 2800 rev/min. The amount of water extracted by centrifugal force depends on the position of the perforated drum (whether perpendicular or horizontal), the diameter of the drum, and the revolutions per minute. All independent spin dryers have an upright drum. The amount of water left in the clothing varies between 30% and 75% of the dry weight of the clothing, and, in general, more water is removed by the independent free-standing spin dryer. Spin dryers are available with a 1 kW heater.

The tumble dryer (2–3 kW), which is time controlled, rotates the clothes in a stream of warm air, so that they may be made bone-dry.

Ironing

Rotary ironer
The rotary ironer may have an independent motor, and be suitable for standing on the table or on the floor.

It is necessary to have a 13 or 15 A socket available, since the loading of this type of ironer is about 1200 watts. The temperature is regulated by two thermostats.

The ironer consists of a metal shoe having a heating coil arranged so as to give an even distribution of heat in the shoe. The roller is of metal, padded with felt, hessian and a washable covering. A foot control puts the roller into motion.

Press ironer
The press ironer is constructed with a flat ironing pad and a heated shoe, which, when brought down on the article to be ironed applies a force of 300 lbf, operated by a lever.

The temperature is thermostatically controlled.

If a stool of convenient height is available, it should be possible to remain seated when using either of the foregoing appliances.

Hand irons

Most irons are now fitted with thermostatic control. They may all have features such as a thumb rest, an enamelled cover-plate, chromium plate, a built-in light and a recess in the side of the sole plate to facilitate the ironing of garments having buttons. Also, cord suspenders of various kinds, which prevent the flex from becoming entangled during the process of ironing, may be obtained. All thermostatically controlled irons, and most irons not so controlled, have fixed flexible cords, thus dispensing with removable connectors. The position of the flexible cord may be interchangeable to allow easy conversion for right- and left-handed ironers, or it may swivel. The construction of the element is often as in the next paragraph.

Construction of non-heat controlled irons

Some of these irons are still made, and many are in use. They are fitted with a heating element of resistance wire, properly insulated, between the sole plate and the pressure plate which is under the cover plate. The loading varies according to the weight of the iron, a 4 lb iron being usually 400 watts.

Where the connector is not built in, it should be removed from the iron, not by pulling the flexible cord, but by holding the connector itself, since the strands of copper wire in the flexible cord are held in position by small screws, and these will become disconnected by constant pulling.

Travelling irons

Lightweight travelling irons are available, which often have folding handles, and which can be used on different voltages.

In the type illustrated (fig. 15.3), there is a double element, and the connector is fitted on the terminals in a different position depending on the voltage of the supply.

When the iron operates at 100–125 volts, the parts of the element are connected in parallel: when at 200–250 volts, they are connected in series. Some travelling irons are fitted with two completely separate elements sandwiched together, each element operating over a given voltage range.

Automatic heat-controlled irons

A variety of heat-controlled irons is available. The thermostat control is quite simple and consists of a bimetal strip which actuates a silver contact, according to the setting of the control knob and the temperature reached. One end of the bimetal strip is clamped to the sole plate,

ELECTRIC HOME LAUNDRY

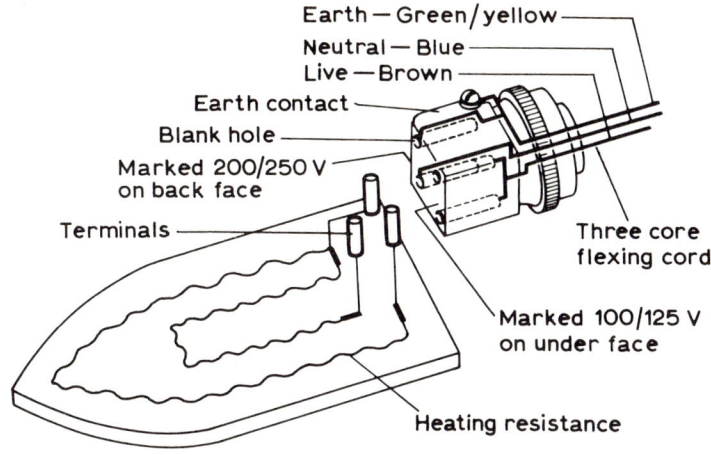

Fig. 15.3 Diagram of connections to a travelling iron.

and, as this gets hot, the strip bends, pressing the arm which carries the contact, and thus breaking the electric circuit to the element. The temperature at which the actual break of circuit occurs is controlled by the cam placed at the end of the control rod.

Steam irons

Domestic steam irons are thermostatically controlled hand irons, not press ironers. They may be used both as steam irons and as dry irons. The steam is delivered at a comparatively low temperature (about 230°F—110°C), from holes in the iron sole plate. It condenses on the cloth, which is cold, and is immediately pressed by the rest of the heated sole plate of the iron. Some steam irons are also able to send out a fine spray of water.

The steam is produced by water dripping, a drop at a time, on to the heated sole plate (fig. 15.4). The iron need not be emptied before switching over to dry ironing.

The loading of these irons is about 1000 watts. They should be fitted with a 3-pin plug, and used on an earthed circuit. At no time does the water inside the iron come into contact with the element.

The constant use of hard water will naturally result in a deposit of mineral salts within the iron. Descaling fluids are obtainable, but the formation of scale may be prevented by using distilled water, or, in the absence of air pollution, rain water. If only tap water is available, it may be demineralised by shaking with some special crystals.

241

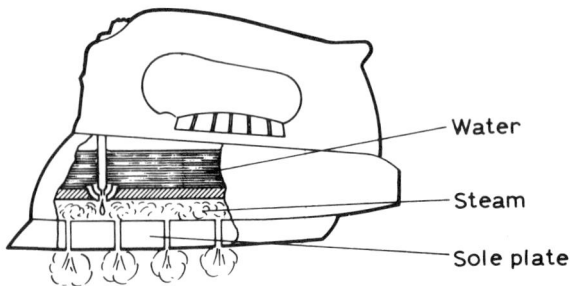

Fig. 15.4 Flash-boiler (drip) type steam iron.

Washboilers

Domestic electric washboilers have a loading not greater than 3 kW. The wash container is usually made of tinned copper or anodised aluminium, and has a capacity of 5–10 gal (23–46 litres). All tinned copper containers, and some aluminium ones, are enclosed in a sheet steel casing, which may be stove enamelled, vitreous enamelled, or galvanised.

Most washboilers are fitted with clamp-on heating elements, which are arranged as shown in fig. 15.5. Some models are, however, fitted with immersion-type elements inside the pan, in which case, provision is made to keep clothes from touching the elements.

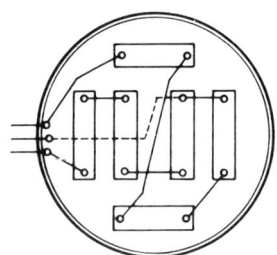

Fig. 15.5 Diagram of wiring of mica strip elements clamped to boiler bottom, to give three-heat control.

A three-heat switch or an energy regulator is provided to control the heater, and, in some washboilers, a boil-dry protection device is fitted, which automatically switches off the current if the boiler is switched on while empty, or allowed to boil dry.

Chapter 15—Questions

1. (i) Describe briefly the four most generally used types of electric washing machine. What type of washing action is produced in each?
   (ii) Name four different types of electric irons, and describe briefly the construction of any one iron.
2. (i) A prospective customer is thinking of replacing an existing twin-tub washing machine with a fully automatic model. Describe the advantages of the automatic washing machine that you would point out to the customer, and the advice you would give about using such a machine.
   (ii) Explain why it is essential that any washing machine is connected to the electricity supply by means of a 3-core flexible cord and a 3-hole socket.
3. List the main features of a washing machine suitable for a small family. State the capacity, and, if there are no other means of heating water apart from the washing machine, estimate the probable cost of using the washing machine for a load of 20 lb of clothing, etc. with electricity at 0·8p per unit.
4. (i) What type of washing machine would you recommend to a woman in a wheelchair?
   (ii) What type of iron would you recommend to a person with disabled hands (poor grip)?
   Explain why your recommendations are suitable.
5. A heat-controlled electric iron does not function. State what faults could have arisen and how you would check for three of them. Why is it not considered good practice to run an electric iron off a BC holder?
6. The most modern type of controls used in an electric washing machine are ....
7. Home Laundering Consultative Council markings are found on the following types of products:
   (i) .... (ii) .... (iii) ....
8. Which of the following electrical appliances removes the most water at the least cost:
   (i) tumbler, (ii) cabinet, (iii) spin dryer, (iv) wringer?
9. A common electrical loading for a domestic steam iron is ....
10. In a washing machine with a horizontal drum, use a .... washing powder.
11. After passing through a spin dryer, the amount of water remaining in the clothes is between ...... % and ...... % of the dry mass.

12 Thermostatically controlled irons do not have removable connectors.

True   False

13 How is it possible for a travelling iron to be used at either of two different voltages?

16 Commercial Equipment

Food Preparation Machines

All the machines used for the preparation of food are operated by an electric motor, the power varying according to the total mass of the food to be prepared at one time, and the number of revolutions per minute at which the machines operate.

Mixers

Mixers are used for the mixing of all cakes, doughs and batters. Beaters suitable for the mass of the mixture are fitted, and bowls are available from 10 to 140 quarts (11 to 159 litres) capacity. They are operated by $\frac{1}{8}$ h.p.–5 h.p. motors, with 3 or 4 gear controls and push button start (fig. 16.1a).

Attachments are available for slicing, shredding, grating, mincing, chipping potatoes, straining and sieving food, and for mashing potatoes.

Free-standing machines, operated by a separate motor, can also be obtained to carry out the above operations when large quantities of food are being handled.

High-speed mixers

These machines are used only for bread, pastry and confectionery mixes. All the ingredients are placed in the bowl at the same time, and the bowl is closed during operation, it fitting closely to the under-surface of the unit (fig. 16.2b), or having a lid fitted over the top. Unless the bowl is in the closed position, the machine will not operate.

This type of mixer saves up to 95% of the time taken by a conventional machine for certain types of mixing. For example:

    in a *high-speed* mixer, puff pastry is mixed in 20 *seconds*,

    in a *conventional* mixer, puff pastry is mixed in 15 *minutes*.

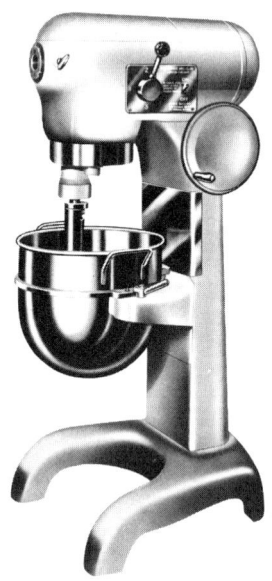

Fig. 16.1a Conventional mixer.

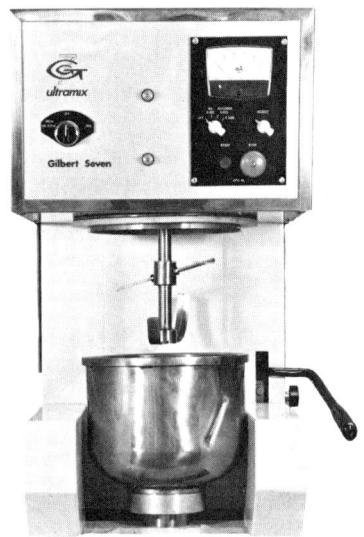

Fig. 16.1b Bench model high-speed mixer.

COMMERCIAL EQUIPMENT

Other Motor-driven Machines

These are available for the following purposes: (i) potato peeling (bench or pedestal mounted), (ii) slicing meat, cheese, bread or rolls, (iii) steak tenderising, meat sawing and cutting, (iv) coffee grinding, (v) bread slicing and buttering, (vi) silver burnishing.

Waste-disposal Units

These operate on $\frac{3}{4}$ h.p.–5 h.p. motors, and the principle is the same as that described for the domestic units. Generally the units are free standing (fig. 16.2), and plumbed to the water supply and drainage system. These machines are usually sited near the washing-up area, or in a central position in the kitchen.

If bottles or cans are to be destroyed, special equipment, operated by an electric motor assisted by hydraulic action, must be installed.

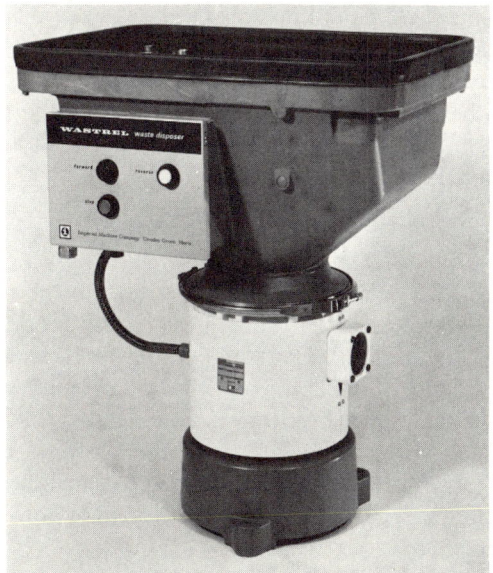

Fig. 16.2 Waste-disposal unit.

Refrigerators

Commercial refrigerators, whether the 'reach-in' type or the 'walk-in' cold room, are operated on the compressor system. In the larger cabinets and all cold rooms, a fan is situated at the back, to assist with the distribution of the cooled air. In some specialised instances,

247

moisture is introduced to eliminate the need for covering prepared food for short-term storage. Normal storage temperature is 40°F (4°C), usually with separate cabinets for meat and fish storage at 30°F (-1°C). Refrigeration units are also installed into serving counters and display units. Specially designed units, for cooling bottles, milk, and soft drinks, and for iced water dispensing, are available.

Frozen-food Storage Cabinets ('Conservators')

Conservators vary in size from approximately 13 ft^3 (368 litres) to large 'walk-in' rooms. They are used for the storage of commercially frozen foods, with temperature settings, varying according to the type of food to be stored, from 0°F to 24°F (-18°C to $-3\cdot4$°C). Like commercial refrigerators, these are operated on the compressor system.

Freezers

These are of a similar size, and operate on the same principle as frozen food storage cabinets, but they are used for the freezing of fresh food, where a maximum temperature of -5°F (-21°C) is recommended. They can also be used for the storage of commercially frozen foods. Where large quantities of ice are required, e.g. in restaurants, separate machines are available for this purpose.

Blast Freezers

The pre-packed and portioned food is loaded into the blast freezer, which is usually designed on a tunnel basis. Fresh food is loaded on to trolleys and put into a freezer tunnel at one end, and removed at the other end when frozen. These tunnels vary in length according to the output required. A rapid reduction in the temperature of the food is achieved, as the cold air is forced around the food by means of high-powered fans. An average time for food to reach the deep frozen state is two hours. The food is then passed into low-temperature storage until required.

Ovens

General-purpose oven
A general-purpose oven is a large conventional thermostatically-controlled oven of similar construction to the type described on page 197 but made from heavier and more robust material (fig. 16.3). It is used for roasting and general baking purposes.

COMMERCIAL EQUIPMENT

Fig. 16.3 Oven and tapered-heat top.

Pastry oven
This is a shallow oven with a large shelf area with thermostatically-controlled elements at the top and the bottom. These ovens are stacked in tiers, according to the baking capacity required (fig. 16.4).

Fig. 16.4 Two-tiered pastry oven.

Forced-air convection oven
This modern method of oven construction works on an intake of air which is channelled by a fan over high-loaded elements, and then

circulated around the oven cavity. This system achieves completely even heat distribution. The advantages are that, although a slightly lower temperature is used, less cooking time is required, food shrinkage is reduced by 25%, and a larger output of food per cubic capacity is obtained.

Micro-wave oven

Micro-waves are electromagnetic radiations like light and radio waves, which all travel at the same speed, but have different frequencies and wavelengths. The micro-waves have a frequency somewhere between those of radio waves and visible light. A magnetron at the top of the oven emits the micro-waves, which are evenly distributed through the oven cavity by a fan.

In these cookers, the micro-waves are used to cook the food. The principle is different from the conventional cooking method. Micro-waves do not heat the oven cavity but penetrate the food directly, causing the molecules in its structure to rub together and create friction, which produces the heat required to cook the food. As the micro-waves penetrate the food, both the inner and outer layers are cooked simultaneously, unlike the conventional method where fierce direct heat is applied to the outside of the food, thus browning it, and the heat is then conducted inwards. During micro-wave cooking the food is not browned at all. Using micro-waves, the food is cooked very quickly in minutes or, in some cases, seconds. It can also be used for quickly defrosting and reheating foods.

Important points to remember are as follows.
   (i) Micro-waves are reflected by metal, so foil containers, silver or stainless steel should not be used for cooking utensils, as they will affect the cooking of the food.
   (ii) Micro-waves are transmitted through materials such as glass, heavy gauge plastic, china and paper, without heating them. Thus, when these are used for cooking utensils, they do not burn, but remain cool and can be easily handled.
   (iii) Micro-waves are absorbed by foods to a depth of about $2\frac{1}{2}$ in all round—any deeper cooking is carried out by conduction.

The degree to which the waves penetrate the food depends on several factors.
   (a) The density of food—the denser the food the more difficult it is for the waves to penetrate.
   (b) The shape of the food is important: the thicker it is the longer it will take to cook. Food should be uniform in size and thickness, so that one part is not overcooked whilst the rest is still

COMMERCIAL EQUIPMENT

cooking. This is an important consideration when preparing meals to be reheated.
(c) Cooking times depend on the quantity of food. A definite amount of energy is generated by the oven, and the more food placed in the oven, the less energy is available for each portion. The cooking time is increased to compensate for this.
(d) The starting temperature of food affects the cooking time. Thus, food in a chilled state will take longer to cook than food at room temperature.
(e) Plates and containers should not reflect the micro-waves.
(f) Foods which are moist must be covered to help retain this moisture. The loading of a micro-wave cooker may be 3 kW or 5 kW, according to size, with an energy output of 1·2 kW or 2 kW.

Combined micro-wave and forced-air convection oven
This combines the two principles previously described, thus providing the advantages of high-speed micro-wave cooking with browning of the food.

Steaming oven
These thermostatically controlled ovens vary in construction to provide steam at normal, slight or high pressure. The steam is produced by immersion-type elements in a water tank. The higher the pressure of steam obtained the shorter the cooking time required.

Hobs

Boiling tops
Boiling tops are produced as an integral part of an oven unit, or as a separate boiling table (fig. 16.5). The totally enclosed boiling plate described in the domestic section is controlled with an energy regulator, and is usually rectangular in shape, although the sizes vary.

Solid plates with tapered heat
Solid plates with tapered heat give extremely fast heat in the centre, graduating to simmering heat at the edges. Two double pole ON–OFF switches are fitted, one controlling the centre and the two side plates, and the other controlling the intermediate annulus (fig. 16.3).

Griddle plates
These are smooth cast-iron plates with embedded elements, thermo-

Fig. 16.5 Boiling table.

statically controlled. As the cooking process is carried out directly on the surface, a gully is provided to collect excess fat.

Grills

Salamander grillers

These are available with open or sheathed elements, controlled by variable heat switches, which give control over the whole grilling area, or by multi-heat switches, which divide the grilling area into sections under separate control (fig. 16.6).

Fig. 16.6 Salamander grill.

Infra-red grills
See page 211, domestic section.

Griddle grills
These have two smooth cast-iron thermostatically controlled plates, one above the other, the top one being half the size of the lower, to enable food to be cooked on both sides simultaneously, while open griddling can be carried out on the front half of the lower plate (fig. 16.7).

Fig. 16.7 Griddle grill.

Toasters

Rotary toasters
The toasting racks, which are connected to a chain driven by a motor, are passed between radiant heating elements, thus ensuring even browning on both sides at the same time. A time switch, known as a 'variable colour control switch', is fitted, and has to be set to obtain the required degree of browning of the bread.

Automatic toasters ('pop-up')
Two open-type elements, controlled by a time switch to give adjustable colour control, are fitted perpendicularly into a frame. A pilot light or bell is sometimes fitted to operate when toasting is completed. Single units producing two slices of toast and multiples of two can be mounted to form larger units.

Fryers

The shallow fryers are heated by thermostatically controlled elements clamped on to the base.

The modern improved deep-fat fryer is heated by thermostatically controlled sheathed immersion-type elements (fig. 16.8).

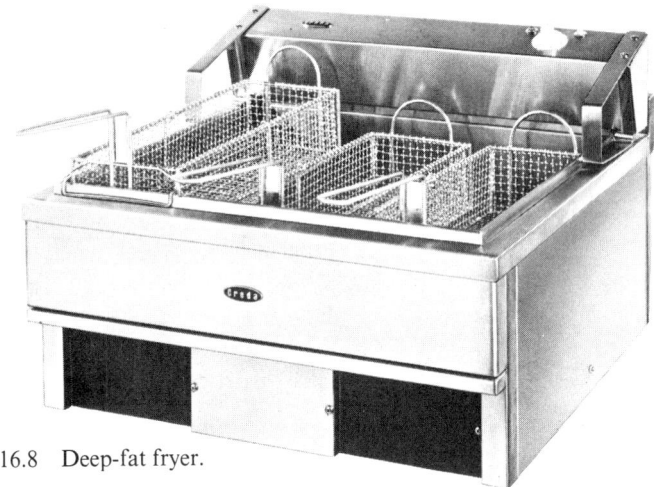

Fig. 16.8 Deep-fat fryer.

Boiling Pans

Tilting pan (bratt pan)

These are usually of heavy construction, from about 6" to 10" (15 cm to 25 cm) deep, and 24" to 30" (60 cm to 76 cm) square. A tilting mechanism allows the pan to be moved from the horizontal to the vertical position for ease of emptying (fig. 16.9). The thermostatically controlled heat, from embedded elements, is spread evenly over the base of the pan. A safety cut-out comes into operation when the pan is tilted. This is a multi-purpose pan for frying, braising, boiling and stewing.

Boiling pans

These pans, used for boiling and stewing operations, have a heated air, water or steam jacket, which enables thickened foods to be cooked without sticking or burning. The larger models are supplied with a draw-off tap (fig. 16.10). These pans are available with clamp-on elements at the base, and they are suitable only for vegetable boiling.

The smaller models, often termed tilting kettles (fig. 16.11), empty in the same way as described for the bratt pan.

COMMERCIAL EQUIPMENT

Fig. 16.9 Tilting pan (Bratt pan).

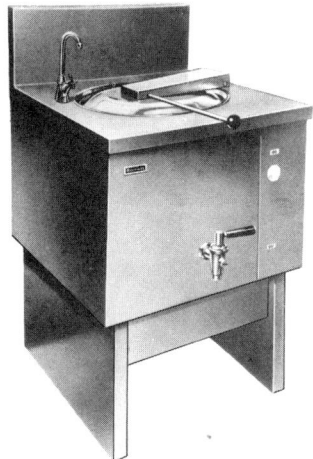

Fig. 16.10 Boiling pans.

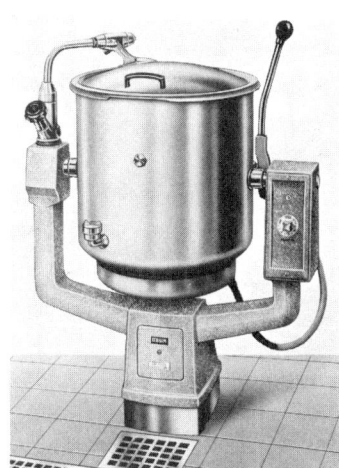

Fig. 16.11 Tilting kettle.

Beverage Equipment

Water boilers

These are normally of two types: (i) the pressure-type, where the boiler is situated under the counter unit, with only the discharge point above, and (ii) the expansion-type, where a self-contained unit is on the counter. These boilers are controlled by thermostats and produce a continuous flow of boiling water in a few minutes from cold.

Steam injectors can be fitted to pressure boilers for instant heating of small quantities of liquid.

Café sets
These are an extension of the boilers above, with side urns attached for the storage of hot milk and coffee making (fig. 16.12). These side urns are also available as separate units.

Fig. 16.12 Counter café set.

Coffee makers
These work on the same principle as the domestic filter or infused method, the commercial type being made in sizes appropriate to the supply required.

Hot-cupboards
These are used for keeping food and plates hot. There are varying designs and sizes, and the hot-cupboards can be supplied as separate units or as an integral part of the service counter. They are usually fitted with sliding doors for easy access. When used for food display, there are glass sides and doors, and an illuminated interior. A temperature of 180°F (80°C) is recommended, and a pre-set thermostat is normally fitted. The top of the unit can be flat and heated, or a water or dry-heat bain marie may be fitted.

Bains Marie

There are three types of bains marie.
  (i) *Open water bath.* This is heated by thermostatically controlled immersion heaters, and used to keep bulk quantities of sauces, etc. hot before and during service.
  (ii) *Dry-heat type.* This is usually an integral part of a service counter, with specially designed stainless steel lidded containers of varying dimensions. These fit into a heated cavity, where the thermostatically controlled temperature is maintained by the circulation of hot air.
  (iii) *Automatic water bath.* The design of this is similar to that of the dry-heat type, except that the heat source is steam which is generated by an immersion-type element in a tank automatically supplied with water.

Heated Plate Dispenser

These may be free standing or fitted into a service counter. The plates are piled into a heated cylinder containing a spring-loaded mechanism which is so calibrated that, as soon as one plate is removed from the top, the pile rises to bring the next plate into position.

Modular Equipment

This versatile system of appliance planning can be designed to suit most types of catering operations. The measurements of hob units, fryers (deep and shallow), griddles, bains marie, and grills, etc. are such that they are interchangeable with base units such as forced air convection ovens, general purpose ovens, and hotcupboards. This system started with small equipment which was used in view of the customers, i.e. in steak bars, etc. It has now extended to large-scale equipment in school meals kitchens and industrial installations.

Dishwashing Equipment

Recommended temperatures of water for all types of machines:
  140°F–160°F (60°C–71°C) for washing,
  180°F–190°F (82°C–87°C) for rinsing.

Spray-type dishwashers
These machines (fig. 16.13) operate with fixed and moving jets of

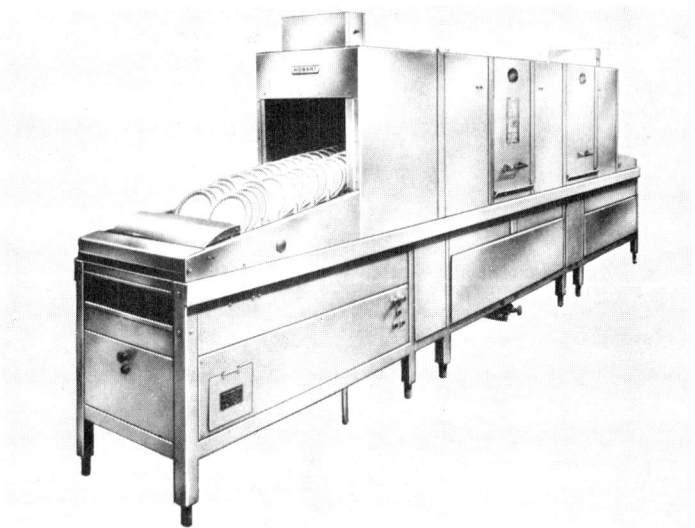

Fig. 16.13 Spray-type dishwasher.

water to spray the crockery, both for the washing and rinsing processes. The machines are operated by one or more electric motors, varying in power according to the size of the machine.

Immersion-type heaters with thermostatic control are used in tanks built into the machines, when sufficient hot water is not available. Automatic water-softening, detergent, and rinse-aid feed can also be incorporated, and for good results it is important that detergents suitable for the hardness of the water should be used. In larger machines, automatic conveyor belts are used for moving crockery. The maximum capacity is 12000 pieces of crockery per hour.

Immersion machines
These machines have one or two tanks for washing and for rinsing. An impeller agitates detergent and water in wash tanks, and the crockery is moved by hand from one tank to another.

Brush-type machines
Separate tanks are used for washing and rinsing. The crockery is cleaned by insertion between revolving brushes, before being placed in racks and immersed in the rinsing tank.

Glass-washing machines
These operate in a similar manner to spray-type dishwashers, the

washing and sterilising sprays playing on to revolving racks, or on to a moving conveyor.

Washing and sterilising sinks
These are twin sink units where the wash sink is supplied by water from an independent heater, whilst the rinse sink is fitted with an immersion heater to raise the water temperature for sterilising.

Water Heating

Self-contained water heaters as described in the domestic section, with capacities from $1\frac{1}{2}$ gal to 100 gal (7–450 litres), are available for commercial purposes. In a 100 gal heater with 9 kW loading, the water is fully heated from cold in four hours. If a well insulated storage tank of sufficient capacity for the day's requirements is in use, the supply can be connected so that it operates on a reduced price off-peak tariff, to effect a saving in the running cost.

Space Heating

There are two main categories of heaters:
    (i) direct-acting, which are charged on a standard tariff,
    (ii) thermal-storage, which are charged on a specially reduced off-peak tariff.

The most suitable direct-acting heaters for commercial use are (i) convectors, (ii) wall and ceiling heaters, and (iii) fan heaters, which are suitable where quick heating for short periods is required, e.g. in dining areas.

Thermal-storage heating systems are (i) floor warming, (ii) storage radiators, (ii) fan-assisted storage radiators, and (iv) Electricaire.

The principle of these systems is the same as described in the domestic section, the size of the installation varying with the cubic capacity of the premises to be heated.

Ventilation

This vital part of any catering installation is a system of ducting and hoods, controlled by electrically driven fans. Heat, steam and stale air are extracted and replaced with fresh air, without causing draughts. Good ventilation systems have to be specifically designed for each installation.

Ventilation must not be confused with air conditioning, which is a more sophisticated process involving cleaning, cooling, heating, and drying or humidifying of the air.

Floor Cleaning

Machines for carpet cleaning and shampooing, floor polishing and scrubbing are operated by electric motors, sizes varying with the amount of cleaning required. These can be separate units, on the same principle as domestic cleaners and polishers, or one central power unit with a system of ducting with connecting suction points in each room. In the latter case, a cleaning arm is plugged in where required, and the dirt is sucked away to one central refuse holder, usually outside the building, to await collection. This method is suitable for large hotels and hospitals.

Vending

Beverages, snacks and complete meals are sold by means of this automatic system of catering.

Beverages
Depending on the type of machine, the output can be a selection of hot beverages, cold beverages, or a combination of both. The ingredients for each beverage are held in separate plastic containers, and a predetermined quantity is released each time the coin is inserted, and the appropriate button is pressed. It is usual to use dehydrated concentrates, with the exception of tea, where the leaf variety is sometimes still used. A mains water supply and an electricity supply from a 13 or 15 A socket are necessary for the operation of the machine.

Snacks
These machines vend pre-packaged confectionery, fruit, biscuits, etc.

Complete meals
The meals are pre-cooked, and therefore, in this case, the vending machine is refrigerated. When a coin is inserted in the machine, the food is released with a time token attached. The food is then placed in a micro-wave oven, the time token is inserted in a slot at the side of the oven, and the food is automatically reheated for the correct time.

Vending machines require regular cleaning, especially in the case of beverage making, where all the ingredients are discharged through one chute, and flavours can mix if care is not taken.

COMMERCIAL EQUIPMENT

Equipment	Loading	Capacity	Type
boiling pans	6–15 kW	10–14 gallons (45–64 litres)	free-standing or pedestal
Bratt pans	12–18 kW	from 125 ft^3 (3500 litres)	free-standing
dishwashers	motors up to 2 h.p. heaters up to 24 kW	max. 12 000 pieces of crockery per hour	free-standing or sink-mounted
floor cleaners	$\frac{1}{2}$–150 h.p. motors		free-standing or central installed units
freezers	from $\frac{1}{4}$ h.p. motors	from 13 ft^3 (370 litres)	free-standing
fryers	from 2 kW	5 lb (2·2 kg) per hour output per kW	free-standing
griddles	from 2 kW	from 17″ × 14″ (430 mm × 375 mm) cooking area	counter- or oven-mounted
grillers	2$\frac{1}{2}$–7 kW	from 210 in^2 (1340 cm^2)	free-standing, counter- or wall-mounted
hobs			
rectangular plates	2 kW–4 kW	8″ × 6″–22$\frac{1}{2}$″ × 11$\frac{1}{4}$″ (200 × 150 mm–560 × 280 mm)	boiling table or oven-mounted
tapered-heat plates	2·4 kW centre 1·5 kW sides 4·8 kW intermediate annulus	10″ (250 mm) centre plate 18″ (450 mm) diameter annulus	
hot-cupboards	max. 1 kW per foot run	20 plated meals or 240 stacked plates per foot run	plain 2′ (60 cm) back to front
hot-cupboards (bains marie)	max. 1·5 kW per foot run	10 plated meals or 120 stacked plates per foot run	bain marie top 2′ (60 cm) back to front
mixers			
conventional	$\frac{1}{8}$–5 h.p. motors	10–140 qt (11–160 litres) bowls	bench- or pedestal-mounted
high speed	1$\frac{1}{2}$–60 h.p. motors	7–280 lb (3–130 kg)	
ovens			
convection	from 3 kW	from 1$\frac{1}{2}$ ft^3 (42 litres)	free-standing, counter or tiered
micro-wave	3–5 kW		counter- or wall-mounted

Table 16.1 Average loadings and capacities of commercial equipment.

Equipment	Loading	Capacity	Type
pastry	up to 8 kW	600–1000 ft² (55–90 m²)	free-standing or tiered
general-purpose and roasting	3–20 kW	3–30 ft³ (85–850 litres)	free-standing with hob or oven only, tiered or side by side
steaming	4½–12 kW	from 3 ft³ (85 litres)	free-standing, counter or tiered
plate dispenser	1–2 kW	up to 6 doz plates or saucers	trolley- or cabinet-mounted
refrigerators	from ¼ h.p. motors	from 13 ft³ (370 litres)	free-standing, counter-mounted or 'walk-in' rooms
space heaters	approx. 15–20 watts per ft² of space		
toasters			
automatic 'pop-up'	3 kW per 6 slice toaster	200 slices per hour	counter
rotary	5½ kW	540 slices per hour	free-standing
waste-disposal units	¾–5 h.p. motors		free-standing
water boilers	3–15 kW	24–480 pints (13–270 litres)	under or on top of counter
water heaters	from 1 kW	from 1½ gal (7 litres)	wall- or floor-mounted

Table 16.1 Average loadings and capacities of commercial equipment.

Chapter 16—Questions

1 Describe how each of the following are operated and state the main use of:
   (i) the conventional food mixer, and for what operations attachments are available,
   (ii) the high-speed mixer.
2 By which system are commercial refrigerators operated and what are the reasons for:
   (i) fitting a fan into larger models,
   (ii) introducing moisture into the cabinet in some models?
3 What are the differences between
   (i) a conservator,
   (ii) a deep freeze,
   (iii) a blast freezer?

4 (i) Describe a general-purpose oven and a forced-air convection oven.
 (ii) Compare the construction, use and advantages of the above.
5 List the different types of boiling plates used on hobs, and explain how they are controlled.
6 Describe the differences between:
 (i) a salamander grill,
 (ii) an infra-red grill,
 (iii) a griddle grill.
7 (i) What is the function of a bain marie?
 (ii) Describe the various types of bains marie available.
8 What are the differences in construction and use between:
 (i) a rotary toaster and an automatic toaster,
 (ii) A Bratt pan and a boiling pan?
9 How does the use of modular equipment affect kitchen planning?
10 Write a short paragraph on each of the different types of commercial dishwasher available.
11 Please tick the appropriate answer.
 (i) Do high-speed food mixers have attachments for slicing and shredding? Yes...... No......
 (ii) Are commercial refrigerators operated on the absorption system? Yes...... No......
 (iii) Is the blast freezer ideal for the storage of frozen food?
  Yes...... No......
 (iv) Does the combined micro-wave and forced-air convection oven brown food? Yes...... No......
 (v) Is less cooking time required in a forced-air convection oven than in a conventional oven? Yes...... No......
 (vi) Can metal containers be used in a micro-wave oven?
  Yes...... No......
 (vii) Are deep-fat fryers fitted with thermostatic controls?
  Yes...... No......
 (viii) Are waste-disposal units suitable for destroying bottles and cans? Yes...... No......
 (ix) Can a Bratt pan be used for frying, braising, boiling and stewing? Yes...... No......
 (x) Is it advisable and practical for ventilation systems to be specially designed for each installation?
  Yes...... No......

17 Electric Shock

The conditions governing the flow of electricity have been explained in previous chapters, from which it will be understood that, in order to establish and maintain a current-flow, the circuit or conducting path must be complete. If, therefore, the circuit includes an individual, he or she will receive an electric shock.

Accidental shock usually occurs by touching a live conductor while the person is in contact with 'earth', e.g. by grasping a water tap, by touching part of a water central-heating system or a bath, or by standing on a concrete floor, etc. The casings or external metal parts of appliances may become live by a failure of internal insulation, or by detachment of conductors from their terminals. The individual handling the appliance may then receive a shock by completing the circuit between the live metal and earth, the neutral conductor of the supply always being permanently connected to earth at the supply sub-station.

Most cases of shock occur by the person completing the circuit between live conductor and earth in this way, as distinct from contact between supply conductors.

The normal method of preventing metal parts from becoming live is to connect them to earth. With portable appliances, this is done through the 'earth' core of a three-core flexible cord or cable (the green and yellow, or, on old appliances, the green core) as indicated in fig. 17.1. With properly earthed apparatus, a fault would cause the circuit fuse to operate, and so automatically disconnect the faulty apparatus.

An alternative to the safeguard of 'earthing' is for appliances to be made of all-insulated or double-insulated construction, and many such appliances are now available.

The diagram also shows another source of danger—the switch on the portable heater being connected on the 'neutral' side of the element, instead of on the 'live' side. Connected in this way, the switch will

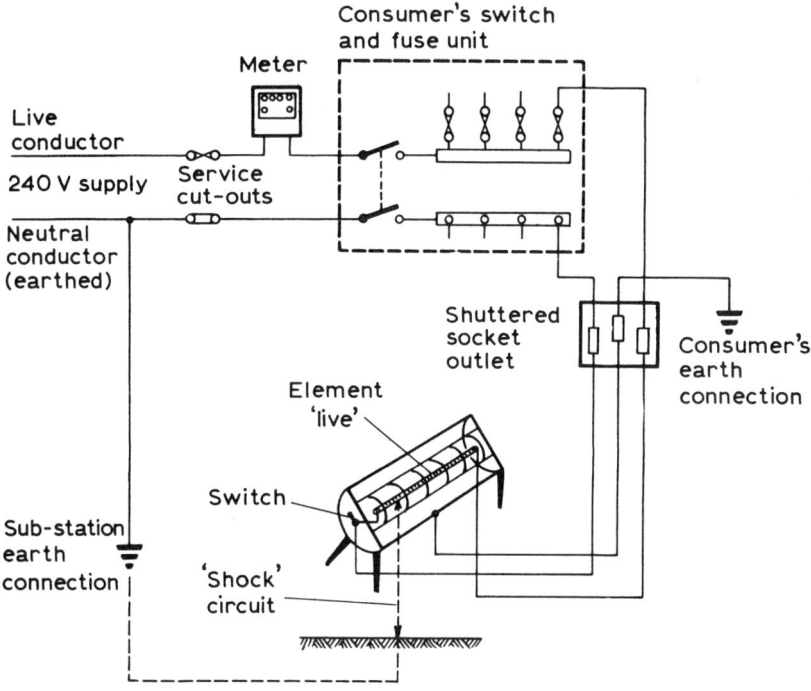

Fig. 17.1 Diagram showing how electric shock may be received. This also illustrates the risk of connecting a switch in the 'neutral' conductor.

interrupt the circuit when in the OFF position, but will still leave the element live. Anyone touching the element therefore (when in contact with earth) would receive a shock, even although the element were cold and switched off.

Appliances should be connected so that switches are always in the live conductor.

The severity of electric shock depends on the amount of current passing through the body. This is governed chiefly by:
  (i) the voltage applied,
  (ii) the area and duration of contact,
  (iii) the skin resistance, which varies with the physical condition of the person,
  (iv) the total resistance of the 'shock' circuit.

As, therefore, electric shock may be possible in certain circumstances, the ways in which it affects a person should be understood, so that suitable and effective treatment may be given as promptly as possible.

If someone gets an electric shock, it is important that whoever goes to the rescue should not put their own life in danger by getting an electric shock themselves. The following simple life-saving rules should be remembered.

Approach the unconscious victim cautiously. If he remains in contact with a conductor do *not* touch him, or you too may be electrocuted. *If possible switch off the current.* In the home, this can usually be accomplished at once by switching off or removing the plug. It is then safe to touch and move the casualty.

In the case of outdoor conductors for public supply, it will be necessary to telephone the local Electricity Board. While this is being done, it may be very dangerous to approach too closely to the conductors, or even to the victim. With high-voltage conductors it is most unlikely that the victim will remain in contact with a conductor, so the current will not continue to flow through him. Furthermore, in cases of this kind, although nearly all the subjects suffer from burns, their heart and lungs function all right, so nothing is gained by heroic but risky efforts to move them before the current is switched off by competent engineers.

Effects of Electric Shock

Muscle contraction
One dangerous effect of electricity is that it causes the muscles of the body to contract (that is to tighten). Should someone grasp a live conductor and form part of the circuit with his body, the muscles which work the fingers may contract, so he is unable to let go. Sometimes, by getting a colleague to disconnect, or by the victim swinging his body so as to pull out the plug, it is possible to get loose. Otherwise a dangerous situation can develop.

Breathing stopped
If the electric current passes through certain parts of the brain, it may affect the vital centres and cause the breathing to stop. Nowadays, it is believed that this type of accident is less common than was at one time thought. Nevertheless, if it does happen, immediate treatment is needed. The victim lies unconscious and not breathing. It may be possible to feel the pulse beating, which shows that the heart is all

right, but by itself that is not enough. What has happened is that the breathing (respiration) has been stopped, and, until it starts again, the victim must be kept alive by someone else causing him to breathe artificially, that is by artificial respiration.

Oral resuscitation (otherwise known as 'mouth to mouth' or the 'kiss of life') is now generally regarded as one of the easiest, and, in many circumstances, the best method of giving artificial respiration.

The method of applying oral resuscitation is as follows.

(i) Remove any foreign material—false teeth, vomit, etc. which may cause blockage of the air passages.

(ii) To open the air passage, tilt the patient's head backwards as far as possible. Use one hand to push the patient's head backwards, and the other to pull the jaws forwards, at the same time slightly opening the patient's mouth.

(iii) Take a deep breath, place your mouth over the patient's mouth and blow. Seal the patient's nose by pressing your cheek against it or by grasping it with the fingers. Give 6–8 deep inflations quickly and then continue to inflate about ten times a minute. Watch the chest during each inflation—it should rise. No movement indicates a blocked airway. Check that the mouth and throat are clear, and tilt the head further backwards, making sure that the lower jaw is held forward. If the victim is a small child, place your mouth over the child's nose and mouth and use smaller breaths.

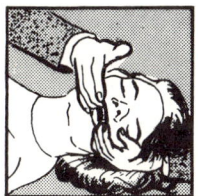 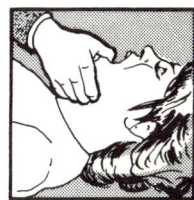 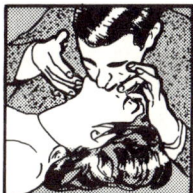

Fig. 17.2   Method of applying oral resuscitation.

Circulation stopped

Most commonly, in a case of electric shock, the current passes through the trunk of the victim, and, in particular, through the chest. In doing so, it may so seriously affect the heart as to stop it from pumping blood around the body. It is important to realise that in this state there is no structural damage to the heart, but that it is only not working properly, and there is no circulation of the blood. The victim will be lying unconscious, probably not breathing, and the rescuer will be unable to feel a pulse either at the wrist or in the neck. The pupils of the eyes will be widely dilated. Although special treatment in hospital is necessary to start the heart beating again, the victim may die within three or four minutes unless the circulation is kept going by first-aid treatment.

Therefore, it is necessary to start straightaway, as a first-aid measure, an artificial circulation which must be kept going all the time until the patient gets to hospital. This can be done by applying external heart massage (external cardiac compression).

Application of External Heart Massage

As soon as a victim is rescued, *start oral resuscitation at once,* and continue without interruption.

Instruct an assistant to feel for a pulse at the wrist or at the root of the neck (carotid artery). If no pulse can be detected, and if the pupils are dilated, *start external heart massage immediately* as well.

Procedure

The casualty must be lying on his back on a firm flat surface.

With two hands resting one on top of the other, press sharply down on the low part of the casualty's sternum (breast bone). Enough force should be applied to push the sternum one or two inches back towards the vertebral column (backbone).

NOTE—Rib fractures or other injuries may be caused by either excessive pressure or pressure in the wrong place. Remember, the lower part of the sternum, and not to one side or the other. Do not press too heavily on thin persons or children.

Repeat about once per second—the exact timing and rhythm is *not* important, but should not be less than once per second.

Continue oral resuscitation and external heart massage until spontaneous breathing and/or heart-beat is apparent, or until a doctor takes charge, or until you can evacuate the casualty to hospital as quickly as possible, continuing oral resuscitation and external heart massage, if necessary, without interruption during movement and transportation. *Never* practise external heart massage on a fit and conscious person.

Summary

These points summarise the treatment.
  (i) Remove victim from contact with the live conductor, without endangering yourself.

ELECTRIC SHOCK

(ii) If he is not breathing, start oral resuscitation at once.

(iii) If you cannot feel a pulse and the pupils are dilated, give external heart massage as well, without any delay.

(iv) Send for an ambulance, and keep up the treatment without respite until the ambulance arrives.

(v) It is difficult and may be useless to apply oral resuscitation or external heart massage if you have not practised before. It is *very dangerous* to practise external heart massage on a fit and conscious person. You should therefore get in touch with a doctor or first-aid training organisation for practical instruction, so that you are prepared should the need arise.

Chapter 17—Questions

1 Describe the action you should take if, on entering a room, you found someone lying on the floor, and in contact with a 'live' part of an electrical appliance.

2 Describe fully the circumstances under which a person may receive a shock from an electrical appliance. Illustrate your answer by a diagram indicating the path taken by the current causing the shock. Why is it important that, when single-pole switches are used, they should be placed in the live conductor?

Appendix 1

Definitions of SI Basic Units

Length (l) — metre (m)
The metre is the length equal to 1 650 763·73 wavelengths in vacuum of the radiation corresponding to the transition between the levels $2p_{10}$ and $5d_5$ of the krypton-86 atom.

Mass (m) — kilogramme (kg)
The kilogramme is the unit of mass. It is equal to the mass of the international prototype of the kilogramme.

Time (t) — second (s)
The second is the duration of 9 192 631 770 periods of the radiation corresponding to the transition between the two hyperfine levels of the ground state of the caesium-133 atom.

Electric current (I) — ampere (A)
The ampere is that constant current which, if maintained in two straight parallel conductors of infinite length, of negligible circular cross-section, and placed 1 m apart in vacuum, would produce between these conductors a force equal to 2×10^{-7} newton per metre of length.

Thermodynamic temperature (T) — kelvin (K)
The kelvin of thermodynamic temperature is the fraction 1/273·16 of the thermodynamic temperature of the triple point of water.

Luminous intensity (I) — candela (cd)
The candela is the luminous intensity, in the perpendicular direction, of a surface of 1/600 000 m² of a black body at the temperature of freezing platinum under a pressure of 101 325 N/m².

Appendix 2

Definitions of Derived SI Units having Special Names

Force (F) — newton (N)
The newton is that force which, when applied to a body having a mass of one kilogramme, gives it an acceleration of one metre per second per second.

Energy (W) — joule (J)
The joule is the work done when the point of application of a force of one newton is displaced through a distance of one metre in the direction of the force.

Power (P) — watt (W)
The watt is equal to one joule per second.

Electric charge (Q) — coulomb (C)
The coulomb is the quantity of electricity transported in one second by a current of one ampere.

Electric potential (V) — volt (V)
The volt is the difference of potential between two points of a conducting wire carrying a constant current of one ampere, when the power dissipated between these points is equal to one watt.

Electric capacitance (C) — farad (F)
The farad is the capacitance of a capacitor between the plates of which there appears a difference of potential of one volt when it is charged by a quantity of electricity equal to one coulomb.

Electric resistance (R) — ohm (Ω)
The ohm is the resistance between two points of a conductor when a

constant difference of potential of one volt, applied between these two points, produces in this conductor a current of one ampere, this conductor not being the source of any electromotive force.

Temperature (θ) — kelvin (K) or degree Celsius (°C)
The units of kelvin (K) and Celsius (°C) temperature interval are identical. A temperature expressed in degrees Celsius is equal to the temperature expressed in kelvin less 273·16.

Luminous flux (Φ) — lumen (lm)
The lumen is the flux emitted within unit solid angle of one steradian by a point source having a uniform intensity of one candela.

Illumination (E) — lux (lx)
The lux is an illumination of one lumen per square metre.

Appendix 3

Multiples and Submultiples for Use with SI Units

Factor by which the unit is multiplied	Prefix	Symbol
$1\,000\,000\,000\,000 = 10^{12}$	tera	T
$1\,000\,000\,000 = 10^{9}$	giga	G
$1\,000\,000 = 10^{6}$	mega	M
$1\,000 = 10^{3}$	kilo	k
$100 = 10^{2}$	hecto	h
$10 = 10^{1}$	deca	da
$0{\cdot}1 = 10^{-1}$	deci	d
$0{\cdot}01 = 10^{-2}$	centi	c
$0{\cdot}001 = 10^{-3}$	milli	m
$0{\cdot}000\,001 = 10^{-6}$	micro	μ
$0{\cdot}000\,000\,001 = 10^{-9}$	nano	n
$0{\cdot}000\,000\,000\,001 = 10^{-12}$	pico	p
$0{\cdot}000\,000\,000\,000\,001 = 10^{-15}$	femto	f
$0{\cdot}000\,000\,000\,000\,000\,001 = 10^{-18}$	atto	a

Prefixes indicating multiplication by a factor of 10 raised to a power which is a multiple of $+3$ are preferred, e.g. kilo, milli, micro, etc.

Appendix 4

Conversion Factors between Imperial and SI Units

Length
1 in   = 25·4 mm
1 ft   = 0·305 m
1 yd   = 0·914 m
1 mile = 1·61 km

1 mm = 0·039 in
1 m = 3·281 ft
1 m = 1·094 yd
1 km = 0·622 mile

Area
$1 \text{ in}^2 = 645 \text{ mm}^2$
$1 \text{ ft}^2 = 0·093 \text{ m}^2$
$1 \text{ yd}^2 = 0·836 \text{ m}^2$

$1 \text{ mm}^2 = 0·001\,55 \text{ in}^2$
$1 \text{ m}^2 = 10·764 \text{ ft}^2$
$1 \text{ m}^2 = 1·196 \text{ yd}^2$

Volume
$1 \text{ in}^3 = 16\,390 \text{ mm}^3$
$1 \text{ ft}^3 = 0·028\,3 \text{ m}^3$
1 gal = 4·546 litres

$1 \text{ m}^3 = 35·315 \text{ ft}^3$
1 litre = 0·22 gal

Mass
1 lb = 0·454 kg
1 ton = 1 016 kg

1 kg = 2·205 lb

Force
1 pound-force = 4·45 newtons

1 newton = 0·225 pound-force

Energy
1 kW h = 3 600 000 J
       = 3412 Btu
1 Btu = 1055 J
1 ft lbf = 1·356 J
1 calorie = 4·19 J

1 J = 0·738 ft lbf
1 J = 0·24 calorie
1 MJ = 0·278 kW h
     = 947·8 Btu

APPENDIX 4

Power

1 h.p. = 550 ft lbf/s   1 W = 0·738 ft lbf/s
     = 746 W   1 kW = 1·34 h.p.

Useful Conversions for Cooking Purposes

1 oz = 28·4 grammes	(approx.	30 g)
2 oz = 56·7 grammes	(,,	60 g)
4 oz = 113·4 grammes	(,,	110 g)
6 oz = 170·1 grammes	(,,	170 g)
8 oz = 226·8 grammes	(,,	$\tfrac{1}{4}$ kg)
16 oz = 0·454 kilogramme	(,,	$\tfrac{1}{2}$ kg)

1 gill ($\tfrac{1}{4}$ pint) = 0·142 litre	(approx.	$\tfrac{1}{8}$ litre)
1 pint = 0·568 litre	(,,	$\tfrac{1}{2}$ litre)
1 quart = 1·137 litres	(,,	$1\tfrac{1}{4}$ litres)
4 pints = 2·273 litres	(,,	$2\tfrac{1}{4}$ litres)
1 gallon = 4·546 litres	(,,	$4\tfrac{1}{2}$ litres)

Extracts from BS 3763: 1970—*The International System (SI) Units* and PD 5686:1969—*The Use of SI Units* are reproduced by permission of the British Standards Institution, 2 Park Street, London W1Y 4AA, from whom copies of the complete standards may be obtained.

Answers

Chapter 1

1. (i) megawatt (ii) millimetre (iii) nanosecond
   (iv) kilometre per hour (v) cubic centimetre (vi) litre
   (vii) kilonewton (viii) megacandela (ix) metre per second per second
   (x) degree celsius (xi) gigajoule (xii) square metre
2. (i) 17·23 metres (ii) 5·835 kilowatts (iii) 0·025 second
   (iv) 6000 kilojoules (v) 3×10^6 cubic centimetres (vi) 0·018 microsecond
   (vii) 0·32 ampere (viii) 0·1582 decagramme (ix) 300 decimetres
   (x) 0·00025 microfarad (xi) 4730 newtons (xii) 16000 millimetres
3. (i) 33·55 metres per second (ii) 2·469 kilogrammes
   (iii) 7·93 metres (iv) 15·02 newtons
   (v) 11820 seconds (vi) 0·60 square metre
   (vii) 15240 joules (viii) 2611 watts
   (ix) 0·299 cubic metre (x) 0·0239 cubic metre (23·86 litres)
   (xi) 838 joules (xii) 9·81 metres per second per second
4. 17·8 newtons
5. 1632 joules

Chapter 3

1. (i) 5 A, 1200 W, 5 h, 4·8p
   (ii) 20Ω, 2000 W, 1 kW h, 0·8p
   (iii) 480 V, 2400 W, 10 h, 24 kW h, 19·2p
   (iv) 10 A, 60Ω, $\frac{1}{3}$ h, 1·6p
   (v) 15 A, 14·67Ω, 15 h, 49·5 kW h, 39·6p
   (vi) 100 V, 200 W, 0·05 kW h, 0·04p

ANSWERS

2 0·415 mm^2
3 5 A, 205 V
4 1·44 kW, 3·456p
5 $R_A = 120\Omega$, $R_B = 80\Omega$, $R_{eq} = 48\Omega$
6 24 kW h, 216 kW h
7 12·5 A, 10·4
8 (i) 0·72p (ii) 0·48p
 (iii) 3·2p (iv) 1·6p
 (v) 1·2p

Chapter 4

1 2·6 A
2 (i) 5·18 kW, 21·58 A (ii) 73·18 kW h
3 1·44 kW, 19%
4 (i) 200 V, (ii) 40Ω, (iii) 1 kW, (iv) 3·33 A

Chapter 6

1 50
6 3 A, 6

Chapter 8

2 £20·13, £32·36
3 £14·99
5 136 kW h, £16·47
6 100 kW h

Chapter 9

6 (i) 40Ω, 1000 W, 2 kW h (ii) 100 V, 4 h, 1000 W
 (iii) 10 A, 2400 W, 12 kW h (iv) 100 V, 5 A, 3 kW h
 (v) $\frac{5}{12}$ A, 576Ω, 10 h (vi) 25 A, 9·6Ω, 12 kW h

Chapter 10

1 4·2 minutes, 0·084p

Chapter 11

2 (i) 45·4p, (ii) 14·1 A, (iii) 17·1Ω

Index

acceleration 6
alternating current 13, 30–42, **4.1–4.13**
alternators 59–63, **6.7–6.11**
ammeters 15–16, **2.7**
amperes 8, 270
atoms 10–12, **2.1–2.3**

bains marie 257
batten holder 125, **9.14**
beverage equipment 255–6, **16.12**
boiling plates 203–7, **13.7–13.10**
boiling rings 211
boiling tops (commercial) 251, **16.5**
brightness 182–3, **12.9**
British Electrical Approvals Board for Domestic Appliances 109
British Standards Institution (BSI) 2

cables 115–19, **9.6, 9.7**
capacitor 40, 104
cells, primary 55–7, **6.1–6.4**
  secondary 57–9
Central Electricity Generating Board 74, **7.1, 7.2**, 94–6, **8.1**
clocks 219–20
conduction 150–1, **11.3**
conductors 14
'conservators' 248
Consumers Association 109
convection 149, **11.1**
cookers, domestic 195–8, **13.1–13.3**
  boiling plates 203–7, **13.7–13.10**
  care of 208
  choosing 208
  griller-boiler 208
  grills 207
  hoods 217–18

278

ovens 198–203, **13.4–13.6**
  sizes of 198
cost of electricity 27

direct current 18–27, **3.1–3.7**
dishwaters 221–2, **14.3** (commercial) 257–9, **16.13**
distribution system 91–3, **7.14–7.18**
drying, methods of 239

earthing 112–14, **9.4, 9.5**
electricity
  distribution of 91–3, **7.14–7.18**
  generation of 78–87, **7.4–7.11**
  transmission of 87–90, **7.12, 7.13**
  Electricity Boards 74–6, 91–4, 107, **7.1, 7.3**
Electricity Council 73–4
electric shock 264–6, **17.1**
  physical effects of 266–8
  treatment of 266–9
electrons 10–13, **2.1–2.4**, 13–17
electro-motive force 16
energy 7
  electrical 24–5

fans 216–17
Faraday, Michael 43, 50
  's Law 50
floor polishers 216
  cleaners (commercial) 260
food mixers 218 (commercial) 245, **16.1**
force 6, 7
freezing units 228–9, **14.7**, (commercial) 248
  cleaning of 229
  preparing foods for 230
frequency 36

INDEX

fryers (commercial) 254, **16.8**
frypans 211–2
fuses 110–12, **9.2, 9.3**

glare 184
griddle plates 251–2
grills 253, **16.7**
griller-boilers 208
grills 207, (commercial) 252–3
  infra-red 211
  salamander 252
guards 165

hair dryers 218–19
heart massage, application of 268
heat, amount required 161–5
heaters
  ceailing 161
  convector 151–2, **11.4, 11.5**
  Electricaire 160
  fan 155, **11.9**
  panel 161
  radiant 152–4, **11.6, 11.7**
  radiant convectors 154, **11.8**
  radiators, oil-filled 155–6, **11.10**
  storage 156–7: floor-warming 157–8, **11.11**: radiators 158–60, **11.12, 11.13**
heating 149–151: conduction 150–1, **11.3**: convection 148, **11.1**: radiation 150, **11.2**
  (commercial) 259
hobs (commercial) 251
hoods, cooker 217–18

Illuminating Engineering Society 184
illumination 180–1, **12.7**, 184–5
illumination meters 181–2, **12.8**
immersion heater 136–7, **10.3**
impedance 39–40
Institution of Electrical Engineers 110
insulator 14
ironers, rotary 239
  press 239
irons
  hand 240
  heat-controlled (automatic) 240–1
  non heat-controlled 240
  steam 241, **15.4**
  travelling 240, **15.3**
kettles 209–10, **13.11**

lamps
  coiled-coil 168, **12.2**
  electric discharge 171
  finish of bulbs 168–9
  fluorescent, circuits of 176–8, **12.3–12.5**
  fluorescent mercury 172
  fluorescent, tubular 174–6
  gas-filled 167–8, **12.1**
  hot cathode discharge 171–2
  incandescent 167
  mercury-tungsten 172
  metal halide mercury 173
  quartz-halogen 171
  sodium high-pressure 173
  special purpose 170
  tungsten filament 170–1
  ultra-violet 173–4
laundry, home 233–4
Lenz's Law 51–3, **5.12–5.15**
light, nature of 179
  and vision 183–4
  fittings 185–8, **12.10, 12.11**
lighting
  commercial 192
  domestic 188–91, **12.12, 12.13**
  shop 192
lighting design 184–5
  lumen method of 187–8
luminous efficiency 179, **12.6**
luminous emittance 183
luminous flux 179
luminous intensity 179

magnetism
  Faraday's Law 50–1, **5.11**
  Lenz's Law 51–3, **5.12–5.15**
  magnetic field: and conductors 46–8, **5.5–5.8**: around a bar magnet 44–5, **5.1, 5.2**: around a coil 48–50, **5.9, 5.10**: between two magnets 45–6, **5.3, 5.4**
  theory of 43–4
mass 4–5, 6
meters, electric 130–2, **9.20**
modular equipment 257
molecules 10
motors
  single-phase 66–7
  3-phase induction 63–6, **6.12–6.16**

279

Oersted 46
Ohm, George 18
   's law 18, **3.1**
ovens 198–203, **13.4–13.6** (commercial) 248–51, **16.3, 16.4**

pans, boiling 254–5, **16.9–16.11**
percolators 210
phase difference 38, **4.11**
plate dispenser 257
plugs 129–30, **9.19**
power, electrical 25–7
power factor 103–4
power stations 76–80, **7.4, 7.5**
   coal-fired 80–2, **7.6**
   hydro-electric 84–7, **7.9–7.11**
   nuclear 82–3, **7.8**
   oil-fired 82, **7.7**
protons 10–14

radiation 150, **11.2**
refrigerators 223–7, **14.4–14.6** (commercial) 247–8
   frozen foods in 228
   hints on use of 227
resistance 19–20
resistivity 22–4, **13.5, 13.6**
resuscitation, oral 267, **17.2**
ring circuit 121–8, **9.9–9.18**
rollers, heated 219
rose, ceiling 125, **9.13**

safety 109–115
salamander grillers 252, **16.6**
sewing machines 219
shavers 220
spits 212

tariffs 94–104
   area-board 96–7
   bulk supply 95–6, **8.1**
      commercial 102–3, **8.2**
   domestic 97–102
temperature conversion 146–7, 202
thermostats (oven) 199–202, **13.4–13.6**
   (boiling plates) 205–6
tilting pan 254, **16.9**
toasters 211 (commercial) 253
transformer 67–70, **6.17, 6.18**
transmission system 87–90, **7.12, 7.13**

unit, cost per 27
units 1–9
   CGS and MKS 2
   derived SI 5–9, 271–2
   Imperial 1–2
   multiples and submultiples 273
   SI 2–5, 270

vacuum (suction) cleaners 214, **14.1, 14.2**
velocity 5, 6
vending machines 260
ventilation (commercial) 259
voltmeters 15, 16, **2.7**
volts 271

waffle irons 211
washboilers 242, **15.5**
washing machines 235–7, **15.2**
   automatic 238
   cleaning of 238
   one-tub with wringer 237
   solid-state control 238–9
   twin tub 237
washing powders 234–5
waste disposers 222–3 (commercial) 247, **16.2**
water heaters 137–43 (commercial) 259
   cistern 140–1, **10.6**
   combined system 141, **10.7**
   free-outlet (non pressure) 138, **10.4**
   indirect system 142–3, **10.8**
   low-pressure 139–40, **10.5**
water heating
   cost on 143–5
   installation of 135–6, **10.1, 10.2**
weight 4–5
wiring circuits
   ring circuit 121–8, **9.9–9.18**
   traditional circuit 119–21, **9.8**